A SUNDAY PILGRIMAGE
Six Days, Several Prayers and the Super Bowl

ALSO BY
Anthony L. Gargano
Co-author of *The Great Philadelphia Fan Book*

Middle Atlantic Press books may be purchased for educational, business, or sales promotional use. For information please write: Special Markets Department, Middle Atlantic Press, PO Box 345, Moorestown, NJ 08057.

Middle Atlantic Press Web site: www.middleatlanticpress.com

Second Edition

2 3 4 5   08 07 06 05 04

Cover Design: Christina Gargano-Lupo
Interior Design: Royalty Press
Printed By: Royalty Press
Cover Photo: Permission granted by Associated Press

A SUNDAY PILGRIMAGE
Six Days, Several Prayers and the Super Bowl

Anthony L. Gargano
Co-author of *The Great Philadelphia Fan Book*

Foreword by Andy Reid

Middle Atlantic Press
Moorestown, New Jersey

ACKNOWLEDGMENTS

A bevy of people helped this book come to fruition. My gratitude is extended to the entire Philadelphia Eagles football club. I've worked around numerous franchises in sports, and the Eagles truly are the Gold Standard in what they project. From the front office to the coaches to the players to those who work tirelessly behind the scene without any fanfare.

Special thanks to Derek Boyko, director of football media services, one of the fine people in sports. Always professional, courteous and considerate of our insidious motives as media, Derek simply gets it.

The same can be said about the rest of the department, most notably Rich Burg, dedicated father and media guardian of Donovan McNabb, and Bob Lange.

Thanks to those at Middle Atlantic Press, Bob Koen, Blake Koen and particularly Jim Di Miero, who helped shepherd this project and put up with my tantrums and whims and incessant begging for two more weeks, which turned out to be two more months.

Thanks to the wonderful people at Sportsradio 610-WIP, including Station Manager Marc Rayfield and Program Director Tom Lee, whose idea it was to send us on this journey in the RV, program assistant Jill Speckman, colleagues Angelo Cataldi, Al Morganti, Rhea Hughes, the First Lady of Philly Sports, Joseph A. Weachter, Jr., Howard Eskin, Glen Macnow, Mike Missanelli, Garry Cobb and Ray Didinger.

Thanks to Larry Platt and Bob Huber from Philadelphia Magazine, who sent me on assignment for several pieces on the Eagles, and helped hone my writing and reminded me of what journalism is supposed to be.

Help also came from interns Seth The Kid and Zach, and family and friends and sounding boards, Christina Gargano-Lupo, my talented sister who designed the cover and understood my vision, Anthony R. Gargano, Florence Gargano, Mary Tomasetti, Michael Deangelo, Joseph Benvignati, Robert Marino, Anthony Buchanico and Ike Reese.

Thanks to the fellas for making the pilgrimage to the Super Bowl a lifetime memory: Joseph Tomasetti, Vince Portaro, David Rodden, Steve Martorano, Nick Martorano, David Breitmaier and Paul Nagle.

Finally, I extend appreciation to those who inspired this book: The impassioned fans of Philadelphia, by far the best in the land.

DEDICATION

For Joey, my brother,

God has blessed me with many friends in this life, none greater than you.
After all these years, you're still my hero.

CONTENTS

FOREWORD
BY ANDY REID

I MUST TELL YOU A STORY. I must tell you the story of that morning in January 2001 when single game tickets went on sale for our first playoff game against the Tampa Bay Buccaneers. We were still at the Vet and I had been working all night, catching a few hours of sleep on the couch in my office, and I emerged, the sun barely up and awake, to a throng of people braving the bitter cold for a chance to buy seats. They stood out there, lining the ramps of the stadium, some for most of the night, and it was colder than football cold but they were undeterred. And when they saw me, they cheered and hollered and began doing EAGLE chants, and what I saw was something profound: The Passion of Philadelphia. It was overwhelming. I bought them hot chocolate and doughnuts and I wished I could have brought them all into my office to keep warm, though they're a tough bunch, football players in spirit.

I knew it then and I know it now: I'm very fortunate to coach football in a sports town like this, a town that loves the game the way I love the game. When I got here in 1999, I knew the reputation of the Philly fans. How they care deeply, so deeply that they will let you know it, good or bad. The first night I was in town, I went out to dinner at a restaurant in South Philadelphia called Frederick's, a place I would frequent often in the coming years, and a priest at a nearby table yelled over to me, "Hey, Coach…BOO!!!!!"

The Father then smiled, and said, "Just wanted to make you feel at home."

It didn't take long for me to feel at home here. When it comes to sports, this is a big city with a small-town atmosphere. It's almost a college atmosphere. The fans will fill the stadium whether the teams are winning or losing. I think back to that first year when we were building the foundation of our success and not winning a lot of games; I looked up into the stands and they were there. There's no front-runner in these fans. What I like the most is that I think we share the same pulse of how things are going. If you're winning, they're feeling pretty good, celebrating the good times with you. If you're not winning, they're booing and you're kicking yourself in the tail. We're in that same frame of mind.

We connect.

I was with the Green Bay Packers when I first learned of The Passion of Philadelphia. Reggie White was with us and I remember being at the hotel and the people gathered around the lobby. It was part Reggie, but also part the people loving Reggie. It showed me the loyalty of this city. That's carried over to this football team. People don't just follow this team. They study it. They love it. They live it. When people start willing things to relatives that are Eagles related, that's when you know it's getting close to a religious state. Our fans want to be engulfed by the Philadelphia Eagles.

It's the support that resonates the most, whether it's at home or on the road. It's a great feeling to come into the hotel and see all of our fans there. It's a feeling of comfort. Then we arrive at the stadium and they're all lined up with their Eagles jerseys and cheering the bus. It feels like we have reinforcements. Our fans were out of control at the Super Bowl. When we arrived in town, they were already there on the sides of the road and the main highway chanting and cheering. I'm sure the police in Jacksonville were blown away by the reaction of the fans. The stream of people became even thicker the closer we got to the hotel. As the week transpired, our people came flooding in until they took over the town. The Super Bowl felt almost like a home game. Amazing!

As you read this book, I want you to remember the journey. Embrace the memories and those with whom you shared them. Football can be a beautiful game, as well as a hardscrabble one. It brings people together: families, friends and football players.

I want to thank you for all of the cheers and the chants. I want to thank for being a part of this special journey. Above all, I want to thank you for being the lifeblood of The Passion of Philadelphia.

INTRODUCTION

I shall begin by the river's edge because there are moments, however fleeting, when we are gripped by a great understanding.

It can happen at the oddest of times, places, whereabouts, though it usually attaches to an event, a profound event. It just washes over you, too, without asking. Suddenly, the randomness by which we live makes sense without resolution of the riddle, the restlessness that governs us momentarily quelled. Call it what you will – clarity? The coalescence of contentment and clarity? It lasts as long as a déjà vu and is equally mysterious, a kind of cosmic snapshot.

I guess I shouldn't be all that surprised it occurs here by the river's edge, where the flock has now been moved to song, spontaneous song that sounds almost Elysian. Mind you, these are not, sans the priest and the nun that stands before me, choir people or professional churchgoers with voices enhanced by their tribute to God. If anything, most of them have been paddled by patois, inheriting, like I did, a thick, muddy accent distinct to Philadelphia. Alas, they are simply touched by something, thus proving our inherent need for creed in any form. The entire scene that has played out over the weeks leading up to this moment along the breezy banks of the St. Johns, beneath a makeshift party tent beneath a winking Southern sun in a makeshift town, engenders this feeling.

Perhaps it's not the pilgrimage that we are conditioned to know. The end is not Fatima or Clonmacnois or some other monastic place.

There is no quicksand or hissing snakes to overcome in this journey, and the only treacherous road to travel in the literal is Interstate 95. What rises up in the distance is not some divine relic that might heal the infirmed or awash those in genuflect with good earthly fortune but a stadium. It is a nice enough stadium, relatively new, but terribly standard, without lore or legend, storied inhabitants, or any profound significance, except that the land once housed the Gator Bowl, and still annually hosts what the university types dub the world's largest outdoor cocktail party.

Oh, certainly it is pilgrimage.

There is an exalted purpose and spiritual significance, which is at the core of any pilgrimage. People don't gather like this with such emotional outpouring without exalted purpose.

So know this is a modern-day pilgrimage for sure; modern-day meaning at a time when we are not addict-obsessed by religion or our cosmic purpose. There are too many diversions or distractions nowadays, which is not an editorial statement of either good or bad but an observation of simply what is. Please add the backdrop of what brought us here, both in the physical and back in Philadelphia in spirit, as a chief diversion, particularly, though not exclusively, for the stereotypical red-blooded male. Without exaggeration, sport is the lifeblood of our existence. Whether as participant or spectator - and we are really doing when viewing, even if it's simply cursing - sport provides us with our core needs.

We struggle over the role religion plays in our civic life, color our states to signify our raging rift over morality meets spirituality, while all the while sport has completely usurped the separation of church and state. After all, where does the real praying occur on Sunday? What produces the real piety? Where is faith most abundant, attaching to an almost tangible form, particularly at the start of every new season? Where else do we find the blurring of the social barriers and the only real perk for social standing is a better pew? Where do we gather and root for rapture?

"So sung they, and the empyrean rung With Halleluiahs," Milton once wrote, describing what now could easily be the stands following a touchdown.

Some may scoff, perhaps dismiss with disdain, damning it heresy. But shall they peer through the obvious and peel away preconception and see what I see? Shall they see the convergence of souls? Shall they see people drawn to one another, their spirits uplifted, energized, galvanized, Born Again, however fleeting, however the means? Am I foolish to believe something that brings us together should not be deemed a trivial entity? Who would be so blasphemous to say otherwise?

So allow me to cease with my defense and admit to you our destination is THE River City, Jacksonville, a town more Georgia than Florida, one that realized water is the holy element in life and real estate and that the ultimate path to American acceptance is through professional football. The river that snakes through downtown and the ocean that hugs the nearby coast make for pleasing aesthetics for an otherwise artless place. Jacksonville, however, might as well be anywhere in this world. For Jacksonville is only relevant to this story because it obliged to play host to our revolving Mecca called the Super Bowl.

I
WEDNESDAY

The city aches this time of the year. It's postholiday, and longing for spring is to wish your life away because it's too far off. Like the streets, blotched with blackened ice, peoples' spirits are typically freezer-burned and hardened by too many sunless hours. But on this morning, in the dead of a Northeast winter, the mood colors the town pastel.

The clerk at the convenience store where I buy my newspapers greets me with a cheeky smile. He's from a far away land and he's wearing an Eagles jersey from a discount sporting goods store. "Only five days to go," he says before asking the same question he's asked me before every game since September.

"Think we can win?"

My reply is standard but enthusiastic: "Most definitely."

The use of "we" by the clerk from southern India speaks to the inclusive nature of this phenomenon. Who am I to couch my reply with caution that the Eagles are playing this era's dynasty, the New England Patriots, who have won two of the past three championships of the NFL? I co-host a sports radio show in this city and all people want five days before the game is to sustain faith. Besides, deep down, I am like the clerk and all of the others who call Philadelphia home, and would prefer to embrace optimism on the day I leave to cover my boyhood team in the Super Bowl.

One of the things we cherish most about sport is its direct link to our youth, particularly if, like mine, childhood was pleasant. I rationalize that sport is born unto human frailty and choose to ignore its flaws, as I would do with people I treasure. It's been too great a constant and companion in my life, and otherwise, I wouldn't feel the way I do now, overcome with boyish exhilaration.

A wave of gratitude overcomes me: How fortunate to make this my profession. When I was twelve, I slept on sheets that were decorated with the logos of every team in the NFL. My bedroom with the shaggy red rug was that of a typically red-blooded Philadelphia boy: a replica Eagles helmet on the bureau, Phillies batting-helmet lamp on the bed stand, Sixers wastepaper can, plastic figurine of Bobby Clarke on top of the small black and white television. The walls were adorned with posters of Julius Erving, Ron Jaworski, Rocky Balboa, Bo Derek emerging from the ocean with a see-through shirt, and various pennants, including the one celebrating the 1980 Eagles Super Bowl team with all of the players' names on one side.

That was the only other time the Eagles played in the Super Bowl. The story has been the same since then, one everyone around here knows by broken heart. They have always been promising, always good enough to devastate their fans in the end. Like the Buddy Ryan run, where the boastful, blustery coach commanded the best defense in the league, only to succumb because of a quarterback's broken leg or a quarterback's inability to read defenses, because, perhaps, he wasn't coached that well.

Even those with a heart like tree bark have to concede the fate of the Eagles' last three seasons to be excessively cruel. Three NFC Title Games, three crippling defeats, including two at home. The first one could be explained and easily excused as the Eagles were unripe, playing on the road and offering a hearty showing, leading at halftime before eventually succumbing to the spitfire Rams. Now the second one? That was the one, definitely, positively the one. Bet the mortgage, re-fi, and double down. The Eagles were home for the last game ever at Veterans Stadium, playing a team that shrank outdoors in the elements, a team they beat easily in the regular season. No way, Tampa Bay, could they lose.

Stone. Cold. Mortal. Lock.

No one saw it coming, especially after the game's opening, the fighter jet flyovers followed by the quick touchdown for the lead and an outpouring of emotion that would rival Rapture. Those are the worse kinds, where you plop from a mountain peak and can't brace yourself.

So it came down to three, the holy number. It's got to be a charm, eh? The Eagles had struggled in their first five games last year going 2-3. Fans howled. Then Brian Westbrook saved the season with a dramatic punt return for a touchdown in the swampy Meadowlands. They won nine straight to amass an unlikely 12 victories and home field in the conference. Still, injured bodies mounted, piling up in stacks like old magazines. It looked as bleak as a Wisconsin winter in the playoff opener against the graying Packers, the Eagles unable to stop the run, which is a slow and agonizing way to perish with, the offense relegated to watching helplessly on the sidelines. They got a final turn as the clock burned to nothing, but a sack of quarterback Donovan McNabb left them with final down and forever. Out of the ashes thaumaturgy fell upon Lincoln Financial Field, as McNabb slung a pass to Freddie Mitchell deep over the middle, in the smallest of seams in the Packer D, a skosh over the sticks. Fourth and 26 was born, the football equivalent of water into wine. The Eagles scored to force overtime, and won it after Packers quarterback Brett Favre threw the worst interception of his Hall of Fame career.

Fourth and 26 just had to be divine. The season, such a tumultuous ride, mimicking the play of the oft-maligned McNabb, had to possess some special meaning. After all, it always happens when you least expect it, eh? So while the flock carefully quelled its Bowl bliss, belief billowed. The opponent in Title Game III was the Carolina Panthers, a bushwhacker team whom the Eagles had beaten in the regular season, without a proven quarterback or playoff track record. The game proved the cosmos hath no compassion, as McNabb got hurt and the offense stalled like a '74 Maverick.

Failure's foam somehow turns sweet when it's finally purged, like now with the realization that all of that worry over the week that preceded the fourth straight NFC Championship Game was undue.

There was no way in Philadelphia hell the Eagles were going to lose to the Atlanta Falcons, no matter the perfect storm of an impending snowstorm, Michael Vick and the usual bad phriggin' luck.

So here it is, no letdown, the heart whole again and filled with anticipation, one of God's greatest gifts and perhaps the main reason for football's prodigious fancy in this country. Anticipation provides purpose, gumption to engage in the mundane, if simply to sustain. It truly is the bridge of life because it bridges the time between rewards, whether a holiday or a birthday, a vacation or a football game. The brevity of the season and the week between each game allows a story-line to develop and us to pine for the action, though the two weeks between the conference championship game and the Super Bowl can feel like an entire calendar year. While anticipation makes the days passable, it also makes them longer, almost strenuous. The first couple days are easily manageable because the residue of bliss from Title Game lingers playfully. Soon, however, the feeling burns off and is replaced by restlessness.

By Tuesday, some nine days following the Eagles' win over the Falcons, the town is agitated. For most, today will be more of the same, especially since the team left on Sunday morning and seems as far away as the game. But I am fortunate. Today's the day I begin my pilgrimage – in the literal, of course, for my pilgrimage began when I was a boy and fell hard for this game and this team, which, then, donned white helmets with green wings. Simplistically, though not without charm, they became my boys because they were from where I was from. I loved my home city so it was only natural that I become a raging homer. To this day, I still cling to that myopic view when it comes to sport. I believe it is a traitorous act not to root for the home team.

Forgive us for seeking diver-
sion. It's ugly out there, with a
war waging and the decay of
humanity, which is really how
it's always been. The signs of the
apocalypse littered the earth
when man inherited it, which is
hardly comforting in our own
time of need. We hunt for comfort and so it's completely
acceptable to blow off a day's
work and belly up to a sports bar midday, midweek to talk Super Bowl
and see off the Caravan.

So Tony Luke's is packed for our final radio show of the week at
home. Tony Luke's is a sports bar across the street from the famous
Tony Luke's sandwich shop, which is utterly Philadelphia, with its eating area under an awning because we eat lunch standing up in
Philadelphia, and lunch is always chopped beef or cutlets of chicken
nestled in a good roll. The bar is located in South Philly, under a highway and not far from the docks, and its décor denotes a standing sub-
marine more than a classic pub or corner tavern.

Out front awaits the white RV in which we will journey. The traveling party will consist of my radio partner, Steve Martorano; his sev-
enteen-year-old son, Nick; my cousin, Joey; our lifelong friends, Vinny
and Boo; and our two producers, Skinny Dave and Big Bubba.

Tony Luke's is decorated for a party, with green and white streamers and "Go Eagles" placards, and the wait staff, too, is wearing Eagles
jerseys. The patrons match. Mostly from the adjoining neighborhood,
they are festive and quite welcoming. Like Boston and Chicago and
the boroughs of New York City, the people make Philadelphia. They
possess hardened hides and warm middles, and are always eager to help
one of their own. Today, when Steve announces on radio he's feeling
ill, a doctor drops by to write him a prescription for an antibiotic. The
doctor prefers to remain anonymous, as he wears sunglasses and blends
into the crowd and motions to Steve on the sly to see him. He will call
Steve the next day for a verbal checkup.

One by one, kind people who would like to ride along vicariously in this journey approach the perch where we are broadcasting, dropping off gifts for the trip. Usually, it's homemade red wine in nondescript bottles or elaborate Italian pastries. Part of it is the nature of doing talk-radio, particularly on a radio station like 610-WIP, which is driven by the listeners and plays the role of town square. Unlike Steve, my chosen profession was print journalism, not broadcasting. Truth be told, I still possess an ink-stained soul but what I adore about radio is its warmth. Writing provides natural barriers, where you can hide behind your inner voice and have little contact with the reader. Talk radio is direct byplay, nearly as close as touch. You feed off the vibe of the callers and the listeners and the town. They know more of you and about you. You become a companion, whether they like you or dislike you. You are a constant voice, and anything consistent is usually comforting.

I dare say that I prefer it when radio is this way, when the show is light and airy and the masses are happy and hopeful. I know it's not what truly sells, even when it comes to sports. It's always the screaming and bickering and shock, shlock. But this is a welcome change, as I see Steve huddled at the bar with the doctor, a woman named Candy and her girlfriend. Because of her name, I thought Candy was a stripper, but she turned out to be a retired school teacher who taught Eagles defensive end Derrick Burgess in Maryland. Turns out, the middleaged women decided to leave their husbands for the weekend and join the Caravan. Turns out, they are the bigger football fans in the family.

I see faces that smile in the room. There's Mister Al, who looks like a sheik and I can see him in a fine pelisse with a one-girl harem, a spitfire redhead named Gen who adores him. Mister Al is well into his fifties, hit-man scary-looking and though he walks with a cane because of two bad hips, physically imposing at six feet two and two hundred and sixty pounds of well-proportioned flesh, which exhales an older man's strength, life's strength, just before the body begins to disintegrate with old age. It's his mien that ruffles most, the glistening olive-washed bald head, dark goatee and eyes that droop just a little, as if in judgment. He's a case study for looks that lie, and an accent that perjures, partly because he's tumble-dry friendly and partly because he's well read, scholarly in fact, a college man back in the day – Widener, attending on a basketball scholarship. He's also the son of a once prominent bookmaker, dubbed the "Midtown Sportsman" by the local gossip columnist. He assesses the Eagles' chance through the sharp eye of someone who knows what he's talking about. He talks of putting a wager on the team, quite assuredly.

I see a local cop, Joe, whose nephew also named Joe, is a star running back for Lafayette College, a Roman Catholic High School boy who has a shot at playing in the NFL. Joe and his partner, hard-working Philly cops in their early-thirties with families, neighborhood guys who wanted a job with good benefits and a chance to do the right thing, once watched part of an Eagles Monday Night Football game over my house. It was a quiet night in the city and they are big football fans. I offered them a beer that they declined due to the on-duty thing.

I see Jerry, a city guy who left for the deep breath and space of Jersey, an educated man who called the day of my first show and extended kind, encouraging words that helped buoy my confidence when I struggled with nerves that stilt diction already cursed by my own gravelly accent. A witty fellow with girth, he's the kind who pins nicknames that stick, the good-natured ball breaker who loves an audience. "Green Shoes," he calls to Steve, because one afternoon Steve wore shoes with a green tint, though they were really a deep forest color.

Steve nods the way he does, this sort of knowing nod. Steve always looks like he knows everything, partly because he knows plenty and partly because he's forever processing, his runaway mind flashing like the time on an alarm clock after the power comes back on. I think he's completely devoid of being surprised.

I see these people before me, professing devotion to this football team in their own sort of way, lifers from young to old. With that, comes devotion to each another. Tony Luke's is equal food and beverage, so there are children in here, including a sweet teenage girl who needs a kidney and has the courage of a soldier. She'd rather talk about the game and how she hopes they win because of her father. She's smiling, and in the background there's the din of chatter and laughter, ever inviting, like a family cookout, even if it's mostly strangers. The scene is familiar to me. I've always liked pubs and sidewalk cafes and corner joints where the old ladies' entrances are now side entrances, sweating stale beer. I like stadiums and arenas and movie theaters and the polished downtowns of cities for the same reason. I simply like places where people gather, as long as they are not heavy with despair or burden billowing from the doors.

I must get ready to leave now. The television cameras are here. It's a good visual, the local sports radio team ushering out the door of the sports bar and into a big old RV, destination Super Bowl. Skinny Dave, who is rock-star skinny and unkempt and whose deal is that he's a music guy in a jock world and buys his clothes from second-hand stores, packs up the equipment. Big Bubba, who's really, really big, some six feet, six inches and four hundred pounds, but a big man's athletic, slips behind the wheel. He looks the part of driver, the Mitchell and Ness trucker hat perched on his head shields an amiable, cheeky face with shards of a reddish-brown beard.

The rest of the crew arrived moments earlier. Steve's wife, Marie, dropped off Nick, who's a handsome kid born of good genes, with chiseled features and a sleek build from youth and free weights. My faction huddles together. Joey, who just kissed goodbye his wife, Karen, and his young daughter, the angelic Domenica, is my only first cousin. He's been an older brother to me and my sister, and he could be my twin because we have the same mannerisms and similar build and dark complexion. Boo, whose real name is David or Brian, whichever is fine, depending on whether it's a client or an acquaintance, as I've never called him anything but Boo in the near thirty years I've known him, fidgets next to Joey. He's a partner with his brother in a thriving Center City law practice and he's an active father of three small children, so these sorts of boys' weekends provide an oasis, plus he will be the biggest sports fan in the RV.

My friend Vinny, an airline executive, flew in this morning from Appleton, Wisconsin, where he has lived for fourteen years. He cares more about the journey than the game. While Vinny and I have kept extremely close, traveling extensively through the years and working on various writing projects together, this is his opportunity to keep close to the hometown group. Vinny's father, Armando, a proud, hard-working man who came to this country from Italy in his teens and still maintains an accent and views his forty-year-old son as a boy, dropped him off. He now stands amid the send-off smiling, shaking his head. I can almost hear him: "These guys, crazy guys. Vincie, when are you gonna get married?"

I see Jimmy Head, one Jim Hethrington, Boo's brother John's longtime friend whom we have since chosen to play the sage-like character of the group, the one wise from life's travails and this town's many football heartbreaks. A fanatical Eagles fan for many years, Jimmy Head has never lost that first-time feeling with this team.

Jimmy Head, an eccentric one who dons a full mane of hair, strikingly white, liquid paper white, that belies a rather youthful-looking face that bears both his Irish and English heritage, is one of only two of my friends who calls the show on a regular basis. The other is the great Ace, or Angelo Borgesi, a man whom I admire deeply because he made all the right choices in life, however hard it was to walk away from the easy money that may come from a neighborhood's hustle, instead opting to hustle four legit jobs at once: atop the Walt Whitman Bridge, helping with his uncle's restaurant, doing mortgages with his brother and rehabbing houses. They call him Ace because he's always been, well, Aces, just an Ace of a guy.

While most of Jimmy Head's calls have to do with him being a frustrated showman and a hoarder of a free time, the deeper thought is that football, more succinctly, this Eagles team, is the only the aspect of his life that is not encrusted by cynicism. How he would call each week in the spring and offer the countdown to the opening game of the season, fighting himself for wishing away part of his suddenly dwindling years. How he would analyze each upcoming game with a coach's eye and idiom, then end it abruptly by pronouncing the Eagles will win 42-7. How he is so methodical in his approach to fandom, right down to his viewing habits, wrought with superstition.

Together at a bar where I did the road pregame shows, we once watched the Eagles play the Giants in the last game of the season, the year Donovan McNabb broke his leg and A.J. Feeley rode to the rescue with five straight wins. Now I usually don't like to watch a game in that sort of atmosphere, the cluster of people and noise making it difficult to concentrate appropriately, but the crowd upstairs was rather thin and I try to follow a strict rule: Never miss kickoff. So Jimmy Head, sitting across the room from where I did the show, remained watching and refused to join our table because the Eagles were playing well. The Eagles were lining up for a game-winning field goal, a chip shot of a kick, especially for the usually automatic David Akers. Right then a man nearby who had watched the entire game asked for his check and got up to leave to signal the game's ending. Just as Jimmy Head began to scold the man, Akers pushed the kick wide and the Eagles went on to lose in overtime. Jimmy Head spent the entire postgame postmortem that lasted one more beer swearing the Eagles would have won had that man waited for the proper time to ask for his check.

Jimmy Head is very Philadelphian, and so his final words to us are, "Don't jinx 'em!"

We pile into the RV and plop down around the picnic table, peering out the window. The people wave goodbye and the TV crews roll their cameras. I reach my hand through the window and slap five with some of the fine strangers.

"Bring us home a championship," someone yells out.

The thought immediately comes to mind, "Who the hell are we?" The players are in Jacksonville. We will have as much to do with the outcome as these people standing on the curb. But that is stating the obvious. At this moment, we personify the event, which seems untouchable by the masses, encased by the barrier of bigness and television and hype, which is how sport, particularly a happening like the Super Bowl, has evolved during the great boom over the past twenty-five years. For the most part, the participants that once lived among us are now gated away, an economic moat separating them from the city they wear on their jersey, which is fine for them because only a liar or a fool wouldn't embrace that opportunity, but it chips away at the charm of sport. While television attempts to bring us closer, with cameras planted into the turf or in a nook of the locker room, it is strictly in a sort of hands-off, voyeuristic way. Sport has become a museum piece. So at this moment, we represent the flesh, the flesh unto the flesh, the conduit in which the masses can relate.

Bubba wheels the RV out of the parking lot and makes a left on Oregon Avenue, leaning on the horn. A handful of cars with fans that embrace the idea of a road trip follow dutifully behind. Boo pops open a lukewarm Coors Light. Joey and I start to wrestle playfully, something we've always done when we're excited, something that boys do because that is how they outlay their emotion and something that men do because they still want to be boys. The journey in the physical, which will take us down Interstate 95 and an overnight pit stop in Durham, North Carolina, to do Thursday's show, has begun.

Boo calls it "The Caravan of Destiny."

THE FATHER AND THE SON

I give you fathers and sons since they are the lifeblood of football, the vehicle on which it travels through time, sustaining through love and lore, the fabulous lore. Football represents at least one precious heirloom a man will pass to his boy, sans his surname. How easy to remain true to our nature as men then through a game that transports emotion through physicality.

Men, primarily, though not exclusively, connect through sport. It provides an excuse to communicate because deep down we'd prefer not to go that deep, whether it's with a stranger or with one of your own. Sports presents a cushion for conversation.

For men, more profoundly, though not exclusively, sport bridges gaps between and among generations. It creates a common thread and shared experiences, which is the bond to any human relationship. So it's a no-brainer that Nick Martorano joins his father for the championship game the way Steve Martorano joined his father for the Eagles' last championship some forty-five years earlier.

Life is a series of parallel lines. Steve is sick now the way he was sick then, a boy of twelve with the unknown ahead of him, looking into the future only deeply enough to hope for enough health to witness in person the Eagles play the Packers. Steve's family was a football family at a time when baseball held America's heart. Upon release from the army, John Martorano played semipro football in one of those tough-man leagues that were so prevalent at the time. Men played for teams sponsored by their work, and it was not uncommon that a special player was given a job because of his talents. John was fast and flashy, and when Steve was old enough, his uncles would tell him tales of his father's exploits. Most children can't imagine their parents young and vibrant, and Steve thought the stories to be greatly exaggerated. "By the time I started paying attention, he never got off the couch," he recalls.

But there was this one and only time he caught a glimpse of the man his father used to be. The local Little League sponsored a game between the parents, and John Martorano strode to the plate. He batted left-handed and this surprised his son because the man did everything else right-handed. It was a welcome surprise, as though he had discovered something about his father, as though he somehow knew him better because of it. The kids were umpiring the game, and Steve stood behind second base and marveled at his father's long, smooth swing, real compact and level, and the fact that he looked like a ballplayer. This also relieved Steve, because the biggest fear of any boy is that he is shamed, particularly athletically and particularly by one's family. I can recall the same relief when my father refereed in my basketball league and didn't get any of the calls wrong, that he simply knew the signal for traveling and looked good and fluid with a whistle.

So John Martorano draws a walk and coolly trots down to first base. "Next thing I know," Steve says, "he's stealing second. He barrels into the shortstop covering and hooks into the bag and rips every tendon in his ankle. He's totally pissed. I called him out. I tried to look even-handed. That was the last time I saw him do anything athletic."

John Martorano and his brothers-in-law were among the first football fans. In the fifties, they would fly to Cleveland to catch the Eagles play. When the Eagles played the Giants in Philadelphia and the game was blacked out, a common occurrence in the grainy days of the NFL, John and his wife's brothers would drive to the part of central Jersey that picked up the New York television market and rent a hotel room and play cards and watch the game. "These were the guys," Steve says, "that when people in the stands said, 'What's the spread?' they'd say three in the paper, but downtown's getting four."

Both of Steve's uncles had season tickets in 1960. They brought him to three games during the regular season, including the opener against Cleveland, when Jim Brown ran all over the Eagles, like he always did. The Eagles caught fire in the middle of the year, and that's when, according to Hall of Fame writer and historian Ray Didinger, this "football thing" tipped in Philadelphia, meaning it bled to the masses and became its own phenomenon. The Eagles had been averaging close to twenty thousand fans a game and after beating Detroit on the road, sixty-five thousand attended the following game at Franklin Field. "All through the year," Steve says, "my uncles kept saying, 'We're gonna get to see a Championship Game.' When it became clear, I started begging. See if you can get tickets. Please, please, see if you can get tickets."

The day of the Championship Game drew near, and that week Uncle Albert called. "You know what?" he began somberly, "I tried real hard. I couldn't get an extra ticket. You go with your cousin, I'll stay home."

Dogged by dilemma and regret that he had to do the right thing, he told his Uncle Albert, "I can't take your ticket, Unc. I just can't."

With that, Uncle Albert's voice suddenly pitched high. "Relax," he said. "I'm just bustin' your chops. We're going to the Championship Game."

The game was to be played the day after Christmas, on a Monday afternoon, because, after all, in 1960, we were still a God-fearing nation. In 2004, the NFL played a regular season game on a Christmas

Eve and two more on Christmas Day.

The day before Christmas, Steve felt sickness on the horizon. You can always feel sickness looming, the faint difficulty in swallowing, your throat getting scratchy, your energy dipping, the body becoming weary. Steve tried to ward it off, telling himself he would be fine. But over the coming hours, the flu socked him with force. Christmas presents didn't allay his fear of missing the big game. By the next morning, fever had taken his temperature to 102. John Martorano sat his son down and told him, "This ticket is worth a lot of money. I can sell it and give the money to you. Whaddya say?"

Steve declined. When you're twelve, no amount of money is fair compensation for missing the big game. "See if you can get a hold of the doctor," John said to his wife. John paced the room. He usually left for the stadium by eleven o'clock on game days and it was closing in on noon.

"Take him over," Steve's mother said after hanging up the phone. "He'll see him."

In those days, the family doctor's office was in the doctor's house. The doctor examined Steve and shook his head. The kid was extremely sick. "But," he said, "we'll get you through this. You may never see another Championship Game again."

Steve thought this comment odd, if not completely ludicrous. "I'm thinking I hope he knows more about medicine than football," he recalls. "I think he's nuts."

So father and son went to that game. They arrived late in the first quarter and the boy heard the player introductions while walking across the South Street Bridge to the stadium on the campus of the University of Pennsylvania. He felt the bridge vibrate from the noise of the crowd. The day was unseasonably warm and the sky clear, the stadium rising in the foreground amid the roar of all those people; the experience intoxicated the boy, momentarily flushing his sickness.

When you're twelve, Game Day takes on a mythical feel, its enormity flooding your senses. For me, that moment came while walking up the cement ramps of Veterans Stadium with my father for the 1980 NFC Title Game against the Cowboys, bundled up in the bitter cold, jostling with the crowd, inhaling the smell of the ballpark, wondering what it would be like if my team won, nervous over the outcome.

I've been to thousands of games since, and part of that thrill always returns. It's what I love about being a sportswriter, the travel to these different stadiums and arenas, each with their own distinct personality. Sans a few, the details of the games have faded from memory, but walking into those places, especially the ones in football towns or those on college campuses where there's always verve and vivacity, I will bronze every detail: how Arrowhead Stadium looks from a distance, smoke from burned-out barbeque grills billowing into an overcast sky, grey swallowed up by grey, above what looks to be a rippling pool of blood because they all dress in deep red in Kansas City; how it smells like the woods outside of Cameron Indoor Arena clear Carolina night, I swear, a faint hint of cherry tobacco in the clean air, how what it's like walking through the great walls of Notre Dame Stadium, no matter what you feel for the university, is not unlike how you feel entering the great gothic cathedral for Mass.

"I remember being terrified they might lose," Steve says. "I'll never forget my other uncle, Uncle Rudy, making an offhanded comment that made me feel better. 'Van Brocklin is gonna pass this team dizzy,' Uncle Root said, and all of my doubts vanished. He said it with such certainty. It wasn't bravado, merely a statement of fact."

The boy held his breath on that last drive by the Packers. They were a machine, pushing steadily up the field with short throws. He rooted for the clock to move faster. Time always slows to a halt when your team is clutching a lead at the end of a game. Finally, mercifully, the boy willed the legendary tackle by Bednarik against Taylor and saw the men rush the field and bust up the goalposts and hand out pieces of them like Halloween candy. The boy felt grateful to be there in person. The game wasn't broadcast on live television, rather tape-delayed later that night, and he could relive every single moment in the newspaper the following day. A couple of years later, the doctor's words ringing true, the Eagles having traded Jurgensen began to decline, the boy had off from school and took the bus to Philadelphia to visit the Public Library and again read and relive on microfilm the news clippings from that day.

So it was a foregone conclusion that some forty-five years later the man now would take his son, who is the spitting image of his father in a football uniform, down to the pose, on this journey to the Super Bowl. They shared a moment like this once before, two years earlier, when the Eagles played the Buccaneers in the second championship game. Tickets were again an issue. But this time he had a friend, Steven Horn, who offered him his tickets. Of course, he couldn't accept. Only a cad would take another man's tickets. But Steven insisted. He told him, "God wants me to give you these tickets so you can take your son and be there together."

"He trumped me with God," the man would say later.

The man couldn't wait to tell his son. He thought it to be the perfect bonding moment, and though the outcome played out differently than they hoped and wished, it certainly was. They shared the walk up the Vet's cement ramps, terrified that the Eagles might lose. They shared getting to the stadium earlier, bundled together in their seats high atop the field, and pointing out to each other at the same exact time Hugh Douglas, sleeveless in the biting cold, jogging around the field by himself. They shared the first two minutes and the moment of utter rapture. And in the end, they shared consolation.

"When Rhonde Barber picks off the pass," Steve says, "Nick looks at me and says, 'Let's go.' Just like that. I knew then that he knew what it was like to root for these teams. He had been initiated into the club."

When it comes to sports, Nick is different from his father, in fact, from me too. The innocence regarding sport has waned in Nick's generation, the players becoming as remote as rock stars and movie stars, their contracts and their ways, real or imagined decadence, too much the focus. Nick will probably never truly ache from his team but he wouldn't admit it if he did because he's seventeen now.

Yes, it's different now. Two years in a boy's life is ten in a man's. It's been a good year for father and son. They've grown closer, through the pratfalls of adolescence and through high school football. During the undefeated season by Connestoga High, where the son played fullback, the father probably became one of those fathers, though not in a bad way, mind you. "That's my boy" is something every man should say with a fulsome nod, even if it's about his daughter.

So it just made sense to take Nick out of school and pack him along. This trip that they share, particularly because it's a road trip, with other guys, guys whose ages are in the middle of theirs, marks the perfect conclusion to this stage in their relationship. For soon, Nick will be off to college and begin his own life with his own agendas. "A trip like this will never happen again," remarks Steve. "If we do it again, he'll be less a younger member of the group and more just a member of the group."

THE BAKER AND HIS BOY

A boy is busting out of his skin today. He's been the toast of the fifth grade at GAMP Elementary School all week upon sharing his good fortune and the elevated status in the hallway has been fun. But he can't stop looking at the circular clock the size of a hubcap high on the wall of the classroom. It calls to him silently, the way a candy bar does. He won't be here Friday so he's got about thirty-six hours left before the time of his young life, just him and his father, away on the road as two men, and the football game. Pretty cool that his first game in person ever is this game. No, it's beyond cool.

The boy learned of his surprise just this past Sunday, when he called his father at work to say hi and tell him that he loves him. Someday he'll understand how it came to pass.

See, the boy's father woke up in the middle of the night for work the way he always does when the song from the radio shook the sleep from him. The bread business is not a sleeper's occupation, not if you want a semblance of a life or catch the end of a ballgame. It's been a difficult time for him of late, splitting up with Roe after all these years, moving out of the house, worrying about the kids, how they're handling it. They're at a bad age for this, eleven and ten, as if any age would be a good age for this. He sees Santino and Gia almost everyday, spends good chunks of healthy time with them, but it's not the same when everything's intact and they're sleeping down the hallway. It's been months now since he took that drive down the Atlantic City Expressway to grieve the death of a marriage and cried from the first tollbooth to the shoreline. It's been long enough not to dwell but to cope. No, no, it's not the end of the world anymore. He lives with his mother now, which is fine because mothers in this neighborhood are quite doting and she's alone and could use the company, and it's closer to the bakery. But it's a shock to the system, being in your forties, your routine blown sky high, having left your house, your things, your space and your domain.

So he's in the car for the shortest of commutes, one of a couple city blocks, and he's barely thinking because nobody thinks at four in the morning when it's the start of your day. The radio plays in the background, some oldies station. The song is "Cat's in the Cradle," and, though he's heard it plenty over the years and he doesn't particularly like it all that much, he begins to dissect it. It's about a father who doesn't have time for his son when the son reaches out to him. Then the father grows old with the hurt of remorse in his heart and reaches out to the son, only to have the son tell him that he now doesn't have time.

The owner of a popular business, Lou Carangi is a quasi celebrity in his world. It's that way in the neighborhood when your place is a sort of hub, a daily stop for people, including some of those who work for the football team. He looks the part of celebrity baker, nattily dressed out of work, handsome and thin, with a full head of black hair and the Roman nose. Business is good, thank God, confirmation that he made the right choices in life, like before he had the business and he dealt bread to the casinos in Atlantic City and a neighborhood gangster offered him money to use his clean profile as a way in and he politely turned the gangster down by putting five grand in an envelope with a note that said rather formally, "Thanks for thinking of me regarding this opportunity, but I must pass."

Right now he has to fight the urges to chuck it all, sell the bakery and move to south Florida, where he has an investment property and some good friends and the possibility of "that life," you know, the beach and the serenity. He can rationalize all the way to A1-A, say what he wants, that he'll fly up on weekends to see the kids, bring them down during summers. Deep down, he knows what'll happen. He'll let a weekend slide, then two and three, and life will interfere and time will pass like it always does and he'll drift apart from his kids. Then one day he will wake up an old man and reach out for his children and they will be grown and they won't have the time or the inclination to see him and he will hear that song on the radio and it will haunt him.

It's important to note that at this time Santino is probably closer to Lou and Gia closer to Roe, which makes sense, as the law of gender usually applies during a situation like this at their ages. So on that iced-over early morning, exactly one week before the Super Bowl, he couldn't wait for Santino to wake up. He would tell him about the tickets and the trip to Jacksonville, just the two of them. It would be costly financially on both ends, particularly because he wouldn't be at the bakery on Super Bowl Sunday, a big day for pizza and strombolis and rolls for all of those sandwiches, because he is his best worker. "I'm thinking I can't leave the business, I shouldn't leave," he says. "But that song melted me. It's like the commercial: Lou Carangi at the bakery: an extra thousand dollars; Lou Carangi at the Super Bowl with his son: priceless."

Lou apologizes if it all sounds too corny, which is totally absurd, the notion of too corny when it comes to father and son, I swear, the devil's work. What's priceless is the memory the son will carry with him like his father's genes. Someday he'll recall fondly the plane touching down in Jacksonville and waiting at the carousel for the bags and driving forty-five minutes to the condo on the beach in St. Augustine, on the same grounds of the hotel where the Patriots stayed. There was a steakhouse in the complex, and he even ate next to some of the enemy players who were nice guys. When you're eleven, dinner at the steakhouse, being in the company of all of those men, dressed up like them on a Saturday night, glomming a sip of your father's wine, is memorable, especially after spending a cool, cool kid day at the NFL Experience with all of those interactive games.

Santino will recall fondly game day, taking the water taxi to the stadium at noon, more than six hours before kickoff. He'll talk of the bigness of the stadium and being in his seats and his father pointing out how the winds might affect the game, how David Akers, the Eagles' kicker, couldn't make a forty-five yarder on one end of the field and was booming them into the screen from well over fifty from the other end. He'll talk of how one of the best friends of Deion Branch, the Patriot's wide receiver and the game's MVP, sat in front of them and that was so annoying. The whole game Branch killed his team and he had to listen to those guys cooing, as though they were the ones out their on the field. The whole game, slapping hands, bumping chests, wailing, "That's our boy! Look at him, yeah, yeah, Deeee-oooon. Go, baby. Yeah, baby."

He'll recite The Meatball Story, how his father used up all of the juice on his cell phone trying to hook up a buddy with a container of meatballs flown in that morning on a private jet from Fort Lauderdale. That buddy was the Eagles' equipment manager, John Hatfield, who thought it important that Lou take his boy to the game and hooked him up with game tickets for face value. Lou thought it a nice gesture, knowing John's long day and his obsession for the meatballs at Martorano's Restaurant in Lauderdale, which is certainly reasonable because Martorano's meatballs are the size of softballs and might just be better than those of any apron-minded grandmother who buys her bread from Carangi's Bakery. Lou knows everyone at Martorano's, a popular celeb spot with strong Philadelphia ties, though none to my partner Steve despite some confusion over the years, and he knew one of the guys who works there was flying up for the game and had him bring three containers of meatballs, sharp provolone cheese, soppraset-ta and some bread. The plan was for John to run out from the locker room and meet the guy outside the stadium, with Lou the contact. But they missed one another from two-thirty until ten of six due to the maze of security. Two different FBI agents demanded to check the con-tainers and stadium security wouldn't allow their entry, so the guy finally laid them down on a curb outside one of the gates and went into the game.

In the end, he'll talk of the time he spent with his father, just the two of them. That's been the net good from all that's happened, mak-ing the memories, like spending the day swimming in the heated pool on a chilly day by Florida standards, his father waiting with a towel when he got out, then buying some souvenirs the next morning before they left, then telling the fifth grade at GAMP all about his journey.

The father, meanwhile, smiles an indelible smile. "With this whole thing, I've become that much closer to him," Lou Carangi says. "He's probably the closest thing in my life to me. When there's a problem, whether work-related or in my personal life, I rally around him and the love between us. For some, I guess, it's their best friend or spouse or parent. For me, it's him. I don't care if it sounds corny."

THE TALE OF THE TWO BUTCHES

I can see them now, huddled together by the elevators of the swanky golf hotel by the beach, Big Butch doling out the evening orders over the faint sound of chamber music and Little Butch nodding dutifully, a visual display to his father that he is paying perfect attention. Like Little Butch could ever fog out during a Big Butch colloquy, partly because he admires the man the way he always has, an unwaning, "my-namesake, my-blood" devotion. He embraces the soubriquet "Little Butch," though he is slightly taller than Big Butch with decidedly more girth, best described as powerfully husky.

You might recognize Anthony Buchanico without knowing it if you've watched the Eagles play on television. He's the mustachioed man entrenched to the right of the coach, gentlemanly trim, particularly for sixty, with blown-back salt and pepper hair and hooded eyes that dart continually from side to side, always on high alert. Throughout Butch's entire life, his job has been to be vigilant. It began when he was a boy, growing up the son of a numbers writer in the Old World neighborhood he never left, fearing those angry knocks at the door, and continued to the day he stunned his father and the hustlers on the corner and became a beat cop in a city that was a cauldron of racial turbulence in the '60s and '70s. He left the force as Sergeant Butch, decorated in medals and the kind of reputation every man with a worthy soul should achieve, to head up the Philadelphia Mayor's Office security detail for Ed Rendell. He remains vigilant as security chief for a professional football team, technically a retirement job, though it's absurd to call it that. The gig is twenty-four/ seven with more brush fires than San Bernardino in a drought, which is why I dubbed Butch "Mr. Wolf," the tuxedoed-Harvey Keitel character in *Pulp Fiction* who cleaned up dirty messes for the mob with an artful, Florentine flare.

I can hear Butch's booming voice: "You have no idea. It's the NFL, for chrissakes. Serious as a heart attack, this shit."

To most fans, professional football is an idea, a notion that you embrace, somewhat imaginary, at least what you think transpires behind the curtain, as though it's some otherworldly existence. From the howling coaches to the riotous players, they take on the appearance of mere images that flash before you, flat, fictitious characters that somehow don't exist as people outside of three hours on a Sunday and the daily sports pages. Even while you know otherwise from a rational standpoint, perception confounds reality.

So here's Butch now engaged in player bed check. It's one in the morning, the curfew Coach Andy Reid set for his players for Super Bowl Week, and it's Butch's job to make sure they comply. So, armed with hotel security, he will direct Little Butch to take the rooms to one side of the elevators and he will take the others. They will knock on each door, open it with a master key, and hoot something like: "Sweetheart, you here?"

The player will grunt something inaudible.

They will respond, "Goodnight, babycakes, sweet dreams."

While it all sounds so summer-campish, please note that the NFL's great boon has been accompanied by great contaminates. How easy it is to corrupt young men with raging libidos and swelled egos, with fast fame and quicker riches, with immodest ways and an armor of invincibility. How easy it is to attract the parasites, the social climbers, the swindlers and the charlatans, the ticket hounds and the memorabilia freaks, and the gamblers and the drug pushers and the harlots. How easy it is to attract a crowd, even if it's comprised by those whose motives are not impure; perhaps they are in need of their own fulfillment, however honest, however emotionally crippled you may think that is, or maybe they clutch the hand of a pie-eyed child. For Butch, a crowd is a crowd, and didn't the throng that greeted the team upon its arrival at the Marriott Sawgrass Hotel surprise even him? People lined the winding access road all the way up the driveway and through the lobby, and they whooped it Deep South Revival style.

Keeping order is Butch's primary function, though he also must play father hen to the players, priest and protector, keeper from mayhem. Before every season, Butch holds a meeting at training camp with only the players and he warns them of the pitfalls that await. He tells them in detail the places to stay out of and the people to avoid, and he makes it clear that if they break the law there's nothing he can do. He makes a point to stare into the eyes of the rookies and the younger players when he speaks, ever so colorfully to keep their attention. He is blunt: "Use your fuckin' head. If you're goin' out and you're going to drink and I know you are, get a fuckin' driver. Don't be stupid. And if you're driving and you're stopped by a cop, be polite. Turn down your fuckin' stereo and speak to him in 'yes, sir, no sir' fashion. There are some cops who would love to take in a Philadelphia Eagle. Know your surroundings! Know where you are. Know the room. If you're out and somebody shady buys you a drink, take it, thank him politely and walk the fuck away. Those of you who are single, be smart with the broads. You don't want to be My Baby's Daddy. Wanna see your paycheck disappear? Get a paternity suit slapped on you. When you're dealing with the public, wear your baseball cap right and save that jive shit for when you're hangin' with your buddies. Remember you're a target."

And before every season, Butch hopes that some of that message resonates, that it's there somewhere in their mind when a situation arises. And a situation will always arise. It's why he dreads the phone, especially the calls that come deep into the night. Yes, yes, they will come. Perhaps there's been a fight or a drunken driving charge or a domestic incident.

The job is a bit easier now, compared to when Ray Rhodes coached the team. While Andy Reid picks his players via a formula that includes one's principled fabric – though let it be known that virtue shall never trump talent – Rhodes took chances. He was lenient and laid-back, a fatal flaw from being a longtime assistant when it's your job to befriend your position group, and the players run amuck. Never was it more apparent than before the Eagles playoff game in San

Francisco in 1996. The night before the game, a group of players rented a limo and cruised a seedy section of town dubbed Ho Road and picked up two prostitutes and brought them back to the team hotel. Following a squabble over payment, one of the prostitutes claimed she had been raped. Butch, in his first year as director of security, was awoken in his hotel room with the news. After a nightlong investigation with local detectives, her story sounded spurious, especially when she urged Butch to talk to her pimp and the pimp mentioned something about the media. Sure it was a shakedown. She left after giving detectives a fake name and address, and police deemed the charge bogus. The Eagles lost that game 14-0, and afterwards the players hurried to the chartered flight to avoid the possibility of being detained.

After the incident, Butch made two immediate changes during road travel: No one other than team personnel would be permitted on the hotel floor where the players stayed and he was sure to keep a stash of what he calls WAM dollars, an acronym for "Walking Around Money."

So much has changed since then. In fact, an entire wing of the hotel is quartered off now, including banquet halls where the team will hold meetings and eat their meals in a cafeteria-style setting. The Super Bowl presented a more difficult challenge because of the enormity of the game and the swarm of fans, guests and media. Butch notified the local police the week prior to the Eagles' arrival and used a map of the hotel to devise his security plan, which included a daily police escort with motorcycles and a helicopter for the team to and from practice and media events. In fact, every time the team reached a certain part of the bridge that led to Jacksonville the helicopter would be at eye level. It helped that the team stayed forty minutes outside of Jacksonville and traffic was snarled to and from the center of town, which meant the players were just about isolated from nightlife and potential conflict.

There have been many infamous occurrences involving players during Super Bowl Week, most notably Falcons defensive back Eugene Robinson, a self-proclaimed Christian, getting caught with a prostitute the night before the game. During a players-only meeting, the Eagles' veterans made it a point to recount those stories and urge their teammates to stay out of trouble. "Don't do a Eugene," hooted Hugh Douglas. "Don't wanna see yourself on SportsCenter in the back of a police car. Say no to Eugene."

The only thing close to an incident during the week was an erroneous report that Donovan McNabb was spotted coming out of the gentleman's club. "He was sleeping in his room," Butch would say later. "I know, I saw him. He was rooming with Nate Wayne and I talked to both of them that night."

Butch is watchful. It's that cop thing. It's always close by with Butch. Once a cop, always a cop, especially a city cop. It's in you for life, something you can't delete. It goes beyond indelible memory. You can forget the mornings after a fifteen hour stint that you came home and stripped to your underwear on the front step because you didn't want to bring death into your house.

You can even forget that day the hysterical woman flagged you down on the street and shrieked that her husband had gone berserk and chased her out of the house with a butcher knife and you escorted her back to her home and the place was in shambles, broken glass littering the floor and blood smeared on the walls and every piece of their life smashed systematically: picture frames, smiling faces through horrible, jagged cracks, expensive china, lamps, dining room chairs, assorted knickknacks. And you tiptoed up the stairs with your gun drawn calling out his name and he wasn't there. You begged her to stay with a relative before you left because you just can't abandon the streets to stay with someone for a day or a week or however long it takes to keep them from harm.

"Whatever you do, hon," you said, "don't go back into that house without a cop with you."

And later that night you were at the morgue and you opened a drawer with a body in it because that's what you did to keep sane and you pulled back the slivered scalp with the long hair that veiled the corpse's identity (they always cut the scalp and drape it over the head) and that woman's face stared at you solemnly. And it didn't matter that you were a hardshell cop who'd witnessed the darkest of humanity. You went berserk and the tears swelled and you tried to fight their violent rush and you shook the woman's lifeless body and you shrieked, "No!

No! No! No! I told you not to go back into that house! Why didn't you listen to me?

Why? Goddammit, why?"

And you cursed and sobbed your way home and then hugged your wife, Joanie, a cask of innocence, without her knowing why. You can lock that all away, put the memories in a casket and bury it in the center of the earth. But it doesn't change the fact that you're forever changed, your makeup, every cell and life particle, forever altered.

Little Butch knows this. Why of course he would follow with great pride his father's path into the force. With Big Butch working long hours, always scratching for overtime, and having only sisters and a lovely, doting mother, Little Butch looked at his father almost as a mythical figure, part dad, part deity. When you're ten, your father always looms larger than life, and now put him on a horse, upright in his dress blues and leather boots, and the gleaming butt of a gun protruding from his holster, manning a corner on South Street, protecting the city from scoundrels. So it made sense that years later he took the police exam, though at the time it was simply to appease his father. Little Butch, who had graduated from St. Joseph's University with a marketing degree but without a true calling, had become another wandering youth, hustling the odd dollars as a club DJ and construction worker, sleeping through the afternoon, answering the late-night whisper of the street. Before any of this talk, Big Butch had sized up his son the way most parents do and deemed him a promising boy, capable of choosing a vocation free of red-faced labor, and what father wants his son in harm's grasp, anyway? Especially one who knows how wrenching the city-cop life is, how it plunges beyond the obvious danger, how it's an endless trek through sludge, how that hardens the core and desiccates compassion. I recall a recent exchange with another cop friend of mine: I asked him how his day went, and he responded in an eager tenor that he was the first to arrive at an apparent suicide plunge from atop a Center City office building in the middle of lunchtime foot traffic, and how the person's head had been severed completely at impact and rested along the curb by a parked car ten feet from the body. I think he used the word *cool.* I was taken aback momentarily. Such a monstrous way to view an ultimate tragedy. Then you realize there are certain professions where the only way to sustain sanity and buffer torment is to divorce emotion.

Anyway, Butch thought, there is nobility in cop work. More importantly for his son, there is stability in cop work. Later, after Butch Jr. graduated from the Police Academy in 1990, the twinkle in Butch Sr. would appear: Pride.

Damn, the kid reminds me of me.

Butch has four children with Joan, and he beams when he talks of them all. Angela and Monica and Joanna are his angels, he likes to say. But there's a special kinship that develops with your only boy, particularly when he's the oldest and you're in a house of women.

So how grand a gift to share something like this! Someday they could swap stories as men and as members of the same brotherhood and as two generations of Buchanicos.

And they would. Butch Jr., now with his own wife and his own four children, had risen through the ranks to become a Sergeant assigned to the Counter Terrorism-Homeland Security Unit of the Philadelphia Police Department. And they would do so over a glass of homemade red wine and sliced pepperoni and provolone cheese on a breezy late afternoon at the seashore, while the women enjoyed the beach with the children.

BUTCH SR.: There was that time in West Philly when we busted into a rowhome that hosted steep card games and we drew our guns and the thugs drew their guns and we stood there in a Mexican stand-off for what seemed like an eternity. Nobody flinch, I thought, or bullets will rain. I clutched my chest to make sure my safety vest was there, tight and secure. "We're cops," I said. "We're cops. Put down your weapons." Turns out, a rival gang had been knocking off card games in the neighborhood and they thought we were there to rip them off.

I was there during the MOVE standoff when Mayor Wilson Goode bombed his city. I was there during riots and I was there during shootouts and I was there during raging fires and I held the dead, and I held babies taken out of drug houses.

BUTCH JR.: I was there in the Tasker Homes and helped take down the Young Guns, a bloodthirsty gang that once killed a guy over a piece of chicken at a barbeque. I delivered a baby in those projects amid the sound of automatic rifle fire after the mother staggered out of the Last Stop Bar on 31st and Tasker. I took a gun off of an assailant during a firefight at four in the afternoon on 20th and Morris. I handled a robbery turned hostage job at three in the morning on 16th and Parrish. Two men were holed up in a Chinese store with the clerk while SWAT lit up the night with gunfire and I was wedged between a brick wall and a firehouse door. They were killed. I recovered $192,000 in a trash bag in a woman's bedroom shoe closet and seized $5,000 from Indianpolis Colts star wide receiver Marvin Harrison's alleged cousin and Harrison showed up at the station and was a complete gentleman. I think Marvin learned a bit of a lesson that day. When the Eagles hosted the Colts, Marvin pulled me aside and thanked me.

It only made sense that when Big Butch needed trustworthy help with the football team for a meager day's pay that he call upon Little Butch. To stand on a field that you once deemed an exalted stage and look through the thicket of helmets and shoulder pads and butte of flesh and see your son manning the other side of the bench of your childhood passion. How could you quell the rush of memories?

Football was always your sport. You remember when your father got tickets to see the Eagles play the Rams at Shibe Park and in the stands you were so captivated that you would watch any game you could when you weren't playing. There were those semi-pro games at the field near where you grew up and you would study each movement as though you were a choreographer. From then on, you would espouse the belief that football is the game of life, one that teaches you self-preservation, teamwork, patience, instinct, physicality.

You recall your own obsession, which was utterly comical. How you would watch the Eagles games with your son on television clutching a Sears catalogue – or was it JC Penney's? – so you could hurl it against the wall when the inevitable letdown occurred. How you would laugh with him over the Pumpkin Pie Story. It was Thanksgiving and the whole family was at your house and you watched the Dallas Cowboys play and rooted for them to lose because you held an irrational, blind hate for that team. Everyone's finished eating dinner, the soup, the macaroni, the turkey, so enormous and garish that even the dog got a taste, and you're in your recliner with a piece of pumpkin pie and the Cowboys' quarterback Clint Longley, the one-holiday sensation, throws a touchdown pass and you had a forkful of pie in your hand and you made that angry face with the pursed lips and shook your head and you look at your wife Joanie and she scolded, "Don't you do it. Don't you drop it." For a moment you think otherwise. Then you let the pie fly straight on the rug and stalk about the house muttering, "I knew it. I fuckin' knew it." And the whole family thinks your crazed and your father-in-law asks Joanie if you had a bet on the game and she shakes her head no and he shakes his head and says, "It's worse than I thought, hon."

Your son recalls that very moment and countless other times you would scream at the television and throw things and curse the ref and the coach's family, and look at him and say, "Do as I say, not as I do." Your son loved it that everybody thought you were unbalanced – yes, that's what they'd call you – and he understood you. He loved it that you would let him stay up until halftime of the Monday Night Football game to see Howard Cosell's highlights and how the next morning you'd write the final score of the game and a brief description of what happened next to his schoolbooks.

Your son recalls that Saturday many Decembers ago when he sulked because he couldn't go to the Army-Navy game, but you had detail for the game on your police horse and you called home and told him to meet you in the North Lot of JFK Stadium. You tied up your horse and dragged him by the arm into the stadium, right onto the field, told him to be quiet and to go along with you and then you made some sort of spectacle in front of the Navy cheering section at the 50-yard line. Something like, "C'mon you rotten little bastid. Let's go! Outta here!" Somehow you knew the Navy cheering section would boo you, deem you a true meanie cop for kicking out the poor scamp, and so you played along. "You want him? You got him." The good Navy boys motioned that the child sit with them ten rows from the field and watch the game and you went back to work, and retrieved him when the game was completed.

Your son recalls so many moments. How you led the second Flyers parade on your horse and he got to play big shot with his buddies standing on the corner of Broad and Shunk whistling, "That's my father. See him?" How you came home one day and announced you had purchased season tickets to the Eagles and you let him open the envelope every year and tear apart the tickets that came in an uncut sheet. How your ritual for the games went like this: You would leave at 10:30 with fried meatball sandwiches with fresh tomatoes and a hard roll and drive the short distance to 13th and Bigler, park (because you could do that sort of thing then) and walk to Veterans Stadium, and that time during the stroll to the game "things" were discussed, things like behavior and schoolwork. How you'd work the sports complex, sometimes the field for the Phillies, sometimes the penalty box for the Flyers, and you'd always bring him home trinkets, an autographed baseball or a broken hockey stick.

What your son, however, will recall in the future, long into the future, when you have passed and all that will be left are your footprints in this world, is how you sought him out during the End Moments of the NFC Championship Game, the one the Eagles finally won. The Sweetest Game Ever. How there was 40 seconds left and the outcome was known and you walked three quarters around the bench to the front of it and grabbed your son and you had tears in your eyes and you hugged him and you said, "Dad" – which is what many fathers from the neighborhood call their children – "we're going to the Super Bowl!" We're *finally* going to the Super Bowl!"

Andy Reid told Butch the Super Bowl might be a letdown. No, no, not because he could foretell doom. Because it's hard to better that moment of finally – (deep breath) – finally scaling that wall to the great wall that had been the NFC Championship Game, and doing it at home in front of your people. Every soul who was at Lincoln Financial Field that night felt apart of it in their own special way, and there was Butch on the field looking up into the sea of jubilation and being warmed by it in his own unique way. For while it was the players' feat and the coaches' feat, they all come from different places. By God, he was born into the notion of the Philadelphia Eagles, and after all of those years of throwing things at the television, he played his own little part in this first Super Bowl in 25 years. Even Butch Jr. admits that he has been wooed by other teams, first the Vikings long ago, then the Broncos, but that his father had always remained true.

The father wished he could have captured that moment in the cup of his hands. It's why he made sure he took that NFC Championship trophy and held it for the others, the families, his own, the players', the attendants that worked the locker room. As if to say, that trophy, what it represents, is all of ours, Butch Sr. made them touch it and cradle it and take pictures with it.

"It's like a group of snapshots," Butch said. "It's almost like when you look at a pretty woman. It's a series of snapshots. You're looking her in a way that you really see her. You're just watching her. There's something about her. You're slipping a million looks – click, click, click, click – you might fall in love. One look and you fall in love. All of those games, those memories, those moments, flashed before me. I felt in love.

"Of course, it was a fleeting moment in that I had to get to the stage for the ceremony. I had to get Andy and make sure he can get to the stage and that there's a chair on there and then I gotta dance him around so FOX can see him. Then I gotta grab TO and get him to the stage. I gotta make sure the ceremony is clean on our end. Everything happens so fast."

I can see them now, huddled together entering the elevator that will take them to the players' floor where they will commence with bed check. It will be a quiet night, thankfully. Just like the night before, the one that happened to be Butch's 60th birthday. He had to escort Andy to a news conference that day and then he met some of his co-workers for dinner at Jacksonville Beach and they had a cake for him. When he returned to his room, the coach had sent him a birthday package: a giant bottle of Ketel One vodka and three martini glasses. Two were empty, and a third one had olives in it and a pair of pantyhose because there was that time when one of the girls from sales jokingly asked if I wanted try hers on.

It's not odd that Andy Reid would do that, firstly because he's not as prudish as you might think, secondly because Butch is the great dis-armer of men, no matter their stature. I recall the story he told me of when, accompanying Rendell to a major political function, he first met Hillary Clinton, right before her husband's second election, and how he jokingly told her, "Don't worry, I'll get everyone in South Philadelphia to vote twice."

Without pausing, she shot back, "Butch, I'm from Chicago. Is that all you vote here?"

Months later, he would encounter Hillary Clinton again at the White House. He wondered if she would remember him.

"Butch! How have you been?" she said immediately, and kissed him right on the cheek.

"Hillary," Butch said, "you're the best, baby."

Rendell shook his head.

Butch Jr. will celebrate his birthday, his 39th, on Super Bowl Sunday and tonight they hope it will bring the gift of a lifetime. "I was at Broad and Pattison when the Phillies won and it was insane," Butch Sr. said. "I led the second Flyers parade on my horse. I was there on Broad Street the night the Sixers won. I was there when Villanova won. Nothing will top it when we win. Nothing. That's what scares me."

2
THURSDAY

It's raining Thursday morning in Durham, winter's reach south making it cold and hard, the kind of rain that begets sleet and sickness. The same storm that forced the early part of Super Bowl Week indoors in Jacksonville, except of all things the Eagles' practice is running up the coast. The weather matches the way we feel, sloggy from a long day before and too much beer and wine, and eating only snack foods.

"Trail mix," Vinny called it.

We arrived at the hotel in North Carolina early in the morning, enjoying the ride the way men do when they are in the company of only men. There is a freedom that comes with this sort of trip, especially for the family men. Hours of no agenda and good company always makes for a good time. So we played poker, and Nick, who thinks he's a shark because he plays all the time since poker is all the rage in high school these days, lost 80 dollars.

"Take his money," Steve ordered. "Kid's gotta learn the hard way."

We played video football, the newest Madden game that Bubba brought along, and played Eagles versus Patriots over and over. I was, of course, the Eagles and got trounced. Bubba and Dave, the late twenty-somethings who took their act from the movie *Swingers*, were the most prolific. Boo, too, fared well, which is not surprising because we used to have Madden wars on the old Sega-Genesis system in the basement of his first house on Latimer Street in Center City and he kept the hobby as a way to unwind after work. In our twenties, we'd hunker down there when Boo's wife, Emily, was out, order pizzas, drink Heineken and smoke cigarettes which we technically weren't allowed to do in the house. Now, in the basement of his sprawling home in Delaware County, he plays with his son, Joseph, a funny sight because Boo, whom we also call Big Boy because he's 6 feet 2, and goes 250 pounds, sits in the too-small chair next to his small boy and urges him to shoot down the alien spaceship in the Star Wars game.

With Dave having relieved Bubba from behind the wheel, Bubba was free to roam and have a beer, and so we thought only natural to pit Boo and Bubba in a one-time only, steel-cage chugging match. Boo likes to swank over his younger days at Lycoming College how he was the anchor of his fraternity beer swilling team. Over the years, for our own amusement, we would goad Boo into downing a beer or two, which was actually a very impressive stunt. In a matter of seconds, and maybe two gulps, the contents would disappear into his gullet and he would scrunch the can with his hand.

Oh, the byproducts of higher education.

Of course, Bubba, with his enormous size, boasts a similar prowess. Plus, he says, he's closer to his Temple days than Boo of his Temple Law days by about 7 years. A good heavyweight bout indeed, and we each pick our man in the race, because men love competition, no matter what the competition. Bubba appears to win a close call, but like with any competition among men, there is a dispute. Bubba began gulping before "go." So now it's one more for the beer belt, and this time, Boo wins rather handily. Bubba prattles on with some excuse, but concedes the championship title.

Mostly, we did on the ride what men do in each other's company: break balls and tell stories. Bubba got it over his size, Skinny Dave, whom we also call Zworkin, the character he plays in his weekly Dungeons and Dragons game, over of his geek tendencies, Vinny over his handheld Global Positioning System. Chances are if Vinny is not in the conversation he's immersed in his GPS, offering constant updates on our ETA or little known geographical facts. Meanwhile, Joey, whom I call the Style Guy, a play on the columnist for Gentleman's Quarterly magazine, because he's got the exquisite taste of a fine gentleman, which belies his modest upbringing, brought one thing with him other than his overnight bag: wine glasses. Heaven forbid we drink out of water glasses by the sink, or worse yet, plastic, which reminded me of the scene from *The Pope of Greenwich Village* when Paulie, after getting his cousin, Charlie, or more phonetically, "Cholly," fired from their restaurant gigs for getting Walter The Cook drunk and backdoor dealing entrees, held up a bottle and two tumblers, and said, "Hey, Chalooch, let's drink some cognac and watch the sun come up like gentlemen." That was always our favorite movie, though I usually played the role of the eccentric Paulie, played by Eric Roberts, while Joey was the pressed and cool Mickey Rourke character.

The fabric of conversation on any guys' trip is either music or quoting movie lines. Most women do not understand how we can watch the same film, or parts of the same film, again and again. Our television habits are that of a child at an amusement park. If there is not a suitable sporting event to watch, we employ the click-and-stick method, which is thumb through the channels at warp speed until we find the gem that washes away our glazed look. It could take 3 minutes or 30 and a three-time run through the 500 channels, until finally, say, up pops *Pulp Fiction*, right at the part where Butch and Marcellus Wallace encounter the hillbillies in a creepy basement and Marcellus is saying how he's about to go "to work on the Holmes here with a pair of pliers and a blowtorch," or any point of any of the *Godfather* movies, even "Three," and know that we refer to the films separately and singularly as, "One," "Two" or "Three." I must say that Steve does an excellent Frankie Five Angels.

Steve is not in the mood to entertain this morning. Wine and cigars, of which Steve freely consumed, as if in spite, only dulls a virus for so long. The next day it flares back angrily, with twice the symptoms. So Steve looks the color of a newspaper found in the attic and he moves in slow, creaky motion and he has this sort of pudding face, which gently forces a half smile to greet the perky hotel staff that greets us like visiting dignitaries. "Darlin'" type girls in their twenties they are, with genuine smiles, all wearing their nametags on Eagles' shirts. They have decorated the common lobby area from which we will broadcast our show. It has a cozy, chalet feel, with its comfy couch set, brick finish and fireplace with large mantle that holds coffee and cakes and sodas and a cheese plate. There is a "Welcome Eagles Fans" banner that spans the entire room. Green and white ribbons drape from the ceiling.

The room fills rather quickly with onlookers, most of them Philadelphia expatriates who found out we were in Raleigh from their friends or relatives. If you must leave Philly, Raleigh-Durham is a fine place to settle with its lush green landscape and mostly temperate weather and affordable housing. It's the Shallow South, just north enough to welcome Northerners, and its three universities, Duke, North Carolina and North Carolina State, all within a few miles on Tobacco Road, provide some culture, meaning there's more to do than just the Multiplex. One onlooker, an emergency room doctor at Duke, is a Duke grad, and it made sense for him to stay. Originally from South Jersey, he misses home and we provide a taste of it, and, forgive me, a much better one than the cheesesteaks the hotel put out for complimentary hors d'oeuvres. Though a sweet and valiant effort, nothing kills a cheesesteak worse than some strange, mayonnaise-based dressing. The doctor, probably in his mid-thirties, wears his Eagles jersey tucked into his jeans. I don't have the heart to tell him that is major violation for jersey wearers. All the while, Steve is melting into his high-back chair. The doctor feels good that he can examine Steve and write him a prescription and do his part to save the day.

Steve tells himself it's a good omen that he's this sick, the way he was 45 years ago when the Eagles last won a title. I tell Steve he should fill that prescription and leave the show early and rest. Later, Steve would tell me he honestly thought he wasn't going to make it to Jacksonville and that his plan was to catch the RV on the way back home.

The show moves quickly, as it always does when the town is swept up. Some days, usually in the summer, when everyone is at the shore and the Phillies are floundering and football training camp is still weeks away and the phone board is dark and I really have nothing to say, five hours can feel an eternity, though, truthfully, it never really feels like work. And when it's like this? I feel, somewhat undeserving.

Three o'clock arrives before I can stop it and we have some time to kill before we head back on the road. Bubba sent the RV out to be detailed at a place near the hotel. Eight guys in close quarters for eight hours with beer and wine and cigars on a bumpy road can reek up an RV.

THE GUYS: THINK DINER

We are now just four lifelong friends lounging in a hotel room in North Carolina. The hotel is made for extended stays so the room is really a two-bedroom, two-bath apartment with a full kitchen and living room, furnished for business comfort, very practical, very relaxing. The window looks out on the leafy grounds of the hotel, and I think I can easily stay here for a month and write. I'm sprawled on the couch, while Vinny and Boo sit in the adjacent armchairs and Joey leans on the counter of the nearby kitchen. Joey talks of cooking steaks for dinner, which would be an excuse to open the one really good bottle of wine that my buddy who owns Traino's Wine and Spirits with his brother in Jersey stocked for us. I am overwhelmed by a sense of déjà vu, though it's probably not really déjà vu because we have spent so many moments like this one over the years.

So many years now, it hits me, because we are talking about one of the many trips we've taken before, a ski trip in the Catskills, and Boo says it was the year U2 released "Achtung Baby," one of our favorites, and Buster Douglas beat Tyson. It comes up that he's now been married for thirteen years, and that number gnaws at me.

"You've been married thirteen years?" I say.

"Yeah, cuz," he nods. "Believe it?"

Silence overcomes the room, as though it just dawned on all of us at the exact same time that we're thirteen years older. Time is a sneaky sonofabitch, which is not exactly a revelation. Throughout life, there are three or four moments like this one, when you wake up and it's been that many years. Funny how you never feel it as it's happening.

Yes, I remember Boo's wedding like it was breakfast. Actually, I really remember the rehearsal dinner, kidnapping him outside the restaurant in Joey's car, being loud, acting the fool, and Boo trying to maintain decorum in front of his in-laws-to-be, particularly Emily's father, an ordained minister. He's motioning for us to be quiet and Vinny booms for everyone to hear, including Emily's father, "Shhhh! It's the fuckin' Reverend!" And this reminds me of when Vinny and I were in the Vatican the year before and he's on my shoulders trying to see if the Pope is really giving Mass and he blurts, "Ohmygod, it's the fuckin' Pope!"

Tall and thin and forever boyish-looking, Vinny doesn't look like he'll turn 41 later this month. Long ago, while he studied engineering at Drexel University, he turned a part-time job loading bags into the belly of an airplane into a successful career. Because of Vinny, we all got jobs at the airport while going to college, mainly for the free flight benefits. It was our first taste of the world. Joey and I worked for Midway Airlines, and the first time I was ever on a plane was when we went to Chicago for job training. The charm of that trip doesn't escape me, as the first day we're in the hotel room we think the heat lamp in the bathroom is a tanning light so we set up the boombox on the lip of the tub and towels on the cruddy bathroom floor and lay shirtless next to one another side by side. It's the middle of a Chicago winter blast and every fifteen minutes or so we'd compare the skin color of our arms and ask each other, "Did I get anything?"

"Yeah, bo," the other would automatically reply. "You look dark."

While I left to pursue my dream of becoming a sportswriter, Joey nearly made a career out of the airlines, rising to upper management when Midway opened a hub in Philadelphia. He pondered hard a job offer of Station Manager in Los Angeles. The airline industry is volatile, he thought, perhaps too volatile if you want a family. But it went beyond that. A true born-here, die-here Philadelphian who appreciates this city more than anyone I know, particularly Center City with its vast charm and eclectic blend of Federal, Georgian and Neo-Classical architecture and all-around manageable ways, he would never leave, even for a short period. It's not in his blood, like it still is in mine.

Shortly thereafter, Midway drowned, growing too big, too soon, a pitfall of many of the mid-majors. Joey took the death of the airline rather hard, mostly because of the plight of his many co-workers who relocated their families. But he also found his path, as there he met the woman who would become his wife. She believed in him so much that before they were married, she invested a good part of her life savings to help him buy the children's clothing store he worked at all through high school. It is a small, delightful store with an always tasteful and never junky window front located on Passyunk Avenue, a winding city street with quaint restaurants and coffee shops, where old world meets new, and where our mothers long ago used to take us shopping to buy Easter outfits, topped with white leather shoes that always hurt my feet. The store is part boutique and part school uniform business, and has his flare and is a rousing success by the definition that it has granted him the life that he desires, one that revolves around family. We were out recently and I was telling him about a potentially lucrative business opportunity, and he responded, "That doesn't impress me." While my motive was purely innocent – I was only trying to share some of the happenings in my life – I knew what he meant. Success can be defined in many ways. For Joey, it's the freedom to be the best husband and father I know.

Meanwhile, Vinny chooses the single man's freedom for now, amid the loving coos of Armando and Edda who wish their only son would meet a nice girl and finally settle down and move back home from that godforsaken Wisconsin and stop flying all over the goddamn world. In truth, they are co-conspirators, providing him with a choice they did not have when they emigrated from Italy and a sweet homelife hard to duplicate long ago. Edda, a lovely woman in her late sixties who is more comfortable speaking Italian than English, still crinkles her nose at the thought of going to a supermarket. She makes everything from scratch, and what she doesn't grow in her small city yard comes from an organic market. Like many of the homes in South Philadelphia, the basement is a second kitchen, though it's really the primary kitchen, where Edda cooks and the family eats. The upstairs kitchen and dining area is primarily for after-dinner or morning espresso with a splash of homemade anisette and Italian cookies that aren't the cookies you know, their sweetness coming from either honey or cooked red wine. Edda's basement could be a bomb shelter. It winds like a tunnel, and if you wander into the deep end there is a storage area with jar after jar of tomato sauce and cured meats and sharp cheese and gallons of Armando's wine.

Vinny's neighborhood east of Broad Street to Ninth Street was predominantly Italian but second and third generation types, thus his upbringing was unique in that he was usually the only kid whose mother lined his pockets with hot roasted chestnuts to keep him warm while he played football. It's a world away from where he lives now in Appleton, where I first saw an Applebee's and the people are toothy-smile nice. They really possesses a sweet demeanor, despite the horrific climate, and they are good, hearty pro football people. Vinny fits in rather well there, though they think he is a bit of a kook because he's not afraid to be confrontational and he has this vein that pops out in his forehead when he's angry. And because he regales them with stories of our youthful exploits.

"Oh, you're Anthony," his secretary said to me when I first went to visit him, years ago. "You're the one who told Vince about the horse, right?"

I nodded, red-faced.

Oh, Lord, The Horse That Swallowed Its Tongue.

I was the young, foolish one who had told everyone to bet on that infamous horse. I found them on the corner of Gladstone Street, Joey, Vinny, Andy, Boo, Bobby and John, killing time, playing a game they invented, called Scab Ball, where you had to roll a pimple ball across the little street, over the curb and the cracked, uneven sidewalk and make it sit in a weeded box built into the wall. While attending Temple University, I worked as a stringer covering preps for the Burlington County Times in New Jersey, and my editor there, a wonderful newspaperman, was quite the sportsman, a real horse lover. Harvey known for his ebullience dubbed everyone "babe" and had a plenteous head of tight, curly hair that resembled a white man's Afro, received a tip about a horse running at the old Garden State Racetrack. The horse was a bona fide runner but had a penchant for swallowing its tongue midway through a race and subsequently finishing poorly, and Harvey heard that the trainer was going to tie down the tongue with a heavy string.

So I told the guys about my sure thing and how we needed to get to the track right away and how we could make a sizable score because The Horse That Swallowed Its Tongue was to go off at hefty odds. The story was so preposterous that it whipped them into a frenzy, scraping up not-so-spare dollars to bet. When we arrived at the track, I was to wait for Harvey's signal before we pooled our money and made a rather significant wager. With about ten minutes to post-time, I spotted Harvey rising up the stairway in mid-jog from the infield bearing a catbird grin. He flicked up his right thumb and hooted, "Tongue's tied, babe."

Big shot, I thought I was, sauntering over to the 100 dollar window with a wad of cash to choke that horse, which of course is what happened. The horse burst into the lead, clomping with renewed vigor, seemingly without fear of that awful fate of the tongue. Midway through the race, the horse held a substantial lead, and we rejoiced, though not like in Hollywood. In real time, it happens so fast that when the rope snapped and the horse slowed dramatically, the field catching up and finally passing him, we were flushed in a state of doubletake.

Where is he? He won, right?

The Horse That Swallowed Its Tongue did so again, and never finished.

Yeah, I told Vinny's secretary, I'm the one who made him bet the horse.

Over the years, I've tortured Vinny with my ways, from forcing him to pay 60 dollars apiece for two Budweisers in an exclusive nightclub on the Italian Riviera because I wanted to meet girls, to ridiculous competitive binges. One time I was covering a game in Dallas and he met me for the weekend and I invented some silly hotel swimming pool football game using a balled-up sweat sock as the ball and the bottom of our feet bled because neither of us wanted to lose.

That was a regular occurrence when I worked for the *New York Post* and just about lived in Marriott Hotels. Vinny travels for free and the newspaper paid for the room so it didn't cost much. He'd meet me in the city I was in and we'd engage in bar games, mostly pool. We had a bet that the first one to win three hundred eight-ball games would pay for a trip to Italy. He won. I bought him a coconut drink in Costa Rica. In the room, we'd always play cards, usually cribbage or two-man poker or blackjack, and we'd play for sips of beer and we'd have these deep conversation about life's purpose, which culminated one night in a shady bar on Chicago's West Side when we conjured up a story about our group of friends being the reincarnation of the Apostles. We wrote our notes on bar napkins and laughed at them the next day. Since then, we've collaborated on a few screenplays and half of a novel and still cling to the dream of doing it full-time in the Caribbean.

I'd love for him to feel what it's like to get published. I owe him. Vinny drove with me to Chicago when I moved there at twenty-two with only a freelancer's gig and stayed with me for two weeks while I got settled. I had found this health club that offer extended stay, one month for 500 dollars. It was a dump that got raided for drugs short-ly thereafter. I liked it, though, because the basketball court was open all night. Anyway, I remember the night Vinny was supposed to leave. Vinny drove my car, an '88 black Cutlass Supreme (he always drove because he was four years older), and it was raining and there was a road that was closed near O'Hare Airport. I saw the ditch ahead but I didn't say anything. I figured he knew where he was going, though it was probably more the level of trust I had for him. We called a tow truck and got two six packs of Heineken and went back to the room, and I was happy because he had to stay another night.

Boo's talking about his brother Jimmy, who died suddenly after a hard life 14 years ago, not long after another of Boo's four brothers, Mickey, died from cancer, leaving four children. "He was a huge Eagles fan," Boo says. "We're at the Snow Bowl against Dallas in '89. Jimmy Johnson is getting pelted with snowballs and it's me and Jimmy in the seats and I get picked at halftime by Rosenbluth Travel to kick a field goal for plane tickets. I remember I said, 'You go, Jim.' He couldn't believe it. Kept thankin' me, tellin' everybody what his little brother did."

It is a wistful moment, late in the afternoon on a rainy day, all of us tucked away for a few hours waiting to pile back in the RV and leave for Jacksonville. I think of the other guys who aren't here. Joe Ben is nestled back home in Delaware County with his wife, Audrey, and their new baby, Sammy, whom everyone believes was named after Sammy Hagar because he's such a Van Halen freak, or Samuel Adams, because I swear Joe Ben is the only one who can taste-test the Winter Ale from the Spring Ale.

John is in California, about 45 minutes south of San Francisco, also with a newborn, a blessing after the heartache of having to bury newborn twins a little over a year ago. God, he's been out there forever now it seems, close to fifteen years. I couldn't wait when the Mets played the Giants and I could see him, and we ended the night at this Philly cheesesteak joint near North Beach like we used to do back home at Geno's. A burly, barrel-chested character with a football player's forehead which belies his job title as a Silicon Valley software executive, John loves his cheesesteaks, almost as much as he does the Eagles. He would have met us in Jacksonville but his teenage stepdaughter was going through teenage troubles and he wanted to be with her and his wife, Son.

Most of all, John's exterior conceals a truly blessed heart.

John played a year at Temple as a walk-on and fancies himself an expert, though Joey lovingly mocks that he's got pizza board hands because he dropped a big pass in high school. I may go months without speaking to him but when football season arrives I know I'll get the call: "Yo, bo, tell Andy Reid to run the ball more."

God bless Bobby, who's at home with his two small children, Nicholas and Victoria, who lost their mother almost four years ago. God blessed with him strength he never knew he had. One day, life is grand: you're the vice president of a bank and getting your master's degree at night, living the American dream with a house in the suburbs and two kids and a wife you have adored since you were nineteen. The next night you leave to comfort your sister and you return home and Lisa dies in your arms. We were all there the following day. The memory of it is fuzzy, except the anguish, deep and hollowing. I remember Bobby looking for plates and he didn't know what cabinet they were in because Lisa handled everything in the house, and I felt deeply for him. I didn't know what would happen to him and the kids after the immense grief subsided. During the subsequent months, he found Christmas presents in the attic Lisa had bought even though Christmas was months away, almost as if she had foresaw what was to be, he did what he had to do, working and making due, finding his peace only in a darkened movie theater. He'd take the kids to see the same movie sometimes ten times, at times only to nap.

God bless Bobby, who, with the help of others, particularly Joey and Karen, is doing well now, settled into a routine. He bought a summer home in Brigantine and he hasn't lost any of his spirit, which is the best way to describe Bobby, the kind of person you want to be around. He always has a smile, even if it's a devilish one, like when we were kids and he'd dart his eyes back and forth and you knew he was up to no good and you couldn't wait to find out what. Like when we're in our early twenties and we're at a theater in Center City to see "The Doors" movie and it's barely five minutes into the film and Bobby blurts, "Let's get out of here. Let's get quarts and go to the bridge." Nobody responds. On the screen, Val Kilmer's Jim Morrison is in the desert. "Exactly," Bobby persists. "What would Jim do?" So one by one we file out and buy quarts of beer and climb the gate and run along the walkway of the Ben Franklin Bridge halfway to Camden.

Bobby's partner in crime was always Andy, who's now in Boston, which is a shock because Andy never seemed the type to move away. But when Andy's wife Renee was offered a big job there just a few weeks ago, he figured it an adventure, particularly with his stepsons having graduated high school. I've always respected Andy's heart. He regards Renee's kids as his own, and will look right through a quizzical stranger's stare while they're trying to process why this thirtyish-year-old man who is doctor's-coat white and refers to the two black boys in their late teens as his sons.

We go back a long way. I can see Andy pumping his fist and nodding his head about now, as he says he loves the fact he'll be in New England for the Super Bowl. He likes to needle, and his needle is as sharp as his pointy nose. Funny, as a kid, his favorite team was the Los Angeles Rams, mostly because he liked Eric Dickerson and the swirling horn on the helmet and the shoulder pads and their the uniform colors, bright blue and yellow, which made them appear faster and space-age. Back then, in the middle to late seventies, when the Eagles were just starting to get good after years of dismal football, all of the kids had backup teams, choosing from usually the Rams, Dolphins, Cowboys or Raiders.

Tooch has always been an Eagles fan. Tooch, whose real name is Mike though I never, ever called him that, has had Eagles season tickets for twenty years now. He just can't release them. The first year of law school when you're thirty-eight with a wife and two of the most adorable little girls with wide eyes and forever batting eyelashes and a full-time accounting job is not enough to trump his loyalty.

I give Tooch credit. He's always trying to reinvent himself, partly because he is a restless man, always in search of the next challenge. In his late twenties, he left a decent enough mortgage job and went back fulltime to finish school, relying on Debbie's earnings as a hair salon owner and doing tax returns for his brother Steve. Shortly after graduation, he landed a big job with Crown, Cork and Seal, and I remember how nervous he was. This lasted only a few weeks, and once he got comfortable he flourished, and soon he had his eye on the next challenge. He wrestled hard with the notion of law school after the car accident, a nasty one where he was nearly killed. He always thought about it. But after what nearly happened, after a flash of how fleeting life is, he would leave not a stone unturned.

Tooch has always been one of those hypercritical fans, the kind who roots from a dragon's gullet, embodiment of the staunch Philly fan. Like many, he's never totally warmed to Donovan McNabb and Andy Reid, and when they'd lose a game I knew I'd get the phone call Monday morning on the way to work and he'd always begin with a scoffing, "Your boy…" Somewhere during the conversation he'd say, "My God, when you goin' to rip him? Don't let me have to Rush you!" This meant he'd flip the radio dial to Rush Limbaugh, because Tooch lives to break balls. The son of a former Philly cop and a traditional South Philly rowhome Democrat, he rages to the right, though I don't altogether believe when he said last November that he would trade an Eagles Super Bowl for a George W victory.

"In a heartbeat," he repeats.

I treasure Tooch's approach to fandom the way I do Joe Ben's, which is poster-on-the-wall and blame-the-ref benign. Joe Ben freely admits to being a fan and liking it. He'd prefer that he doesn't see the underbelly. Truly it busts his groove. For Joe Ben, it's so elemental. By keeping his head in the sand, he can be transported back in time to his tiny room on McKean Street when the players were bigger than life. Despite what he says this week, how he prays the Eagles will win and it's good for the city, Joe Ben is a bigger Steelers fan. Years ago, I took him to a Steelers playoff game against the Patriots and got him a seat in the press box. I used the excuse that with a tight deadline I could get him to run quotes for me from the Steelers locker room. So I gave him a pen and notebook and directions on what I needed. I dashed to the Patriots locker room and rushed back upstairs to write my story. I had been finished for a good twenty minutes, leaving a couple of holes to insert a decent Steeler quote, and he was still nowhere to be found. Finally, I see him walk to where I was sitting, totally aglow, shaking his head in amazement.

"I gotta tell you, bo," he begins. "Thanks."

Now that's great. I'm thrilled that he appreciates it, but I'm waiting for the quotes. Finally, I say, "Whaddya got for me?"

He stares down at the notepad sheepishly. "Um, nothing," he says. "But I got to shake Bill Cowher's hand while he was coming out of the shower. He was wearing only a towel and he was looking at me like who let this guy in there. The jaw was juttin'. But I told him, 'You're the best, Bill.'"

I have my head in my hands and Joe Ben says, "Don't worry, I took my pass off that said New York Post."

We talk about that moment for the fiftieth time while I'm over his house watching the Steelers play the Jets in the playoffs. His wife Audrey smiles like she hasn't heard the story fifty times either. "Go ahead," she says, "ask him whose picture he has in his wallet. Think it's me or the baby? Uh-uh." I oblige and Joe Ben neatly unfolds a yellowish newspaper photo of Bill Cowher from ten years ago. He shrugs.

Conversely, when I invited Tooch to have lunch with me and Pete Harnisch, then a pitcher for the Mets, we were driving in the car and Tooch blurted, "Pete, when you were with the Baltimore I used to ride you every time you pitched."

Harnisch didn't know what to say. "Sorry 'bout that."

"No," Tooch said, "I meant it as a compliment. You got me out of the hole a couple of times!"

I quickly changed the subject.

Vinny likes to tell the Tooch story from two years ago, when he brought him to a luxury suite at Lambeau Field for the Monday night game between the Eagles and Packers. He dressed in Eagles garb from head to toe and was hellbent on causing a playful ruckus, especially after a few pregame vodka martinis. The Eagles came back and won on the last drive in a thrilling game and Tooch wanted to gloat to the rest of the people in the box, many of whom Vinny worked with. "He was aggressive about it," Vinny laughs, "but they totally disarmed him. They were happy because that meant he had a nice time. They were almost glad the Eagles won because he would have a more favorable outlook on their town."

Tooch couldn't be disarmed when we saw the Eagles play the Packers in Milwaukee years before. I was living in Chicago, and the guys built a trip to see me around the game. It was the perfect football weekend, as we took in Notre Dame against Penn State the day before in South Bend. I covered the game and was the last reporter out of the press box because I wanted my account of that classic game in snow flurries to sing and they were bored and snuck on the field at Notre Dame Stadium to play football. When I finally emerged, happy with my youthful, overwrought prose, they were sitting in my car amid empty fast food chicken bags and dubbed me, "My Left Foot," intimating that the Daniel Day Lewis character could have finished writing before me.

So the next day in Milwaukee, while I'm in the press box, Tooch played the obnoxious Eagles fan (though he objects to obnoxious), swearing up and down. That guy in the Packer jersey deserved to get punched in the face upon the game's unfortunate end with a Herschel Walker fumble and Packer field goal to win it in overtime. "We were going back and forth with Packer fans in the spirit of competition but that dude went too far. When Herschel fumbled, he came down and knocked off my Eagles hat. So I turned around and crocked him. At the end of the game, he came down and put out his hand. I looked at it and I crocked him again. It was one of the best punches I've ever thrown. He fell back and almost knocked over all of the people in line to leave. Like dominos."

"The guy touched me, bo," Tooch insisted. "But it's always the Eagles fan's fault."

FRANK SALVATORE, 74, HUGE EAGLES FAN:
The Last Rites of Skeets

I feel badly for Tooch right now. Soon there will be a hole in his heart, punctured by death without mercy. For Frank Salvatore wasn't just an older relative to the DeAngelo boys, just a sweet uncle on their mother Lucy's side that they loved because he was of the same blood, some family guy who swooped in and out of their lives leaving a birthday bond or two. I tell you the story of Tooch, his brothers, Steve and Scott, and Uncle Frank because relatives become more than just holiday shareholders through the bond of football.

Skeets – as Uncle Frank was also known – always played a part in the boys' lives. He lived barely a block away from them in South Philadelphia and he never forged a family of his own, so he visited the house on Lambert Street often, usually for midweek, after-dinner coffee and cake. In the summer, he'd take Mondays off from his job as a city painter and spend long weekends with the family at the shore in Brigantine, and he'd watch Tooch usually on Sunday nights, often taking him to Atlantic City Racetrack with a wink of Don't Tell Your Parents. But when the boys began to drift into their own lives what cemented their forever kinship was the football team.

Skeets and Steve, the oldest DeAngelo boy, bought three season tickets in 1984, including one for Tooch, the baby of the family that included five children in all. So they had their weekly routine in the fall: Skeets and Steve, who had gotten married and moved to the Pennsylvania suburbs, would meet at the DeAngelo house, where Lucy, his mother, would be frying meatballs for the Sunday gravy. Skeets would yell upstairs to Tooch, "Yo, Mike! Wake up, you bum.

What were ya out all night? C'mon, let's go, let's go, let's go. We gotta game today!"

Tooch would run downstairs in haste, the previous night's revelry still on his breath and the three of them would walk the fifteen or so blocks to the game. Afterwards, they would all return to Lambert Street for Lucy's macaroni feast and talk about what transpired that day at Veterans Stadium.

They kept that same routine for years, through Tooch's marriage to Debbie and the birth of their two sweet daughters, through Steve's thriving CPA practice, through all of good and bad Sundays, right up until Sal and Lucy DeAngelo moved across the bridge to Jersey in '01. Through it all, Skeets never missed a single game.

Earlier this month, Skeets fell ill. His heart rate dropped frighteningly low and suddenly he became very weak, and he needed to be hospitalized. Now he couldn't miss the playoff game on the horizon and he begged the doctors to release him. The day before the Eagles played the Vikings, he got his wish. Before he parked the car, Steve dropped Tooch and Skeets off at the steps of the Spectrum, and Skeets, fighting his condition, stopped to rest as he trudged to the entrance of the Linc. After the game, they celebrated the victory over sodas and club sandwiches at the Penrose Diner.

The following week of the Championship Game, as winter raged, Lucy scolded Tooch: "He better not go to that game. It's too cold for him."

"Mom," Tooch said, "if he wants to go, he's going. We'll pick him up and we'll take him. The man lives for these games and this is his chance to see the Eagles go to the Super Bowl."

They never made it to the NFC Championship Game, the weather too harsh, though Tooch admitted more for him than Skeets. So they talked on the phone intermittently throughout the game, and when it was over, as Andy Reid stood on the stage addressing the delirious crowd, Tooch called Skeets and said, "You believe we're not there? We were there against Tampa. We were there for Carolina. We were there through all of those stinkin' losses by Randall. You believe it, Skeets?"

Frank Salvartore just gurgled a happy laugh. He was that kind of man, the kind who had such a pleasant way about him. Like when they would go to the games, and Steve would yell and carry on when the Eagles did poorly and Tooch would holler at Steve to stop because he made for bad team karma, Skeets would sit back and smile at them. Yes, he got a kick out of the brothers, and thankfully, he would say, we have our friend the anesthesiologist sitting next to us up here, somebody with some medical know-how, because Steve may have a heart attack.

For that moment, following the NFC Championship game, Skeets sounded like the old Skeets.

Soon, he would grow too weak. He went back in the hospital earlier this week with 90 percent blockage. The bypass surgery will take place Monday morning, the day after the Super Bowl. Tomorrow, Scott DeAngelo will visit Skeets in Hanneman Hospital and try to spring him for the game. It'd be nice for all of the brothers and Skeets to watch the game together. But the doctors will not let him go. Odds are, they will say, nothing will happen, but what if Skeets falls ill? Isn't it better that he's here?

Sunday will come and Tooch and Steve and Scott will be on the phone with him the entire game. When Donovan McNabb throws an interception, Tooch will try to make him laugh and say, "Where's Randall when we need him?" And Skeets will gurgle a happy laugh. He will feel badly that the Eagles didn't win. He loved them more than anything in life, other than the boys of course.

Monday morning will come and Skeets will be prepped for surgery and there will be complications. Skeets will not survive. He will pass away on the operating table.

His obituary will begin: "Frank Salvatore, 74, huge Eagles fan."

Frank Salvatore's lady friend of twenty years will pull Tooch aside at the funeral and tell him, "Nothing made him happier than going to the Eagles games with you boys."

Tooch will tell me, "I know everybody has a story. I know everybody is a big fan. But he WAS. All those years going down there, he never missed a game. Literally to the day he died."

THE LEGEND OF THE GREATEST GRUNT

The banquet room at the Marriott Sawgrass, converted into a finely catered cafeteria bustles with hungry men on this Thursday morning, supersized men who crowd the breakfast line panting, with famished faces after a full night's sleep. They brandish plates and silverware like weaponry and their eyes follow each steaming bin of food: bright yellow scrambled eggs, shavings of hashed brown potatoes, plump sausages, long wisps of glistening bacon, giant perfectly squared waffles, half-inch spongy pancakes browned on one side. Next to the bins is a table of fresh grains, a variety of sliced breads, bagels and muffins, and mini cereals, and then a table of fruits and a drink station with pitchers of fresh juice and water and milk and thermoses of coffee, and then an omelet station and a carving station with a hunk of roasted beef. Team meals on the road in the National Football League remind one of a sumptuous Mother's Day brunch without the linen, especially breakfast. Football players always eat breakfast. It's the carbs, a lifeblood prior to a taxing day of practice and workouts.

As we pan the yawning ballroom with the rows of long tables, the players eat in small clusters that resemble your typical high school lunchroom cliques, usually comprised by position. We zoom in on the linebackers, and there he is, Ike Reese, engrossed in conversation with his longtime friend, Jeremiah Trotter, who returned this past season to much glory. Ike has never experienced that kind of glory in the NFL, despite ending last season playing 112 consecutive games, the longest streak by any Eagle over a season. Oh, he's had singular moments of it but never the splendor that sustains, the rare kind that engenders an aura and fame, that forever changes how the world sees you. I recall a moment when we were together and a young boy approached him and he readied his ink pen and a creased, half-moon smile that declares he's an athlete who's approachable, and the boy said, "Excuse me, sir. Are you Donovan McNabb?"

"No," he responded sweetly, "I'm Ike Reese."

The boy shrugged, without diplomacy. "Oh. Is Donovan McNabb coming here?"

"No, he's not, big guy," Reese said. "Would you like an autograph?"

"That's okay."

The boy coolly turned and walked away. So Ike Reese shrugged, without deepening a sigh.

Yes, what can you do? It's your lot in the league, which is not to say it's a thankless one because you've sustained in this league for seven seasons and life is good in the league, but…ya know?

The reason he is wistful now is because he knows what the football fates have planned for him, mostly because of his lot in the league, which could be defined by the league as: Real nice player (nice as in "would you like a nice salad?"), terrific huffing down on special teams, situational down linebacker, great in the locker room. Whether it's entirely true or not, whether he has been typecast as the above throughout his career and that stunted his ultimate successes, doesn't really matter because perception is always reality in the NFL. Ike Reese's contract will expire at the season's end, and he feels it in his gut: he will be forced to leave the only team he has ever known and a city that he has fallen in love with, one he professes shall be his home for good.

Yes, professional football is a numbers game, a money game. Reese has done the deduction: the Eagles have four linebackers whose contracts expire at season's end - Reese, Nate Wayne, Keith Adams and Jeremiah Trotter - and they will look to keep only two. Trotter, the dear friend whom Reese dines with right now, represents the priority-sign, big-ticket guy and Adams, attractive because of his youth and salary, makes two. Thus, Reese has spent this Super Bowl week savoring each moment, slowing each experience to a pause and then a snapshot, as one may do on their first trip to Europe. He didn't care if it seemed corny to bring his camcorder and spend the flight down to Jacksonville interviewing his fellow teammates and coaches, a sort of video "sign my yearbook the last day of school" keepsake, and film the filmers as he descended the portable stairway to the tarmac. He didn't care if it seemed corny that he prattled on about the first time he entered the locker room at Alltel Stadium and saw the Super Bowl emblem next to his name above his stall.

"So many years of watching that game, growing up with it, that game, the biggest in all of sports, and you're finally there," Reese would say later. "Then for us. Can you imagine? All those losses at home, the Tampa game, and we finally got here. Even our coaches were acting the same way the players were, acting giddy. When I look back on it, the Super Bowl was really more then I thought it'd be. I couldn't wait everyday to get up and go to meetings, to go to practice, to watch the news later that night and see that we were the lead story.

"I collected so much stuff so I could hold on to that. I bought all kinds of souvenirs. Regardless of the outcome of that game, I was on that stage, the Super Bowl, performing. That was worth going through all of that. That game, that day, all seemed like a minute of time. I remember I cried after the Carolina game. I was a slobbering fool."

He recounted a conversation he had with his wife, Renee.

"You were a mess," she said.

"Baby, you don't understand. You know how hard it is to get back? Four years in row? It's almost unheard of."

"Still, you were a mess."

But he is feeling pensive now, terribly melancholy. Because it's already Thursday, the week flying by the way vacation does and no matter how hard he tries you can't hogtie time, and the next thing he knows he'll be huffing down the field on the opening kickoff amid all of those collective flashbulbs and then he'll be on the flight home with no sleep and right over to the NovaCare Center cleaning out his locker for the last time.

Because it'll be the last Thursday he'll sit across from his friend Jeremiah Trotter at the team breakfast and gossip about the game on Sunday. Because it'll be the last time he dresses with those guys who were his blood and sweat brothers. Because it'll be the last time he slips on that jersey, his jersey for the past seven years, which now might as well be a body tattoo. Because nobody really likes change.

There is a moment they share during breakfast, a momentary break in the conversation that comes right after they talk of their missing brethren, the players who began this trek to the Super Bowl that really started years ago, whom they feel are cheated for not being here. Brian Dawkins and Ike shared that sentiment a few days ago, and Dawk decreed, "You know, it ain't right. Troy, Bobby, Duce, they're supposed to be here wit' us." And so there is a momentary silence, both of them wondering the same thing: If the Eagles are in Detroit this weekend next year, will guys be saying that about me?

"We looked up from our plates at the same time and looked at each other," Reese would say. "We had this connection. Same thought at the same time. We both kind of half-smiled. Then Trot lightened the mood by sayin' something crazy like he always does."

A story is only trite if it's not yours. It's only a cliché if you didn't have to slog through all of that anguish. If your 22-year-old father, a Marine and the picture of health, didn't die from a heart attack on a basketball court. If you weren't two at the time of his death and that tragedy didn't crush your mother and your family, forever altering everyones lives. If you weren't the second oldest of four boys and you didn't attend six different schools in the first grade. If you weren't shuffled from house to house of any relative or family friend that would take you, your mom and your brothers, or any combination, please. If you didn't have a permanent home and your own stuff, at least nothing more than what would fit with your clothes in a single duffel bag, and you didn't have to worry every night about being in somebody's way and so you tiptoed about making yourself shrink into a knickknack for fear of being cast out yet again and undertaking the same ordeal somewhere else. If you, your mom and your brothers weren't looked upon squarely as a burden, crosses in the flesh for somebody to bear and that somebody who couldn't wait to pat themselves on the back for doing you a favor and never letting you forget that favor.

Familiar as it may sound, yes, yes, The Athlete and His Hardship, Ike Reese doesn't deem his life story hackneyed. Of course, it doesn't feel like a story to him because that would connote fiction, and the reality is that both of his younger brothers are in prison today, one for drugs, the other because he shot someone, and he easily could be there, too. How even if he didn't wind up in jail, it's really a fluke that he's here this morning before a king's spread, down to the grapes that hug their vine. For Ike Reese, for this to happen, the perfect sequence of events had to transpire after he dropped out of high school to drop out of life, another Lost Boy, fast becoming a ghost lost in the nooks of Cincinnati. At that point, after he missed weeks of the tenth grade at a time, at one point 85 out of a 110 days, the principal of the school advised him to just leave. "Why bother now?" he told him. "Just be done with it."

He did nothing all day, hanging with the other strays, killing time, exploring petty crimes, testing how hard he could make his heart. If it's true that one point during our own evolution someone is sent into our life with a hand extended, Reese's seraph wore a whistle in lieu of wings. The man recalled Ike from refereeing grade school basketball games and he pressured him to play for the high school team that he now coached. Ike told him in that brash manner wayward teens speak, "Man, I ain't trying to play no basketball." But the man persisted, hawking Ike, pitching him salvation. Ike finally relented and enrolled in the tenth grade again and played basketball. He went to live near the school with Aunt Geraldine, his mother's oldest sister, and she made sure he got up every morning and that he got his tail to school, begrudgingly at first because Ike's brother didn't go and he griped to Geraldine, "Why do I have to go if he doesn't have to go?"

And Geraldine would scold, "Because you're the one who's going to make something of yourself."

So he went and he liked it because he played basketball and then football his junior year and he really excelled at football. He started getting letters of interest from colleges that spring: Boston College, UCLA, Ohio State. Oh, how that changed the boy's outlook. Just as he dropped his guard, embraced the notion of a path, a truly letter-sweater American one, the Ohio Scholastic Sports Association ruled him ineligible for the season because he repeated his sophomore year and an appeal petition was later rejected. To further confound matters that nice little girl he began dating shortly after arriving his new high school, the one that helped him assimilate to school life, was about to give birth to their baby boy, babies having babies, foot snagged in the downcycle. "I had no plan," he recalled. "I mean, I was crazy. I was happy to have a son and I had no plan."

So he got a job that summer and into his senior year. He worked at Subway, when the chain first opened, and he flapped lunchmeat. He could only work twenty hours a week and he made nickels and he felt himself sinking back into that old life, likely for good. Then George Perles called, Benevolent George of the Big Ten, the coach at Michigan State who believed in redemption and recruiting kids down on their luck, though the practice wasn't totally selfless. Perles believed in sec-ond-chancers and last-chancers because he thought they would bear blind gratitude, feel so goddarn indebted that they would run through snakepits for him, the fear of losing the opportunity for resurrection willing them on every play. "He was right," Reese declared.

Aunt Geraldine was right, too. She knew Ike was the one, from when he was a child, and she never wavered, even during his troubled times when he was a longshot to stay out of jail. She kept telling him he'd be his mother's only hope, the only way to prove the family and its future offspring weren't forever damned, the women doomed to a river of tears and unrequited prayers no matter how many hours they spent in church. Maybe she wanted him to feel the weight of that bur-den, guilt him the right way because she knew he didn't have a wicked fabric and he could actually feel guilt and he possessed something the other boys didn't. Sometimes you just have a feeling about someone.

So he proved truly a product of circumstance, a traditional late bloomer who needed a way, and so everything fell into place for him in college, where he played well and studied well and met the woman he would later marry. He made due the best he could with his son, Michael, whom I saw recently, now a neatly dressed boy of thirteen, a quiet boy who looks like his father, especially in the face, with pro-nounced features, a dark porcelain. I joked with him, and he shyly smiled back, and when he left he made a point to see me, shake my hand in a formal, traditional manner, and said, "Nice to meet you, Mister Anthony."

When Ike Reese looks back at his life now, it all seems to fit. How the romance with Renee came about early in his days at Michigan State and how it was deeply intense and how they broke up when he got drafted by the Eagles because it didn't make sense to bring a girlfriend into the NFL. How he responded when he signed his first contract, even if it was that of a fifth-rounder ("Man," he said, "I thought I was rich."). How he partied his rookie year and how the Eagles were terrible during Ray Rhodes' final year as coach and how it didn't matter then because he still couldn't get over that he was playing in places he had only seen in television. How college was one thing, playing in the Big House against rival Michigan, yeah, yeah, that was pretty cool, but Texas Stadium? Shoot, he watched all those Thanksgiving Day games growing up, and the only thing he took away from his school days was when Ken Blackwell visited his class in the third grade and he told everybody he met "a real, live Dallas Cowboy."

One day in his second year he had an epiphany. "I thought I'd never get cut from the team," he said. "Then a guy like Willie T[homas] got cut and I thought, 'Damn, that could happen to me. You're not on scholarship here. I don't want to end my career five years from now, on the streets somewhere, you know, one of those guys, done spent up all his money, nothing to show for it except the memories in his head.' I didn't want to be one of those guys. I was more or less like, Man, I have an opportunity to make a career for myself if I do the right thing. I try to explain this – there's more to being in the NFL than girls, cars, jewelry. When you're young that's all you see. I wanted to embrace the fans, be more out there, charity events, speaking events, going to schools. When I was a kid, I was always impressed with the United Way commercials. I knew then: I wanted to become a professional football player, not a guy who plays football."

In March 2000 he called Renee's mother and got her phone number out in Los Angeles, where she was attending grad school at Pepperdine, and he told her he wanted to build a life, a real one, and with her. "I told her what I was trying to do with my life," he said. "What I wanted out of life. I told her where I was at. How I had been thinking about her and I didn't want to be out there anymore. I told her I was serious. I became more persistent. I told there was no guarantee as far as my contract. I could get cut tomorrow. I told her the only guarantee is that I want to spend the rest of my life with you. That I wanted her to be my wife."

How he could check off that aspect of life. The next year he became a Born Again Christian. Troy Vincent told him he had been watching him from afar, how he carried himself and heard some of the things he talked about. "You know," Ike said, "locker room talk. You know, women. What I did with them. I remember Troy took me to the side and laid some real deep stuff on me. He told me, 'You will lead people. They follow you. They listen to you. Where are you going to lead them?'

"Once he got his hooks into me, it was over. I grew up a Dolphins fan. I loved Dan Marino. I remember when they drafted Troy, and I'm like, 'Who in the world is Troy Vincent? We need a running back. We drafted this cat out of Wisconsin?' He became an idol of mine. He brought me to a Christian retreat with a lot of athletes. I realized we all had the same problems. Problems with our wives, with our kids, with our families, handling all we've been given, being the guy who everyone in the family looks to for money. Like my brothers with their business schemes. They tell me, 'I got this great idea,' and I'm like, 'Oh, no, here we go. No, you don't.'"

Ike Reese will leave the breakfast ballroom and board a bus to practice, and he will momentarily shake that wistful feeling, losing himself in task. Later in the day, however, after an encounter with a group of fans near Jacksonville Beach, it will return. With that creased, half-moon smile that's honest, born from a blissful state, he will bid them farewell amid backslapping and half-hugs and they will trigger more snapshots of playing in a town that adopted him and that he adopted. It makes perfect sense that he fell hard for Philadelphia, after spending most of life in perpetual reposition. He discovered what home felt like there, the whirling finally having ceased, taking form in the house in Jersey, Renee and the new baby, Michael's frequent visits, their things. Yes, isn't it nice to have things? By things I do not mean expensive articles but the objects of everyday life that connote security and a sense of achievement, just having the setup of, say, the kitchen: The refrigerator with pictures affixed by a magnet from the local pizza shop, the drawer that contains the bills and the checkbook, the calendar board that wipes clean with a rag and has birthdays reminders and the baby's doctors appointments and looks like the one the coaches use at halftime without all of the dates.

He discovered roots in Philadelphia, and it helped the people embraced him. They got Ike Reese, the good grunt who would become another in a long line of beloved grunts, the ace special teamers, the defensive specialists, the muckers and the grinders, the fourth outfielders, the lathered leaders, the effusive kind who always hustled and howled heart to the people and paid homage to them and were grateful to play for them and grateful to play at all. If the people played football, they would all be Ike Reeses, huffing down the sidelines, the glamourless wedge buster or situational linebacker, whatever to do to win.

"I wanted to make a name for myself in the city of Philadelphia," he said. "I tell you when that light went off, I knew I wanted to make it here. I wanted to hone my skills on how I speak and my reputation as a player. I wanted them to know me, and know me as a guy that works hard. That's when I realized what the city of Philadelphia wants from their players. That's when I started listening to WIP, started watching *Daily News Live*, studying them, learning what they want from their athletes. Philly fans like the guy blue collar guys, guys like myself. I never considered myself a prima donna, a guy who's high-maintenance. So I wanted them to know I'm just like them.

"I play with emotion. I know they love that. I wanted to embrace that. This city is a profound sports town, a historical sports town. You know, I think it's cool to tell people I play in Philadelphia, that I'm an Eagle."

So surely they'd fawn over him, compared to, say, the star quarterback, who's always engendered a slight chill from them, who spoke to them through the media in formal sessions and said only the minimum, his guard up and sturdy, whose name was everywhere nationally, appearing in huge marketing campaigns for things like soup and satellite television. The quarterback just seemed further away from them, corporately out of reach, more fable than flesh, more NFL emissary than Eagle. In the offseason, he lived elsewhere, far away in a winter haven hacienda on a man-manicured desert. You can't get further from Philadelphia in spirit or spectrum than Arizona, which does not reflect positively or negatively upon the quarterback, merely defining his heightened stature. To the people, the difference between an Ike Reese and a Donovan McNabb, or any grunt and any star, is one you know and the other you know of.

Last season, Reese enjoyed a scrapbook season. He was the heart of Harbaugh's Homies on special teams, the regular nickel linebacker, a busy assignment because it seemed the Eagles always enjoyed a double-digit lead and the other teams were always throwing the football. He notched a few starts due to injuries and played very well. He made the Pro Bowl, earning the moniker Hawaii 58 (his jersey number), and he co-hosted a popular weekly radio show on WIP with myself and his good friend Jeremiah Trotter, regaling the people with insider stories from the field and the locker room.

And the people howled for him to start permanently, particularly after notching eight tackles and an interception in a defensive-piloted victory Nov. 21 against Washington, a hangover game after the previous week's prime-time walloping of the Cowboys; particularly because they like their linebackers leathery and robust in this town and they didn't get incumbent starter Mark Simoneau, whom they viewed as too light and too slight, whether in the middle like two seasons ago, when he was trampled at the goal line in the Carolina Title Game, or on the outside last season. Whether it was Simoneau or Mike Caldwell, another seemingly lesser player at weakside linebacker who started over Reese a few years back, someone has always stood in his way for the starter's job, though it's probably more a product of him being typecast, the good grunt, a rolebacker. Perception for a player in the NFL is difficult to shatter, and it begins with your draft position, and it's almost a curse to be really good on special teams, especially if you're a former fifth-rounder, like Reese.

Nevertheless, if you play long enough and you care that sincerely, eminence will find you for one twinkled moment. For Reese, it began when he called our show the Friday before the first playoff game against the Vikings, and Steve and I wheedled him into a vow, which when made over the airwaves might as well be in blood because of the propensity to look foolish.

STEVE: You know all those old sports movies where the Babe goes to a hospital to see a sick kid and he hits a home run for him? Well, Ant and I are both under the weather. Would ya score for us?

IKE: I'll get an interception.

STEVE: Hear that? Ike promised an interception for us!

Fast-forward to Sunday: After the Eagles squandered a scoring opportunity and the chance to turn the game into a rout as time expired at the end of the second quarter, the half ending on the lip of the Minnesota goal line with a 21-7 lead, the Vikings took the kickoff and drove right down the field. Score and they would be back in the game, dangerous and high on momentum. They pushed into Eagle territory when Daunte Culpepper tried to squeeze a throw into the right flat. The defensive play called for a center blitz by Reese, but with the middle clogged by bodies, he read the eyes of the Minnesota quarterback and floated back into the passing lane as Culpepper released the ball. Reese swatted it high into the air, followed the shallow pop and hugged the ball into his chest. As he left the field, he held the ball over his head and peered skyward into the stands, as if to say, "Here you go, fellas."

Ike Reese would help fulfill one more pledge that he made on our show: the NFC Championship Game.

"We're going to the Super Bowl," he proclaimed that Friday. "No way we're going to lose. Let everybody talk about Michael Vick. Let everybody talk about the last three NFC Title Games. Let all of the experts pick the Falcons. I hope they do. Because we're gonna prove 'em wrong. Book your flights. Book your hotels. We're going to the Super Bowl and we're gonna turn Jacksonville into Phillyville."

Later, he would address his atypical brashness, talking of a deep intuition, more powerful than a mere hunch. Something in his bones told him. "I just knew," he said. "I just felt it. Before a game, you usually get a certain vibe off your team. Well, we had this confidence going into the game. Nobody was going to beat us. The whole team felt it."

"I'll tell you what it was," he continued. "The head coach. He didn't blink. The cat can stare into the eye of the storm and it just rolls off him. That's what we got from him. He didn't even address the other championship games. He was entirely cool that whole week. He didn't let the player feel a chink in the armor or any sort of worry. I'm tellin' you, it's not overrated. The players feed off that vibe."

So when the final seconds bled away, the game squarely in hand, Reese picked up the giant bucket of Gatorade by the bench, and crept up behind Andy Reid and doused his coach on the wickedly cold night. After all of those wins, it was the first time in Reid's tenure he had ever been given the Gatorade shower, the traditional player-to-coach show of "love ya, bigguy" in the waning moments of a surefire victory. "I had to get him," Reese clucked. "He deserves it. He's never had one the whole time he's been here. Nobody talked about it. I had it in my mind the whole week. I thought, 'I've got to be a part of it. If the game is out of hand and it gets down to a minute or so, he gets the Gatorade bucket.'"

Ike Reese's premonition will come true. Weeks after the Super Bowl, he will wake up a free agent, a loyal man with no colors. He will call his agent and his agent will report that the Eagles are waiting to make an offer, if they make one at all, waiting on Reese's good friend, Jeremiah Trotter, to decide his future, waiting on Keith Adams to decide his future. The agent will report that there are teams interested in him, particularly the Falcons, a young squad in need of veteran leadership, that grunt who will show the others how you win in this league, and that it's best that he visit Atlanta. The Falcons will be hot after him. They will make him an offer, a good one, probably the last of Reese's career.

From a hotel room in Atlanta, he will call his coach who doubles as the Eagles' general manager and he will tell him of the Falcons' courting. He will say what he has to say, that he loves this team and loves playing for him and that he would prefer to stay in Philadelphia and end his career there. Andy Reid will tell him that he cares deeply for him and that because he cares for him he must do what's best for his future and that if the offer is that good, he should take it. It would be an awkward conversation, with a periods of silence. "With that,"

Reese will say, "we gave our just due to each other and said thank you."

Andy Reid will tell me that he "loved that kid" and he hates that part of the job, the frosty business of pro football, people becoming property. "Ike was always one of my favorites," he will say wistfully.

The next morning, Ike Reese will drive up to Suwanee, Georgia, and sign a contract with the Falcons. Shortly thereafter, at about 2:30, he will text message me on my cell phone, while I yammer on the air about the fate of Jeremiah Trotter:

its done. atl. 4 yrs

The following week, he will join our show to say goodbye to the fans. The phone lines will light up in succession, all twelve of them, calls from pensive people. One by one, they will pay tribute to him, convey to him how much they will miss him, how much he meant to this sports city, wishing him well in Atlanta, except when he plays the Eagles. There will be a caller whose voice cracks, and truthfully, I wonder if he's a prankster, a Cowboys fan in subterfuge, mocking the affair. After thirty seconds, it appears he is no charlatan.

"I will really miss you, man," the caller will say. He will stammer and hiccup emotion, nearly breaking into sobs. Finally he will say, "I...I have to go."

"Um," Reese will respond, not knowing how to, "I will miss you, too."

"I got to get off the phone," he will then tell us.

Later, Reese will say: "I had to get off the phone. I was about to start cryin' all over the phone. My wife said to me later that night, 'Were you on that radio cryin'?' She still lets me have it. I'm like, man, it moves you. These people talk from the heart. They ain't just talking. If you got any type of emotion that's stuff that can't help but move you. To hear somebody's voice crackin'? To hear them speak that kind of appreciation? Makes you feel a little uncomfortable, like who am I? I don't deserve that. Thinking about it now, I could get all blubbery. Man, I'm a football player. I gotta maintain my image."

It's all a blink. One moment, you're the captain of special teams, a spokesman and a policy maker in the room, sharing all of those hours with the others, blood-bonding with them through all of the failures and the successes. The next thing you know, you will be lining up against them on a Monday night, the first one of a new season, dressing in a strange stadium with strange faces. It happened to you, like it happened to the others: Willie T and B Mitch and Troy and Bobby and Duce.

"They wanted to go young and ride with Keith," Reese will say. "Cheaper for them to re-sign him. I tried to prepare myself. If you ain't prepared for it, it'll feel like you got your heart ripped out and stepped on. In my situation, here I am, I've always felt like an ambassador for everything they do. I don't agree but as a soldier in that army, it enhanced my professional career. I gotta chance to play in Super Bowl, the Pro Bowl. It hurts. When you become a disposable commodity of a team, it'll kill you if you don't see it before it happens. I saw it coming. I braced myself emotionally."

His voice will trail off. No matter how much you brace yourself...

"My oldest boy, my wife," he will say, "they had so much hope for me remaining with the Eagles. I can't believe it. Well, yeah, I can. I just said...I have to look back fondly. I have to keep those good feelings. I could never wish ill will on the team because those guys I considered brothers. I can't sit back and root against them. I can't start hatin' just because Andy and Joe let me go. I don't want to leave like Duce and Trotter the first time, all bitter. I'm singing that tune. I don't want to be bitter. I had seven years of good football there, the things we accomplished, the joy I had. I did what Troy told me. I was a big brother to the younger guys, Mike Lewis and Lito Sheppard. In my little undercover way, I put my flavor on that team."

SOUTH OF THE BORDER

So we're back on the RV by nightfall. We're hungry and we're tired of Trail Mix but we'd like to get some miles under us before we stop. By this point, we'd just like to get to Jacksonville. We map out the plan: Skinny Dave will drive the rest of the way through North Carolina – Bubba mumbles something about a speeding ticket in the state a few years ago on the way back from golfing with his buddies in Myrtle Beach and he didn't pay it – and then we'll find a decent place in South Carolina to sit down and eat that steak that Joey didn't cook. After years of abusing my body, I've learned one thing: you need protein on these types of trips.

Vinny goes right to work on the GPS to find a spot and he comes up with Peddlers Steak House just over the border and perfectly situated for us, right off of I-95. Skinny Dave follows Vinny's instructions and soon we exit into a splash of neon that bounces off the dark horizon, hooker hot pink and yellow, a sort of mini town that Vinny says looks like Vegas before Bugsy Segal got there. We follow the lights, past a 97 foot blowup of a mustachioed man in a sombrero, into a sprawling truck stop called "South Of The Border," which I would call tacky if it wasn't a truck stop. Since none of us are camper types who refer to the highway as the Interstate, we are surprised to find out later South Of The Border is well known to American roadbeasts, located exactly halfway between New York City and Disney World, where you can buy all the M-80s and rat chasers your pyromaniac heart desires and eight different back scratchers and four different shot glasses and three different mugs and say hello to the giant blowup figure named Pedro, whom they call a mascot and I call racially offensive. I mean, why not have him picking berries? A Google search later finds the official website that booms, "South Of The Border (or SOB, as it's known to insiders)" is a unique amalgam of Dixie and Old Mexico. At first you wonder what all this Mexican stuff is doing in South Carolina, thousands of miles from its natural habitat. But in a remarkably short time you'll accept SOB as Tijuana with the added benefit that its inhabitants speak English and its water is safe to drink." The website also boasts that Pedro is "the largest freestanding sign east of the Mississippi and you can drive between his legs."

The place is shadowy and nearly deserted, sans the few cars in the gravel parking lot of the steakhouse. A darkened Ferris wheel and some contraption called a "Reality Ride" hulk 50 feet from the restaurant, which is oddly shaped, and resembles a spaceship, rather fittingly since this is the type of place where you expect to find a UFO or at the very least people who say they've seen one. Here we come to find out the restaurant is supposed to resemble, in keeping with the slanderous Mexican motif, a sombrero. We are amused by the entire creepy scene and now we must eat here. It's kind of like the time Joe Ben and I stumbled into a Boston bar by the Wharf with two guys who had hooks in place of hands and just had to have beer there. So we pile through the front door, eight ravenous guys from up north following a football team, and we're greeted by long, suspicious stares from the few diners, as though we are the sideshow folk and this is The Palm. The dining room is circular and doesn't go all the way around, separating one side of the sombrero's brim from the other, with the kitchen dead in the center behind a diner-style cash register station and black velvet curtains. The lighting is poor, the kind born from too many burned-out light bulbs instead of romance, and the whole place has a trippy, seventies décor, with a tatty rug and glitter that glows in the dark on the walls and ceilings. The hostess greets us warily and doesn't laugh when Steve and Vinny make cracks about Pedro. She appears insulted. Boo's starving so he attempts to diffuse the moment. "We're Eagles fans from Philadelphia," he says.

She offers a blank response and walks us to our table in the smoking section at the back of the sparse dining room. The restaurant is deathly silent, uncomfortably so. At the table in front of us, a skinny man in dirty jeans and a plaid shirt with greasy long hair and a goatee, eats dinner with his wife and child I suppose. They don't speak throughout the meal, the man engrossed in his plate, beady-eyed and without expression, methodically sawing each forkful of meat. I catch him looking back at us once, a squinty glare of a glance that I return with a sort of curl-of-the-lip look that retorts, "Yeah, yeah, I know about you, pal. You're the kind with dark secrets. I'm watching you, sicko."

I swore I got wicked vibes from the man, and I believe that people emit an aura that tells the story of their soul, though I freely admit to having a pint or two with dinner and a mind's eye that is easily roused.

Of course, our table overflowing with food remains rowdy, as we poke fun at one another, especially Bubba, who orders the fried cheese as an appetizer. Our steaks are fatty, but they'll do. We feel rejuvenated. Steve picks up the check, and we pile into the RV, finally feeling like we are actually going to the Super Bowl. It doesn't dawn on me for five minutes. There's something wrong. We are not moving. Bubba looks perplexed. He turns the ignition key again. Nothing. His hands are slabs with stubby fingers. So this next time he tries to be delicate, slowly turning the ignition key. Still nothing.

"Uh-oh," he burps.

We are now eight guys hovered around the driver's seat, badgering Bubba with the obvious.

"Did you flood it?"

"No."

"Check the gas tank?"

"We just stopped for gas."

"How 'bout the battery?"

"It's not the battery. Everything works."

Bubba plays the accused because he's the driver. He raises his arms to display his innocence. "I didn't do anything," he insists. "I swear it." Now it's not funny. Something really is wrong with this godforsaken parlor on wheelers.

Great.

Just great.

It's 10:30 at night and we're conked out? Here? In the middle of a loony bin truck stop called South Of The Border? In South Carolina? Miles from a real town? I swear, 97 feet up in the air, Pedro smirks, "So you wanna mock me?"

Now, grant you, this is not exactly a major crisis. We're eight educated, able-bodied men with cash and credit cards. But still…

It's interesting when something like this happens how people respond. Bubba and Dave remain huddled around the ignition, still searching for an answer. Boo reaches for the AAA card in his wallet and tabs Vinny to walk to a nearby gas station. Steve calls our boss Tom. He mentions something about heading to the airport but quickly realizes that it's too late for a flight. Then he talks of renting a car for him and me and one of the producers, probably Dave because he's skinny, and the equipment. It'll be tight but…wait, if it's too late for a flight, it's also too late to rent a car. Then he talks of either a cab or commandeering a car, like the cops do in the movies. We are radio pros. Doesn't that take jurisdiction? After all, we must be on the air in

Jacksonville by ten tomorrow morning.

While Nick sits in stillness, Joey shrugs, and opens a bottle of wine. I go sit with Joey at the table and he pours me a glass. I'm thinking, but not really. I stare out of the side window and see a motel that I didn't see before, maybe 200 feet away, the kind that looks the color of a smoker's teeth and boasts free HBO and a honeymoon suite. I can't shake the thought that we've reached our destination for the evening.

Now we wait.

Boo and Vinny return with snacks and bottled water, but no news. The gas station is just a convenience store manned by a clerk who doesn't speak English. "We shoulda brought Pete," Vinny says, referring to his brother-in-law and our friend, a mechanic turned chef/restaurateur who just called and offered to drive down and pick us up, something he'd definitely do. "He could have fixed the RV and cooked us some penne."

About an hour goes by, when Brian the AAA mechanic arrives in his dusty green pickup. Brian definitely looks like he's from South Carolina. Though he's young, probably in his early thirties, he appears older, bald except for a thin layer of dirty blond fuzz, and he wears worn jeans and a jean jacket and walks hunched-over. He speaks like he looks, an accent born in the Carolina backwoods, barely audible and muffled. "Y'all have a dog in here?" he asks as he steps aboard the RV.

"We've got two parrots and some fish but no dog," Steve cracks.

Bubba does his best to explain the problem, and Brian barely nods. I gather he's a man of little words and that he's not a fan of Northerners, particularly the sorry kind who don't know the first thing about fixin'. He lifts the panel of the RV by the driver's seat and begins to examine the engine. After frequent trips back to his truck in silence, his body language suggests that he's not hopeful at figuring out the problem.

We hear the rumble first. Then we see the bright headlights, which appear dramatic in the darkness. Another Winnebago enters the truck stop, only much larger than ours, approaching slowly. Just outside my window, Steve and Boo start to hoot.

"Reinforcements are coming," Steve booms as he waves his arms frantically, marshaling the RV to halt right next to us, as though it's an airplane on the tarmac.

"No," I hear Boo say, "it can't be."

"The calvary is here!" Steve proclaims. "We're saved! By Eagles fans."

Upon further inspection, there is something amiss. The majestic flag that ripples from the side of the RV, like that of a ship designating country, is the wrong color. It's a deep blue, Patriot blue. The driver rolls down his window. "What's the problem, fellas?" he asks, his accent thick and nasally, distinctly New England.

The absurdity of the predicament quickly becomes apparent to everyone. The driver laughs a hearty, mocking laugh. "Broken down, huh?" he says. "Need help, huh? You need *us* to save you."

Steve and Boo are rendered speechless. The driver calls to his passengers, his accent growing thicker, "Hey, boys, a bunch of Eagles fans are broken down over here."

The driver, whose name is Mark, stares at our sunken ship, stuck limp. He looks the typical football fan in an oversized gray Patriots T-shirt that fans and hides his beer belly "Thing looks like T.O. in a cast," he quips.

Mark, who introduces himself as "Maaahk," steps aboard our RV. He sees the PlayStation on the television above the passenger's seat and needles, "Stop playing the version where the Eagles beat the Patriots and the truck will start."

He unfurls that same obnoxious laugh, which is getting a bit on our nerves now, and tells us how his crew left Rhode Island early in the morning and that they are stopping for the night and will continue to Jacksonville in the morning. It is as though we stumbled into an alternate universe. For while there are only six men aboard their expansive Winnebago, one of the guys is named Bubba and he's just as big as our Bubba. But we're whipped in the unspoken game that males play, especially male football fans. Not only is our team the underdog and our Winnebago as dead as roadkill, their RV is much bigger than ours and way more luxurious, with leather couches, a plasma television and a stainless steel refrigerator that has to be worth five grand.

Vinny jokes that we should play band of pirates, armed with honor, and raid their Winnebago. And seize it, just take it from under their grubby Providence paws, and drive it triumphantly to Jacksonville. Along the way we can replace that Patriots flag with our mini Eagles one, a parting gifting from a fan at Tony Lukes, that sits rolled up by the sink.

"Master and Commander," Bubba flexes. "I'll start with this guy and knock his lazy eye straight."

Mark walks to the back of our RV and picks up a piece of the bathroom door that fell off. "What happened here?" he bellows. "Figures Eagles fans would be in something like this."

Defeated, Steve shakes his head. "Welcome to Philadelphia, Jake."

While on the surface harmless, Mark would be the type you can take only in small doses, the kind who refers to his spouse as "the wife" and views a weekend like this as a free pass from his office job and suburban life to guzzle beer and go to strip clubs, who tries too hard to be a guy's guy, as though he's auditioning for a Coors Lite commercial. "At least you're not Carolina fans," he says. "We were at the Super Bowl last year with them and I remember the day of the game we started drinking at nine in the morning and they were all going to church. So we said, 'Fuck you, you're going to get rolled tonight.' You know, just in good fun. But they weren't any fun. They ignored us."

In fairness, Mark turns out to be a fine fellow. He asks if there's anything that they can do for us, and we exchange phone numbers, and the next day he called Steve to find out if we escaped South Of The Border and said they were going to turn around and offer to take us with them. While they speed off in their mighty Winnebago, Mark calls out, "Hey, jerkoffs, put the antenna down and it should start."

We put the antenna down. The RV doesn't start. But just as Brian the AAA Man is about to surrender, he toys with a switch along the foot of the driver's side. He turns the ignition key and we immediately hear the rolling hum of the engine. "Sweet music," Steve says.

"You're the man, Brian," Vinny says.

Brian offers barely a nod. "Yep," he mumbles. "Y'all got a short. Don't fool wit' that wire dow'nere."

Boo hands Brian a 50 that he quickly stuffs into his pocket. He gathers his things and hurries out of the RV without saying a word.

"Probably didn't like the 50 because it had Grant on it," Vinny cracks.

"Now Bubba, don't touch that wire!" Steve orders.

Amid our cheers, Bubba wheels out of the parking lot with authority.

"It's The Caravan of Destiny," Boo exalts.

3
FRIDAY

The Caravan of Destiny is a locomotive through the middle of the night, though to be accurate, the caravan is not really a caravan. We are one weather-beaten Winnebago with a faulty switch, and most of the occupiers have nodded off, all except Bubba the driver and Steve, because he doesn't trust Bubba to drive, which is more a reflection on Steve than Bubba. We lost our few accompanying brethren long ago, when we overnighted in North Carolina, and so the trek through Georgia is a lonely breeze. So much for Southern paranoia, which contorted our open-air invite to travel the roadways together into the act of compiling a militia for a dawn invasion. Earlier in the week, Butchy told me that word had spread through the deep South that a huge convoy of Eagles fans organized by the local sports radio station was expected to muscle through the highways. Butch reported that officials estimated that the convoy could swell to five thousand cars so they were on high alert, particularly the Georgia State Police.

In fairness, the travel antics of the fan base have became infamous in recent years, the Eagle road trippers, I swear, modern-day pirates in search of booty (literally and figuratively) and beer, unleashing their war spelling chant wherever they may roam: E-A-G-L-E-S. A select hardcore has always traveled with the club, especially to games within driving distance, like those against the Giants and Redskins, and rooted on their Birds in a rather collegiate manner. But the staggering numbers that follow this team now have been a recent phenomenon, beginning with a regular season game here in Jacksonville in 2002 through the playoff game in Chicago that January through the landmark Monday night game in Miami two seasons ago in which some twenty-five thousand fans trekked to south Florida through this past year with Chicago again, Cleveland and Dallas marking the popular destinations.

"I'll never forget when I first noticed it on the road," Ike Reese said. "Definitely in Jacksonville. We play here in this same stadium and it sounded like our stadium. I said to one of the guys, 'Man, you hear that? You hear everybody? Sounds like we're at the Vet.'"

So, why?

A large part of it has to do with the obvious success of the Eagles and the fact that it's now cache to follow them. Some of it is about the limited opportunity to see the team live with tickets scarce for games at the Linc. With airfare and hotel accommodations at an all-time low because of so many discount travel websites, sometimes it's actually cheaper to see them on the road, especially when faced with broker prices. People have also built their vacations around following the team, particularly with some of the warm weather destination games. For example, the 2005 schedule will come out this April and the plotting masses will bemoan the fact that the Arizona game will take place on Christmas Eve, spoiling their football/golf getaways.

The Super Bowl, however, is another story.

The Super Bowl is a pilgrimage.

JOHNNY ZAP, SOUTH BEACH AND SADDAM

Meet Johnny Zap, one John Dowdell. He is your classic Eagle Roadie, barely forty, married, just beginning a family, the kind of guy who made his flight and hotel reservations for Jacksonville in November, dialing on a prayer that there would be no Championship Game calamity this time. He put six thousand dollars and change on his credit card back then, some of it to cover the other members of his traveling party, his buddies, the other Eagle hellraisers who would certainly pay him back, right?

Johnny Zap, who is called Zap because that's the name of his pest control business, was on that Miami trip with his boys: Snip (his brother Pat, called Snip because he was never circumcised), Dream Job Quiggs, Tommy Guns, Bill, Anthony, Stoney, Dominic the Cop from Darby and Joey. They were on one of the infamous USAir flights to Fort Lauderdale, part of the unruly cabin, no doubt contributing to the mayhem, though, unlike one of the other flights that originated in Philadelphia over that three-day period, this one wasn't grounded. Oh, the many fans aboard received a few warnings from the flight attendants over their drinking and the continual howling of "Fly Eagles, Fly." It's just they were fortunate the pilot was a fellow Philadelphian who took the intercom before takeoff, mentioned something about protocol and then predicted the score of the game: Eagles 28, Dolphins 24.

The plane erupted in song.

In Miami, Johnny Zap and the boys easily blended among the legion, roaming Ocean Drive with their jerseys and beads and plastic cups of beer, hooting like it was New Year's Eve. The scene was not isolated to South Beach, the throng spreading throughout South Florida, from Fort Lauderdale Beach to Coconut Grove to West Palm.

At the game, they joined the legion in the parking lot with their multiple 12-packs and portable grills purchased at convenience stores, and hooted at the hometown Dolphin fans. Like most fans, they are a superstitious group and one of their lucky props is green troll hair, a sort of straw-hair wig that they painted green, and so they put it atop petite Bill's head and layered beads around his neck upon entry to the game.
And so those in the legion stopped him to pose for pictures and they referred to him as, "Yo, Eagles Troll."

By the end of the game, with the Eagles assured of a victory, the hometown fans having departed in droves, you could hear the chants of "Duuuuuuuuce" for Duce Staley on television resonating through Joe Robbie Stadium. "Miami was easy to take over," Zap said. "It was an absolute drunkfest. That was the week we caught Saddam Hussein and we celebrated with shots."

Johnny Zap and the boys were also in Chicago for the original Eagle Sortie. Because the radio station is a sort of town square, I recall some of the other roadies asking how they could hook up with other Eagles fans. I made a few cursory directives: Friday night, Harry Caray's, 33 West Kinzie, 8 o'clock. I figured at the very least one of the managers at the restaurant was from the Philadelphia area and might offer a little hospitality if any of them actually showed up.

Zap and the boys showed up. So did scores of other Eagles faithful. "We took over the bar," Zap said. "After a few minutes, it was clear it was our place. I remember a guy wearing an Urlacher jersey walked in, took a look around and walked right out, like, What the hell's goin' on? Forget this. We sang the whole time. I went over to the DJ and gave him twenty bucks to play the theme from Rocky and the whole bar went wild. I took an Eagles hat and put it on [legendary Chicago sportscaster] Harry Caray's bust. People were taking pictures with their arms around the bust."

Zap's account for the game went like this: "Next day we jump in our cabs and go to Soldier Field. We're all painted green. It's bone chillin' cold. I pull out some money and we get into their VIP tent for the pregame. I gave the guy a couple of hundred. Free food and free drinks, and he let us all in the tent with all the hard-core Chicago Bear fans. They yelled at us and threw stuff at us. But we held our ground and we stayed. At the end, we won them over, except one guy who tried to trip Quiggs and I punched him. So the Eagles win and now we're leaving the game. Our etiquette is that we don't brag or bust anybody's balls in the opponent's stadium. But this one biker guy, he sees us and he starts right away. We're walking in a tunnel now and he keeps coming at me. Even pushed just so much? So we went at it. I got the best of him."

The victory by the Eagles meant a trip to St. Louis, and so Zap followed dutifully, armed with an understanding with his wife, Jaime: As long as the Eagles go, I go, and I promise to act right, babe. So he sat high atop the Edward Jones Dome, right there in the last row, in the middle of the sea of Terrible Towels, and he hated the towels and he snatched as many as he could from the Rams fans around him, good naturedly he said, stuffing as many as he could into his pocket. "They were nice people," Zap said. "but they weren't real fans."

But Zap didn't go with the boys. He took his dad, bought him the ticket, paid for the airfare and the room. He loved his dad, a hard-working and honorable Irishman named Jack, the kind of guy who always had two hundred and fifty dollars in the bank in case the water heater broke. He didn't gamble, never cheated on his taxes and never stole cable television. A very good athlete for West Catholic in his day, going up against Wilt Chamberlain in high school, and an ardent tennis player as an adult, he believed in the sanctity of sports and if he saw you hanging on the corner with those no-good bums, he'd grab you by the collar and make you play ball or watch ball. Then he'd make you a big jug of homemade iced tea.

Two championships later, Zap took his father to the Carolina game. Paid a 1000 bucks for the tickets. The old man enjoyed watching the games with the oldest of his five children. He enjoyed watching Zap enjoy the game. He took it so serious, not that Jack didn't care. He loved the Eagles, too, since that Championship Game in 'Sixty. Zap thought it nice to be with him, especially after how they lost his mom Elenore, a heart attack next to Jack in the car, her head resting on his shoulders. Jack thought his wife was sleeping. Then he got home. She was sixty-two.

So they sat frozen in the stands that day, and Zap will remember every moment of the game huddled next to the old man. He will remember all the games he watched in his basement with him, all of the guys there, Jaime playing the dutiful wife, emptying the cigar ashes, refilling the chip bowl, Jack forced to sit on the lucky folding chair. One game, Jack asked to move to the couch and Zap stopped him: "Da, you can't. They're moving the ball with you there."

Zap can't watch television in his basement anymore, not after last October, when he entered Jack's house with the key he had and found him slumped. Jack had bronchial pneumonia and Zap went to check on him. He found him already gone, victim of a heart attack. He was sixty-eight.

Forgive Zap for wanting to blow off some steam here in Jacksonville. He will sit in the stadium across the river on Sunday with a buddy of his who also lost his family and say to him, "Bet the old men are proud of us right now, being here."

During the game, Zap will look skyward and say to himself, "Hey Da, how 'bout a little help down 'ere."

And when the game ends, he will rue the result and talk to Jack once more: "Fate slapped us in the parade again, Da."

THE SINS OF THE FLOCK

For a moment, forget Zap. Let's talk of fans embodied by Zap.

You know the rap.

You know how the sports world views these fans: They are the Evil Booers, d'eese, d'ems and d'ose dudes who drink too much, curse too much, complain too much and care too much. They are just too much, the whole lot of them, these soulless monsters, creeps, cretins, louts and unlovable losers who deserve every broken heart and every broken dream that the hand of sports justice has hammered down upon them with great vengeance and furious anger.

By the way, they say, did you know they booed Santa Claus?

And they pelted Jimmy Johnson with snowballs?

And they jeered poor Michael Irvin when he lay motionless on the carpet with a career-ending neck injury?

And they booed Donovan McNabb at the draft?

And they booed Hall of Famer Mike Schmidt?

And did you know, get this, they used to have a courtroom set up in the basement of that horrible stadium named after our servicemen? So many fights and drunks and fights between drunks, such rampant European-soccer lawlessness, they had no choice but to corral the offenders right there on site.

And, did I tell you, they booed Santa Claus?

Over the past week, in media outlets throughout the country, the Philly football fans have been a story, the perfect subplot and sidebar, and rightly so. When Eagles fans outnumber the Patriots fans by a ten to one ratio here in Jacksonville, descending upon this town with the fervor of those who trekked to Fatima, when the city has been without a championship for nearly twenty-two years, the football team without one for forty-five years, coupled with those infamous acts in history and since history breeds perception and perception breeds reality, of course they become a backstory of a rather unsexy Super Bowl with basically two plot lines:

Will the Patriots become a dynasty?

Or will the Eagles finally win the big one?

While one would never condone some of these fans' capital crimes against Sports Nation and society in general, their portrayal as a group has become oh so wearying. The birth of Booadelphia took place decades ago, but when the Eagles became one of the elite teams in the league, the story of the notorious Philly fans again found the forefront of the nation's consciousness. Even the demolition of Veterans Stadium, which many deemed the Third Ring of Hell, didn't stultify the stereotype.

Consider Green Bay Press Gazette columnist Tom Perry's take prior to the Packers' visit to the Linc two playoff seasons ago:

You know there will be some Packers fans who will show up Sunday in Philly. Some may paint their faces. Some may wear Cheeseheads. Some may wear Brett Favre jerseys. Some may die.

OK, maybe that's a bit extreme.

But going to a game in Philadelphia as the fan of an opposing team should come with a surgeon general's warning.

That is because, unlike Green Bay, Philadelphia is a mean-spirited football city.

The writer went on to cite examples of Philadelphia hooliganism:

1) Following a September 1997 game with Green Bay at Veterans Stadium, a Packers fan living in Connecticut wrote to the People's Forum that a fan swiped the Cheesehead she was wearing and tossed it to the lower levels, while security officials looked indifferently. "If that was not insult enough, they did the same to my 10-year-old daughter," the woman wrote. "All she could do was cry and beg for them to

give her back her hat."

2) The since dismantled Municipal Court manned by Judge Seamus McCaffery set up in the bowels of the Vet during game days.

3) The 1999 jeering of Michael Irvin after he was wheeled off the field with a career-ending neck injury.

Perry forgot the booing of Santa Claus. However, Christian Red of *The New York Daily News* didn't in his piece detailing the mood of the city following the NFC Title Game with the headline that yowled:

THE CITY OF BROTHERLY SNUB

On rough streets of Philadelphia, not even Santa Claus can get any love

"While championships have eluded Philly's four teams, there has been no shortage of fan coverage," Red wrote. "Yes, the city that once booed Santa Claus during an Eagles' halftime show has had its fair share of headlines devoted to fan "spirit."

After the NFC Title Game, after the city celebrated the Eagles' first trip to the Super Bowl in twenty-four years with bridled behavior, with a sort of hippie love, without so much as a burning bush, the reaction to the Philly fans' reaction was damning with faint praise.

Consider, John Romano's words the next day in *The St. Petersburg Times*:

> *In the name of celebration, there was concern the city might burn. Instead, it seemed to practically glow.*
>
> *Who knew? Who could have guessed America's most fierce fans would begin the day by weeping as a blind 11-year-old sang the national anthem. Who would have imagined this city of bad attitudes could joyously, and without incident, celebrate into the coldest hours of the night.*
>
> *Who knew Philadelphia had a heart?*

Meanwhile, Michael Wilbon, a wonderful columnist for *The Washington Post*, reminded all of the booing that greeted McNabb way back at the NFL draft in his take following the Eagles' victory over the Falcons.

Wilbon began:

At times the wind gusted to 35 mph, enough to treat a football like a Nerf ball, enough to sail it, hook it or knock it straight down to the ground. Yet Donovan McNabb kept throwing it Sunday, firing it with heat when necessary, daring to loft it with touch when that was called for. The Philadelphia Eagles fans who booed him on draft day in 1999 never thought he'd amount to much as a quarterback, and certainly didn't think he'd be the one who would deliver them from nearly 25 seasons of football darkness. They wanted Ricky Williams that draft day five years ago. Philly fans wanted a running back, maybe even Edgerrin James, but not some quarterback from Syracuse, not some kid from a school with no history of producing great quarterbacks, and certainly not with the second overall pick in the draft.

"It was a booing of the Eagles' strategy, of trying to build around a franchise quarterback," owner Jeffrey Lurie said in the locker room after the Eagles had advanced to the Super Bowl with a 27-10 victory over Atlanta. "There are other strategies in the league. But if you get the chance to build around a franchise quarterback, it's best to do just that."

They couldn't envision McNabb completing 17 of 26 passes for 180 yards, two touchdowns and no interceptions in dry calm, much less in sub-zero weather with the wind howling and the pressure of three consecutive championship-game losses threatening to strangle him and the entire city of smothering love. But that's what McNabb did Sunday to the Atlanta Falcons.

Wilbon fairly pointed out that the man who led the booing – Angelo Cataldi, my colleague at WIP – has apologized numerous times for the bus trip to New York with a group of Eagle rowdies called the Dirty Thirty, including directly to McNabb himself. I know Cataldi, an award-winning former Inquirer journalist and longtime staple of morning radio in Philadelphia, didn't attempt the "editorializing" as anything personal toward McNabb, and since the incident occurred six years, four NFC Title Games and many, many, many sales of McNabb's jersey No. 5 ago, shouldn't it have long since been buried? Also, given that the booing emanated from just a handful of people, is it fair to denounce an entire fan base because of it? And wasn't one of the reasons that moment stood out so was because historically Jets fans owned a monopoly on the Draft Boo, with good reason mind you? Other than perhaps a drizzle of groans over the years, I don't recall McNabb ever being booed wearing an Eagle uniform.

Now this today from columnist Bernie Lincicome of *The Rocky Mountain News* on the Eagles appearing in the Super Bowl:

The hard sell of the Eagles as overdue strugglers in the cruel arena of sports is a natural storyline. It may be the thinnest of scenarios, but it has some recent precedent. This is the year of the long suffering and the worthy, after all, not counting Lance Armstrong and USC.

As much as it would like to think of itself as the real-life version of its most famous fictional citizen, Rocky Balboa, or as football's Red Sox, or a pigskin equivalent of Phil Mickelson, Philadelphia is not.

Oh, sure, the Eagles have not won a title since the big game had no Roman numerals, which makes the math easy…The Eagles finally found a team it could not lose to in the NFC Championship Game, having sent St. Louis, Tampa Bay and Carolina on to Super Bowls. The Eagles were not challengers as much as donors.

It was so cold in Philadelphia on Sunday. How cold was it? Even the Eagles couldn't melt down.

Philadelphia had become the junior-varsity equivalent of Buffalo and Minnesota, who at least stayed on the bus all the way until the end. The Eagles kept jumping off early.

So, why not join the joy and root the Eagles home as the nation did the Red Sox, as it wept when Phil Mickelson leapt at Augusta, as it shrugged when Tampa Bay hugged the Stanley Cup, right after asking what is was for?

Philadelphia is not lovable. That's why. Philadelphia has never carried its losing with any style, any sense of participation in the agony. Sympathy was lost forever the first time Santa Clause was booed.

Philadelphia relishes its reputation as being tough on its sports teams. Hall of Fame third baseman Mike Schmidt said Philadelphia was the only town where the thrill of victory was followed by the agony of reading about it the next day.

It certainly has the credentials for sympathy. Since last the town won a title, Philadelphia has lost Stanley Cups and World Series and NBA Finals and, just this spring, the Triple Crown.

Remember Smarty Jones? Nice Philadelphia story. A city falls in love with a horse. A city that boos injured players, including their own, will be redeemed by a four-legged creature with a small man on his back.

It's one thing to be let down by Schmidt and Eric Lindros and Allen Iverson. But a little compassion, please, for the dumb animal. What was the headline when the beast lost the Belmont? "Smarty Pooper."

No, until Philadelphia can love itself, it is asking way too much for the rest of us to waste our affection on the City of Brotherly Love.

How is a Philadelphia Eagle like a possum? Both play dead at home and get killed on the road.

Go, Patriots, you dull old things. You're all we've got.

Because of such sentiment, Ike Reese felt the need to dedicate the NFC Championship Game victory to the fans with impassioned post-game discourse. "I looked at it like people are always trying to mock the city," Reese told me last week. "Going into the game, I heard some of the national pundits – 'Eagles are gonna lose again and Philly will be cryin' again and Philly merits all the misery it gets.' Well, I'm happy for the fans. They can't be called losers and whiners anymore. And look at the celebration after the game? It was beautiful. There were no mishaps, no burning cars. I loved the way the fans did it."

Now I do not mean to paint a portrait of angels with green faces who toss daffodils at Dallas Cowboys. They all aren't the second graders of St. Andrew's, Joey's wife Karen's class, whom she had call the show from the auditorium and sing the Eagles fight song over the radio. Yes, these fans have committed some unspeakable acts over the years, many that would make the world forget all about Santa Claus. Those who attend the games regularly can be rather earthy, spouting language that would wither a shepherd's staff, particularly toward opposing teams and those poor foolish souls rooting for them. Wishing to contribute to the cause as more than just spectator, many view themselves as sentinels manning the periphery. They are loud and throaty as a group, providing a menacing backdrop to a football game.

"It's brutal," Ravens coach Brian Billick once said of playing in Philadelphia. "There's no place like it. I've been in the league. You go out at the tunnel and they'll yell things at you, and they're personal. These people do their homework. You come out and they say something about your wife they've looked up. They know your wife's name, they know your kids' names, they're pretty brutal."

Part of it is the nature of the game. Football engenders this sort of behavior, and the broadcasts glorify it, down to the commercials. The image of the obnoxious fan dressed in his team's colors in mid-growl is burned into out our mind. Home field advantage is about intimidation. Is there any more validation to a group of fans than when the opposing quarterback must call timeout because nobody can hear the signals? Home field advantage is about a raucous dome in Minnesota with people in Viking hats blowing air horns or the Terrible Towels in Pittsburgh or the Dawg Pound tossing dog bones in Cleveland or the Black Hole in Oakland, with the inhabitants dressed in Halloween capes and skull masks.

In Philadelphia, there are no props. Just raw emotion. Just frothy devotion. Just noise and wicked words.

"The Black Hole in Oakland is tough, but Philadelphia fans would kick the hell out of Oakland fans," Billick said.

"I will defend to my death that these are good fans," Hall of Fame football writer Ray Didinger would chime in. "They've stayed with this team through some incredibly wretched stretches. They got mad and they booed and they never stopped supporting the team. Even while they were booing, they never gave up. They never turned against the team. If they turned against the team, they wouldn't be there. Some years the bandwagon has been a hearse. But the fact is they were in it, hoping to turn the corner and get better. It truly bothers me when people say these are bad fans. You can criticize some of the behavior, but it's really been a small percentage and shouldn't define them."

It's the curse of caring. Rarely do you have rabidity without recourse. The only place in pro football that matches Philadelphia's fervor without consequence is Green Bay, the NFL's version of Disney World, where kids still lend their bikes to players during training camp and carry their helmets for them to and from practice. The one true Bay is truly a charming town, a throwback town, steeped deep in football history, with a cathedral of a stadium and streets like Lombardi Avenue, Holmgren Way and Favre Pass, with convivial, collegiate fans whose biggest worry is getting the (change patois to Midwest nasal) "special sauce" right for the brats.

Yes, the fans in Green Bay have the bite of a puppy, down to their props, Cheesehead hats and Packeroni sticks, bright yellow foam tubes with Packers emblazoned on them, the genesis of the thundersticks you see at NBA games, though they make no noise. It's just another of the many Rockwellian towns of the Midwest with their Main Street and porchfront lemonade sippers, of significance only because it boasts a pro football team.

"The Packers are so much the identity of Green Bay," Didinger says. "People in Philadelphia LOVE the Eagles but Philadelphis is known for a lot of things, not of the least being the history of America. America became America here. That's not true in Green Bay. If there was no Green Bay Packers, who knows Green bay? It's got a cheese factory and a paper mill and a lumber mill."

Meanwhile, Philadelphia is a city, with all of the snarl of a city, without, by the way, the rich tradition of gridiron success of Green Bay. While the Eagles go back, the Packers go way back, back to the beginning in 1919, the birth of the league. While Packers have enjoyed periods of prolong success, collecting twelve titles, easily the most of any NFL team, the Eagles have won three championships, none since '60, one since '49, and will be 0-2 in Super Bowls, compared to 3-1 by Green Bay.

"The Packers have had three distinct eras of greatness," Didinger points out. "You had Curly Lambeau, then bellicose Vince Lombardi, who probably personifies football the most. So you had the Lombardi Packers, then comes Brett Favre, and they win it again. Those three eras set them apart from everyone in the league."

While Green Bay doesn't house any other professional sports franchise, Philadelphia boasts all four and it can't even rely on the other three to ease the sporting temper. The city is currently mired in the longest stretch of any with teams in all four major sports without a championship, a staggering ninety-and-counting sports seasons since the Sixers beat the Lakers in '83.

While the Green Bays win in football and San Antonios win in basketball and Arizonas win in baseball and Tampas win in hockey, Philadelphia must 'Next Year it,' year after year, after year, after year.

Forgive the folks for being a little antsy and hypercritical.

"I'm not sure you can win even if you win," Eagles president Joe Banner told ESPN's Sal Paolantonio shortly after the second title game loss to Tampa. "We had a discussion the other day, asking if we won the Super Bowl, how many days do we get before the criticism starts. We haven't won a Super Bowl, but we have the best record in the NFL over the last three years and played in the NFC championship game the last two years. When was the last time Philadelphia had a professional team do that? It's a long time, whatever the answer is. And I've got to go on the radio to defend us for an hour every other week? It's kind of crazy."

Banner had a point with his words, but he understands the testiness better now, especially now with the flock tossing bouquets in lieu of barbs.

WELCOME TO PHILLYVILLE

I am the first to fall asleep and the last to wake up, which is the norm for me. I admit it, I am a serial napper. I can nod off after a pot of coffee, the afternoon after I get a full night's rest, with the light on, with the TV on, in a noisy place, on a beach in direct sunlight, during any mode of travel, but particularly on a plane, where many times I've drifted off before takeoff only to wake up as the plane rolls to a complete stop at the jetway of my destination city, and I can do it in a matter of seconds. I also know this drives people crazy, like when Vinny and I were hightailing it from Venice to Rome in the middle of the night through massive thunderstorms, and Vinny said he'd drive the entire way and that all he ask is that I stay awake to keep him company. Fifteen minutes into the journey, sinking into the warmth of the small rental car and the sounds of the steady, rhythmic rain and whooshing windshield wipers, I felt my eyes drooping and soon flickering in the great fight, losing badly. Barely conscious, I did my best to hold a one-word-answer conversation for miles, before I exhausted "yeah?" and "really" and "I know" and that fake burble laugh, and Vinny caught on and I felt his stare bore through me. I opened the customary one eye and saw him gawking directly at me and not the road, his arms fully extended, two hands on the wheel and making this rotten-egg face: "You're a real jerkoff."

So now in the Winnebago, sprawled out on the sidebench, I am roused by a sense that we have stopped, then by a thud. Somebody kicks the base of the counter, and says, "Get up. We're planting the sign."

Before we left, a fan had given us a wooden sign enscrawled crudely in black marker with "WELCOME TO PHILLYVILLE," the catchphrase started by Ike Reese on our show. "With our fans? We're gonna turn Jacksonvillle into Phillyville," he proclaimed, and so it became the rallying cry, emblazoned on T-shirts and baseball caps. As soon as we passed the sign for Jacksonville City Limits, Steve had ordered Bubba to pull over along the side of the road, next to a desolate, weeded lot in the shadows of an overpass.

We disembark the RV under the cover of dawn, the sky turning from dark to a deep midnight blue buoyed by the day's first light. Skinny Dave smoothes out a nice plot of land on the edge of the road, and Steve plants the sign for all of forthcoming motorists to see with a squint. We stand there for a moment, encircled ceremonially, admiring the sign, suspending the ridiculousness of this scene (mature, well-rounded adults do not engage in such activity), playing along, thinking collectively: Back home, they would be proud. Boo flashes the look of a marauder who had just marked his territory, one about to be pillaged.

Shortly thereafter, we arrive at the hotel, which causes the staggering double take of whether we are really at the right place. The Ramada Limited is exactly that, a two-floor, L-shaped, no-frills flop stop, located in the shady northwest part of Jacksonville, surrounded by a pebbly lot and a horde of big rigs. Our itinerary sheet boasted among the features of the hotel: "…only five miles from Alltel Stadium and downtown Jacksonville" (via two highways, a bridge and snarled Super Bowl traffic, which made our daily commute begin at a minimum forty-five minutes), "newly re-built property" (re being the key), "swimming pool" (the size of a burial plot, with floaters), "walking distance to Walgreens, Wal-Mart and Winn Dixie and local restaurants" (Arby's and McDonalds) and that great amenity, the "AM/FM clock radio." Granted, I'm a bit spoiled by my days on the road, and while I don't require a cold compress and Bellini upon check-in, or my room furnished with a floral bouquet, I'd prefer one without ungodly stains and the knockout stench of mildew. I fret we've stumbled into an episode of "CSI, SKID ROW," and fear what I will see if the inspector shines that light across the skeevy bedspread.

Of course, this being Super Bowl Week, or Fleece Week for the locals, the room rates at the Ramada Limited have ballooned to 329 dollars a night with a five-night minimum. The Middle Easterner with the dour expression behind the reception desk said in broken English upon check-in, "Absolutely no refund. And we throw you out if you cause trouble."

CARNIVALE de FOOTBALL

The rain is gone but thick cloud cover remains, hulking over Jacksonville, hiding the sun and its warmth. So it's blustery by the river, freezing for Florida, even for the top of the state. But there is great activity on this morning, the town beginning to swell with the score of Friday arrivers. Here, officials have prepared for this day for months now, dressing up midtown like it's Saturday night, adorning the stately bridge that connects the city with smoldering blue and purple lights, polishing the enchanting Riverwalk, a winding boardwalk that hugs the bank of the river, decorating either side of the Saint Johns with streamers and banners, squaring off adjacent sections from traffic, establishing Head-houses and mini foot malls, and erecting tents, so many tents. Tents everywhere. The town is entombed in tents for souvenir shops and beer gardens and snack stands and especially party spots, designated for fans of each team, like the Eagles' Nest and the Patriots' Pen. Jacksonville is more Bible Beach than South Beach and utterly benign when compared to past Super Bowl hosts like Nero's New Orleans, and so the town had to breed many more nightspots with plenty of poles and canvas to quench the thirst of heathen football fans and entertaining corporate cronies. As the new slogan of American hedonism proclaims, what happens during Super Bowl Week stays at Super Bowl Week, unless you're Eugene Robinson or Barrett Robbins.

Yes, for most doing Carnivale de Football, particularly if they are among the non-partisan, be-seen scene, the game is what comes at the end of the weekend, when the mere thought of alcohol curdles the stomach. The trip is for everyone except the participants. I must refer to a conversation I would have with Eagles tackle Jon Runyan about the revelry of Super Bowl Week: "If you're playing in the game, it's not a fun week," he would say. "It's just another week of work. Everybody else is looking to party, and you're looking to get through it to get to the game. By Wednesday, I was tired of dealing with all that crap. I went out one afternoon: I saw my dad and my brothers and had lunch by the beach in St. Augustine. Otherwise, I never left the room. Friday night, I slept fifteen hours. Just never got out of bed. That was actually kind of nice."

Back in the moment, I see a man emerging from a tent with a great big fried turkey breast and a plastic carafe of Lite beer, and still more tents, rising I stand here into the horizon, with more food and more beer and games for the kids, football throws and face painting.

How utterly American. And how familiar. The scene propels us to another time in our history, right around the turn of the last century during the advent of Circuit Chautauqua. What began as a training campground for Sunday school teachers and later for the first correspondence degrees by Lake Chautauqua in upstate New York, Circuit Chautauqua sprouted into week-long assemblies for the masses all across the country, a way to unite community, particularly in rural and small town areas. A series of tents were erected for the assemblies, usually the bed of land next to lakes or rivers or in the grove of trees. They were more food for thought than county fair. They stimulated discussion of the era's religious, political, social and cultural issues with lecturers, many of them renown, covering a variety of subjects from current events to political invectives to evangelical assaults to comical storytelling to life in other parts of the country. There were also performances of classic plays and Broadway hits, and a variety of music, including Metropolitan Opera stars and local folksy ditties, and subsequently top talent traveled from site to site.

At its height in the mid 1920s, Circuit Chautauqua had reached a combined audience of roughly forty-five million people spanning 45 states. Before dying with the Great Depression, it turned out to be that generation's equal to television, linking the masses of a nation in information disconnect.

While promoters of each local assembly championed Circuit Chautauqua as the path to enlightenment and education, as well as self and civic improvement, and Theodore Roosevelt called it "the most American thing in America," it also received heavy criticism from the likes of Sinclair Lewis, who described it as "nothing but wind and chaff and...the laughter of yokels." William James called it "depressing from its mediocrity," and other pundits basically found it bread and circuses for the masses, the brainwashing and brain-numbing of the vast inferior sector of society. They cringed when the local townsman would proclaim in decayed English how Chautauqua educated them, in the same manner today when one talks of being edified by a historical movie.

I see this when I look about the tent that houses our remote broadcast, filling by the moment with revelers in the Eagles' jerseys and caps, thrusting their beers upward in a toast that would last five hours.

> *Fly eagles fly*
> *On the road to victory*
> *Fight Eagles fight,*
> *Score those touchdowns 1,2,3*
> *Hit 'em low, Hit 'em high*
> *And watch those Patriots cry*
> *Fly Eagles Fly*
> *On the road…to…vic…tor…yyyyyy*
> *E-A-G-L-E-S, EAGLES!*

TOM HECKERT - THE SON FINDS HIS PATH

Let us travel to another part of town, where the land becomes lush and expansive. Here on the grounds of the Jacksonville Equestrian Center, we enter a much different sort of tent, one of lavishness and Southern surfeit, where the Other Side of Football convenes cotillion-style, far, far from the beer-swillers and jersey-wearers.

Super Bowl Week is famous for its host-city bashes, featuring Hollywood hoo-hahs and celebrities, athletes and pinup girls, dignitaries and fat paper men, hobnobbers and whores and orgies of food and drink and music. Tonight alone, there are six, among them being the Maxim Party, spiked with the magazine's lingerie models, the Nike Party, the ESPN Party, the Grown Folk's Party hosted by Cedric the Entertainer, and the Leather and Lace Party inside Plush's Leopard Lounge, hosted by Michael Irvin. Tomorrow night is P. Diddy's Party, the Sports Illustrated Party on the beach and the most legendary of them all, The Playboy Party, where Hef will recreate the Grotto for the likes of Owen Wilson and Fat Joe, young Ben Roethlisberger and old Jim McMahon, who will wear still-silly sunglasses and spiked hair.

Now, now, we arrive a much different affair, for it's not dubbed a party but a gala for the civilized and the sophisticates. This is the Commissioner's Gala, hosted by league poohbah Paul Tagliabue, attended by the who's who of the NFL, team owners and executives, coaches and a few sprinkled Hall of Famers, the very wealthy and the very influential. It even wields a theme: "Under the Southern Skies."

Upon entry, a hostess hands each guest a flute of Tott's champagne, and soon the room will widen dramatically, revealing the rite of revelry of the refined. The entertainment, ladies and gentleman, for the evening will consist of a Ray Charles impersonator, a Jimmy Buffet cover band, *American Idol* singer LaToya London and a several-piece swing band. There is a laser show, and a woman dressed as a Greek goddess who squirts water from her fingertips, posing as a statue that moves mechanically, her exhibit entitled "Living Fountain." There is a another woman dressed as a tree, roosted on stilts with her face painted green, the only link to the other side of football.

Move inward, passed the ice sculptures and martini bars and libation stations stocked with the finest of nectar, to be had simply for the asking, and there is the main adult attraction: the spread, very Roman in display, cloth-covered table upon table, heaping immoderation, gluttony for every palate. Should seafood be your temptress, the raw bar offers a seven seas of delicacies: oysters, snow crab, sushi, shrimp the size of kickoff tees. There also sits a carving station with pink-middled slabs of tender beef, a Chinese-Thai station, which features

chicken satay with peanut sauce and a Thai Meat Salad, and a hunkering of Southwest fireside swine and the like, highlighted by barbecued short ribs and pulled pork for sandwiches. If dessert endorses your decadence, pastry profligacy awaits, as well as a sundae stand with three kinds of sauce and three kinds of toppings.

Please step through the to-do, for we

are not here to indulge but to find the man who resembles a boy, youth having smiled upon him, the one who was destined to be here some-day, as receiver not giver of all the glad hands. How could this not be his destiny? It's all he's ever known, from toddler 'til now. Forever at the hip of his football father, the man's life path was emblazoned by arrows and highway signs in neon.

Let us travel that path, back to Adrian, Michigan, county seat of Lenawee County, located about ten miles north of the Ohio state line, supported by auto-parts manufacturing, plastics and aluminum. Yo Adrian, with that quaint, turn-of-the-century feeling downtown, home of Adrian College and home of the Heckerts, Tom and Rose, and their two children, Kim and Tom Jr. Tom is the head football coach of the Division 3 Bulldogs, and the family attends every game, and Tom Jr. is enamored with his father's vocation. After school, he rides his bike to the college to sniff around the fields, wanting to gopher at practice, which makes perfect sense for a coach's kid. But then he is unnaturally drawn to the office, where the science of the game takes place. Soon he holes up in a room by himself with a pro-jector and film of his father's team because it's there to be watched. The film is the 60 millimeter kind, so when the tape breaks he learns to splice it, threading it back to life so he can study some more, honing his eye, an eye that would furnish him a career.

By the way, he is in the fourth grade.

Tom Heckert Jr. went through the natural progression of his path, like many of us desirous in the beginning to play football profession-ally. One's Love of Football is always born from a longing to play the game, as long as possible, the physicality of it I think addictive. And like many of us, the realization always follows, that there is a level we will never reach, our own physicality deeming us out of luck. So Heckert fought his way to playing small-college defensive back at Hillsdale College in Michigan, the way a coach's kid does, strictly on determination, head and coachability. This was necessary for his future, which would involve something to do with the game, most likely coaching, he thought.

By this time, Tom Heckert Sr. had long reached the NFL, serving as director of scouting for the Dolphins, after joining the Browns as a regional scout in 1982 and later the Buccaneers as a national scout. He completed the ascension by grinding through levels: assistant coach at Fitch High in Youngstown, Ohio (1961), two years as a lieutenant in the Army, enrolling as a graduate assistant at Kent State, earning his master's degree in education, head coach at Maumee High in Ohio (1967), assistant at Adrian, head coach at Adrian (1972), athletic director at Adrian (1977). By doing so, he paved the way for his boy with the sharp eye.

Tom Jr., having coached at Hillsdale for two years, was plotting his next move when he went to unpaid work for his father in Miami because he had nothing to do, helping with draft preparations. When it came time to leave, as Tom Jr. stewed over which graduate assistant job to take, Arizona State or Michigan State, head coach Don Shula paid him a visit. Shula was an intimidating figure, legendarily stoic, the kind of man one never approached, particularly if you were a nobody kid, just somebody's son. The rule around the Dolphin office was: If you pass Don in the hallway, do NOT say hello. If stuck in the spot of eye contact, nod politely, deferentially, and if he greets you, only then greet him back, and don't be wordy about it, attempting something lame like small talk, or God forbid, shop talk.

Heckert Jr. didn't let himself think about a permanent job with the Dolphins, as they were a team with few employees in football ops. Shula was old school in that way, keeping tight quarters, entrusting only a few, down to a streamlined coaching staff in an era of you-name-it specialists.

So that morning, Don Shula asked young Tom Heckert Jr. if he wanted a permanent job, reporting to his father. "How would you like to work in personnel?" he asked, and young Heckert, always the courteous, diligent sort, the way coach's kids usually are, accepted on the spot, thanking "Coach Shula profusely for this opportunity."

Thanks to his father, Tom Heckert Jr.'s path had crystallized. "I owe it all to him," he would say later.

The Heckerts worked side by side for ten years, and while the father was a typical coaching father raising his children, always stressing academics and playing life the right way, working for him belied the normally contentious notion of blood reporting to blood. Maybe it's because Heckert Sr. always knew his kid had the eye, from when he was a boy and he'd watch the tapes and he'd utter something that would stop him in his tracks. He was right on, too right on for a child, and he treated his son at work not as a son or some dopey kid but as a fertile mind. Hell, son or no son, he respected the boy's opinion. He called it a knack, and one day at Dolphins headquarters, he told the boy so. The man would say later, "I don't think he would say something to me that he didn't truly believe. He just said when I started that I had a knack for evaluating players, which told me I could do this for a living. It also put more pressure on me, because I didn't want to let him down."

Oh, they would have their disagreements on players, the way all personnel men on the same team do, the way he does now on occasion with Andy Reid. They would argue to resolution, and ultimately conformity. General managers, personnel executives, scouts, evaluators, meat marketeers, men who make their living discerning the talent of other men keep score and their jobs only by how many times they are right. And while those men need to bat an ungodly average for high draft picks, it's the gems they unearth in either the late rounds or on the street that pad one's rep because those players are the backbone of any successful team, either as a grunt or a salary value commensurable to their production.

Heckert's first big notch came with the recommendation of Bernie Parmalee, an undrafted running back out of Ball State who was working as a UPS driver. He studied Parmalee's tapes and swore he saw an NFL caliber player, and urged the running back-starved Dolphins to work him out and ultimately sign him. Parmalee wound up playing nine seasons in the league when the lifespan of an NFL runner is barely four, proving to be a versatile player, blocking, catching the ball out of the backfield, doubling duty on special teams.

Then there was that renown draft the Dolphins had in '97, and Heckert Jr. was in the middle of it. Jimmy Johnson and the staff had targeted two of Heckert's choices, Jason Taylor and Sam Madison. Johnson asked Heckert directly which one would he take in the second round and which one to nab in the third, thus assuring both would still be available. Heckert offered his recommendation: Though Taylor will be the better player in the long run, he's out of Akron and flying a bit under the radar, so let's take Madison first.

"Ohmygod, I had to wait forever for that pick," he would recall. "Talk about anxiety for a whole round. I was squirming on my seat, praying Taylor would be there when we picked again. You don't get it wrong with Jimmy. He woulda flipped out if he wasn't there."

Both players are still with Miami, longtime cornerstones of the Dolphin defense, Taylor becoming a star defensive end and Madison a Pro Bowl defensive back.

Tom Heckert Jr. had never met Andy Reid before he received his phone call. Yes, quite the surprise call. Though all sports people always keep one eye free for job roving and he had a conversation with Butch Davis regarding rumors of an opening in the Browns' front office, Heckert Jr. felt set in Miami.

Then he got the phone call.

Andy Reid had been looking for help, needing to fill a spot to head up the personnel department, and he had talked to Don Shula's son, Mike, about Heckert. The report was glowing, and so Heckert found himself in Philadelphia, spending two days with Reid and while they got along famously from the jump, the last hurdle was an interview that lasted five hours with Reid, president Joe Banner and owner Jeffrey Lurie in which they grilled him with possible scenarios.

Five years later, having recently turned only 39, he's entrenched in the organization, happily perched to the right of Reid. Now he's here at the gala, donning the title Vice President of Player Personnel, gladly being glad-handed by the who's who of this sport as they pay special homage to the executives of the teams in the Super Bowl. The boy with the eye, now a man, says it's quite the ego boost. Particularly here among the old boys, he still looks boyish, sporting a clean face with washed-over features all in the right proportion and a trim build, which will get him momentarily detained by security in two nights. Yes, the Eagles will lose the Super Bowl and Heckert will be on the field, fighting dismay, when he will fight through the mayhem of the postgame Patriot ceremony en route to the Eagles' locker room and a security attendant will stop him. "You can't go in there," the man will say, deeming Tom Heckert Jr. some lackey, probably an intern. Heckert, in turn, will raise his eyebrows. "Excuse me?" he will respond, and flash his credentials, and the man will slink to the side.

It's only fitting that Tom Heckert Sr. is here with Rose to share his son's splendor. The way it works when this country works is the father paves the way for the son, clearing the path for upward mobility. How could Tom Sr. not glow like the Southern sky? The boy's destiny was in his hands for so long, and now, now he's what they call a chip off the ol' block, the ultimate for any father.

"He's the best," Heckert Jr, will say of his father. "He's why I do the things the way I do them. He always tol' me if you work hard, that's all you really need. 'Do your job and don't get lost in the games of the game, being a big press guy, trying to get your name out there. Do your job and you're gonna do well, and your name will be out there plenty.' I watched him do that."

Tonight, he tells his son, enjoy like the Romans! Savor every moment, from the gala through the game. It's why you're in the office at five in the morning every Monday, Tuesday and Wednesday and don't leave the complex until 11 each night, why Thursday's 6 a.m. to 8:30 p.m. shift is perceived a light day. It's why during the season, the only night you're home at supper time is Friday if the team is on the road . It's why you send the intern for takeout four days a week and eat out of a carton with plastic silverware by the flat screen. It's why you're at the complex all the time because you can't watch every tape. Because there's always something to watch, because, you say, "You have to watch the tape to truly tell about a guy. Without watching the tape, you can't tell shit."

It's why you say you didn't feel like you were at the Super Bowl until tonight, spending the bulk of the week far from the revelry locked away in the hotel watching more tapes, getting ready for the draft and free agency while Andy is consumed with the game. It's why you say, "The thing nobody really gets is that when you get this far it puts you behind the eightball for the future. At the end of February, we go to the combine, and it's a big time in free agency. We have to decide who we want to re-sign from our team and who do we want to make a play for."

It's why you spend more time with Andy than your wife Kathy, and among the many reasons you say, "The secret is to marry a great woman and that's no lie. During the season, my wife, she basically takes over. If we need something fixed, she has to do it. Anything with the kids, she has to do it. During the season, she's a single mother. Hopefully, she'll continue to say she's OK with that."

It's why you feel all of that immense guilt because you really don't mind all of the work not even deep down. You enjoy it. It's just when you think of the family, your children, Griffin and Madison, at the elementary school age, you miss them and you feel guilty you're not with them enough.

"My dad kept stressing to understand the magnitude of what it all means," Heckert will say. "Until you sit back and talk to all of the people in the league who never had the opportunity to realize this, that's why you better make sure you enjoy this. You may never get the opportunity again. I remember talking to Marino his second to last year, and he said, 'I went to the Super Bowl my first year and I thought we'd get there all the time. And we never got back.' Like my father, all those years with the Dolphins and they never had a losing record. They were always in the playoffs. And they never got there."

I know what it is now that makes Tom Heckert seem to fit in this game so well. Back to the eyes: he displays a true football squint, which I think makes him look a little stiff in a suit, though technically he is a suit of this game. It's just you can tell that he's a golf-shirt guy, more comfortable with the clicker, holed up in his flip-flops alone in a small room, pausing the tape, running that play over and over again, immersed in the science of the game.

Just like he did way back in Yo Adrian, Michigan, back in the fourth grade.

PETE THE CRAB - A MODERN DAY TOOTS SHOR

I see Pete The Crab with his family, Lisa and the three boys. You can't miss Pete. You know Pete. Everybody knows Pete, Good Time Pete, with that million dollar smile, flashing like the hazard lights on your car, making everyone feel like a superstar, as though they are the sole reason his joints are the most popular haunts in town. He's got it down, my man, better than any priest or politician, especially to the ordinary of us, because what he sells, besides beer and Crab Fries, is acceptance.

Pete The Crab is Pete Ciarrocchi, proprietor of Chickie's and Pete's, now a chain of sports bars, where all the luminaries in Philadelphia go, (even if they are only Philadelphia luminaries), mostly sports figures, media personalities and neighborhood icons. He's in Jacksonville, guest of the Eagles, and he's doing what he does best: salutations.

A cell phone mashed against his ear, he spits them out like sunflower seeds. "Yo, buddy, feel good about the game?" he hollers to someone across the tent, all the while silently shaking hands with another man, offering a wink and a smile, before a quick snap and point in the direction of a guy who just shouted, "Yo, Pete!"

However milk toast the times, Pete The Crab, in his late forties, with a crooner's look, tall and lean, pushed-back hair, a dimpled-chin and a style born from *Saturday Night Fever*, is today's Toots Shor, had Toots never left South Philadelphia for the grand stage of Manhattan. Toots was America's first celebrity saloon keeper, rising to fame in the legendary speakeasy era as bouncer, guardian, manager and tappy owner, the thread of his odd life stitching together the people who made much of the history and mood of the twenties, thirties, forties, fifties and sixties. "He opened his own joint in 1940, and the rest is history," noted author and columnist Bob Considine wrote in the biography, *Toots*. "The greats of the sport world and of the stage and films have frequented his bar and delighted in his steaks, while trying (usually in vain) to match his prowess as imbiber and raconteur."

"Toots," Considine wrote, "must be the only man who was as close to mob lords Longy Zwillman, Big Frenchy, and Owney Madden as he was to Cardinal Spellman, Robert Sherwood, and President Truman. His personality, outgoing and often erratic as a rocket, bridged the sociological gaps that yawned between Babe Ruth and Paul Draper, Frank Costello and Edward R. Murrow, Texas Guinan and the nuns at Marymount, where his three daughters were educated. He was equally at ease, and vice versa, with Sir Alexander Fleming, the discoverer of penicillin, and Casey Stengel, the inventor of the new syntax. He served as catalyst between two distinguished Americans, Yogi Berra and Chief Justice Earl Warren."

So I think of Pete, holding court at the Chickie's and Pete's in South Philadelphia, a stone's throw from the city's sports complex, with the likes of Jon Bon Jovi and then Andy Reid and Joe Frazier and Pete Rose and Pat Croce and Ernie Banks and a City Councilman and a decorated cop and a neighborhood mobster and many of the professional athletes on the local teams and media heavyweights, Angelo Cataldi and Bill Lyon.

I see him sweet talk the room with the flare of a true born barman, paying deference to the men and fawning over their women. After all, the quickest way to win over a man is through his woman, executed delicately in a non-threatening manner. I see him alter his argot depending on the audience, the great chameleon operating squarely in his company's comfort zone. I see him ever the showman, forever buoyant and Christmas merry, because death becomes a bar upon a pall, thus his slogan: It's more fun to eat in a bar than drink in a restaurant. I see him nod to the server, a gesture that there will be no check for that particular table, and when the people invariably object, he raises his palms and says, "Let me get this one. I hope you had a good time at Chickie's and Pete's."

Wonder if you're finally happy now, Old Man Pete? Wonder if you'd finally give your son a pat now instead of all that grief, treat him like a son, with fatherly affection instead of old school fatherly bullshit? Wonder if you would eat your words, Old Man Pete, like all those people do your son's crabs and swallow your pride and admit you were wrong and that sometimes The Son Knows Best? Wonder if you'd even cop to all those times you scolded Young Pete for trying to sell crabs at the bar and forcing him to push the platters, whatever they were? For trying to sell those stupid potatoes, what'd young Pete call 'em – yeah, yeah, Crab Fries?

"Big shot o'er here," you'd tell Pete's mom, Chickie, "wants to reinvent French fries. Wants to change French fries, your son. Belie'e that? Wants to change French fries? And those damn crabs. He won't stop with the freakin' crabs. Wants to serve 'em hot. People been eatin' crabs cold for a hundred years. Now Hollywood o'er here wants to cook 'em."

Wonder if you'd cop to leaning on young Pete like one of those damn drunks against the cigarette machine? Wonder if you'd apologize for never attending one of his football games, the kid making second string All-Public and all, and saying the kid only played football to get outta work at your corner grocery store, the business before the bar? Wonder if you'd apologize for telling the boy that if in fact he put on weight so he could play football he'd better make that team and play on it, 'else he'd embarrass himself and the family and you, and he'd look like an asshole to everyone? Wonder if you would have maybe, just maybe told the boy he didn't have to work every single holiday at the bar, Chickie, the blessed mother, forced to send him a care package with the ham on Easter Sunday and the turkey on Thanksgiving? Wonder if you had to do it all over again you wouldn't make the family, especially Young Pete, the oldest of your three sons, feel like such a burden, and you wouldn't snarl, "I'm doing this for you people. What do I get? Nothin'. Don't spend nothin' on myself."

Wonder if, Old Man Pete, you would marvel at what has become of that little corner joint with the ladies' entrance you bought back in '78 that, had it not been for Young Pete, was destined to be a burned-out corner joint, a place for neighborhood degenerates, depressing slobs waiting to die?

Wonder if you would lament your end and lament that it was ever too fitting, collapsing from a brainstem hemorrhage right there in the bar in '86, the week of Young Pete's thirtieth birthday and the week of the stock market's terrible plunge. You dizzily pointed to the kitchen and Young Pete first thought you were drunk but realized it was too early even for you, and so he carried you out of sight of the patrons and you collapsed into a coma in his arms?

Wonder if you would have told your family where all the money was, instead of leaving them just what was in the register – about 2600 – and a tax audit and a debt of about 60 grand?

Whatever you'd do, change or not, really, it's OK. The boy you called Hollywood still loves your memory, and understands most of what you did now. Plus, Hollywood really is in this town, because when you died, he took over the bar, went from doing 3500 a week to thirty-five hundred a day within a year, and to God knows what with all of the joints combined today.

Remember how he'd sneak serving those Crab Fries when you weren't around? Those stupid potatoes built him a freakin' bar empire, and it's still growing. And guess what? It's not all about the business, either. Hollywood has three sons of his own now, and he's learned to do things with them you couldn't do with him or your other two, tell them the things you couldn't say, father the way you couldn't father, whether it was because of the times and the Northeast neighborhood thing, the old school fatherly bullshit. You know, you help invent the mantra: A father's role is to toughen up his son, hit him hard before the hard knocks do. Somebody's got to do it and it sure as hell won't be his doting mother.

Yes, Hollywood has three boys: Pete, who's seven, yes, another RePete, Blaise, who's five, Anthony, who's three. And guess what? He took them all to the Super Bowl, and you should have seen Youngest Pete in a perpetual state of awe, rooting on his father, because his father was Hollywood down there in Florida, players from the team and big wigs from the beer companies fawning all over him. It was an adorable moment, except Hollywood's a little nervous:

"Him and I enjoyed the same experience together," Young Pete would say of Youngest Pete. "It was incredible. Except I'm 47 and he's seven. How does he top it? It's gonna be hard for him to chase that. From here on out, what does he get excited about? Guess the only way is for them to win it."

Without a formal education, Pete The Crab is a throwback to the great marketer. Though his shellfish is quite tasty, particularly the crabs that he has flown in daily from Washington State and his steamers, there's nothing essentially Philadelphian about his menu, other than maybe the cheese atop the crab-spiced French fries that have become his trademark. What he did was build a brand, take the cult following he had from the original bar in neighborhoods like the Northeast and South Philadelphia and methodically blow it out, in the early days hustling from softball field to softball field to make sure the guys would come back to his place after the game. He built a bigger place on the heavily-trafficked Roosevelt Boulevard with nicer amenities and an outdoor deck, and then went right after the sporting culture. A life-long Eagles fan, he opened a place in Veterans Stadium for games and events, and managed to wriggle the chance to host the Andy Reid weekly news conference, which brought notoriety from the press, which didn't mind the gratis spread he laid out before and afterwards. He hired a down-on-his-luck former umpire, Eric Gregg, and manned him at the bar in the ballpark.

With two new stadiums under construction and the Vet nearing implosion, he went to work on his crown jewel, taking over a super-market in a mini strip mall on Packer Avenue in South Philadelphia, right off Broad Street, and a short walk to the sports complex and the Eagles' practice facility, the NovaCare Center. He opened for the Eagles' first season at Lincoln Financial Field, and made the new place celebrity-friendly with VIP backrooms and plenty of room and hard-ware to host local television and radio shows. He ran shuttles to and from the games, and because of its proximity, the place became the perfect spot for athletes and members of each team to unwind after work. He also hired rookie running back Reno Mahe, a devout Mormon who didn't want idle time in the offseason to be a host. Mahe worked for seven bucks an hour and made for wonderful publicity.

That joint has become the sports hub in town, particularly for Eagles games, and has been awash with local and national reporters over the last couple of weeks for their traditional Philly fan reaction pieces.

So when Pete The Crab left the other day on the bus from the NovaCare Center to the airport with his family and the families of many of the Eagles, like Brian Westbrook's parents and Chad Lewis' wife and children, Jenny Brown, Sheldon's wife, came running over to him excited: "Pete! You know you were in the Dallas Morning News?"

Acting surprised, Pete smiled. "Really? That's cool."

A trueborn barman is a stone attention monger, for the business and for himself. He had already spoken that morning to the Philadelphia Inquirer regarding a trademark story about the NFL and the Super Bowl, the Denver Post regarding Reno Mahe and the Orlando Sentinel regarding the rabidity of the Philly fans, in which Pete said, "No, they're really great fans. They're not nasty. They're not mean. They're not aggressive. They're just good fans with passion and nobody in Jacksonville should be worried that it's the Eagles in the Super Bowl."

Over the past two weeks, reporters from the New York Daily News, New York Post, New York Times, Newark Star Ledger, San Diego Union Tribune, Miami Herald and Sports Illustrated came through the Chickie's and Pete's in South Philly, as well as those from ESPN.com and ESPN television, Comcast Sportsnet, FOX national and FOX local, which set for up several live hits from the Official Eagles Pep Rally throughout the morning of its "Good Day Philadelphia" show.

Pete The Crab can't wait to tell me a story. It's not about the night he arrived at the Marriott Sawgrass and how he had a wonderful time downstairs at the reception party thrown by the Eagles. All of the players and Eagles officials were there, and there he was hobnobbing with all of them, downing Manhattans, flinging all sorts of salutations. Lisa's father is there, and he could play big shot – something that a trueborn barman loves to do more than anything – when Brian Dawkins nearly tackles him with a "Yoooooo, Pete!"

Pete The Crab is also genuine Eagles fan. While he is here because of the business he built, this weekend, even for him, is not about spreading Crab Fries throughout the civilized world. I can recall seeing him on the field that frosty early afternoon of the NFC Title Game against Tampa Bay, wearing his black leather jacket with the Chickie's and Pete's mock turtle underneath, and his eyes were as wide as hubcaps, as Hugh Douglas hoots wildly behind him. "You believe it?" he said. "We're here on the field before the NFC Championship Game? Isn't that amazing? You and I, who grew up two little kids loving the Eagles and we're standing here right now?"

It's his business to follow the Phillies, Sixers and Flyers, but the Eagles? No, the Eagles are his team, down to the fact that he married a former Eagles cheerleader.

Down to the fact that the parish priest he'll pal around with sometimes, Father Paul from Saint Catherine's, is such a devout Eagles fan that sometimes during the season and always during the playoffs he'll sneak in a sentence or two about the team in that week's homily, keeping it in perspective of course, until he's outside of church, and he's at the game with his Eagles hardhat and Eagles gloves and Eagles boxers right over his pants. Pete took Father Paul to the NFC Championship Game against Carolina two years ago, and because it's against the Catholic doctrine to engage in superstition, Pete just had to take him to the Falcons game. Pete went to Mass the Saturday before, the five o'clock service, and he made sure he got in the Communion line manned by Father Paul and Pete had the ticket nestled between his praying palms as he approached the altar. Pete nodded toward the ticket, and Father Paul, without missing a beat, winked at Pete and said, "Body of Christ…"

"So," he says, "you'll never guess where I was last night. I went to a Washington Redskins party, some big, by-invitation-only to-do thrown by [owner] Daniel Snyder. A buddy of mine from Guinness invited us. Lisa and I didn't know what it was going to be. So we had on jeans. I mean, we looked cool and all, but everybody was dressed in tuxedos and suits and evening gowns. Right away, Lisa said, "Let's leave." I said, "Let's stick it out." Lisa had these boots with a rabbit's foot dangling from each boot and people kept commenting on them, saying, "Nice boots!" Because they reminded you of the Redskins' helmet with the feather on it. So she was OK, and then guess what?"

He pauses for effect.

"I get introduced to Dan Snyder and wait'll ya hear how the conversation went."

PETE: Pleased to meet you, Dan? Or, uh, Mr. Snyder?

SNYDER: Dan is fine. I heard about you. You have the third best sports bar in the country. ESPN had you on TV.

PETE: Yeah, it's a great honor. Truly.

SNYDER: Where's your place?

PETE: Philadelphia.

"With that," Pete says, "he turned his head and never looked back at me, and there I was still talking. Then he just started talking to my friend from Guinness. I thought, How rude? He isn't even looking back at me. I already had a few in me so I put my hand on his shoulder, which was very easy to do since he was only a little higher than waist-high to me, and I said, How 'bout that Jeremiah Trotter? Isn't he having a great season? He's going to the Pro Bowl, ya know?

"I give this guy credit, he didn't even look at me. I didn't even notice he took a deep breath and then started talking to my friend from Guinness again. I walked away from him like, Ha! He didn't think that was too funny but I didn't like his attitude."

The Redskins spent a lot of money signing Trotter away from the Eagles the first time and his success has been a thorn to Snyder.

"So I'm looking for my wife so we can jet the party and I see her surrounded by a bunch of executives with the team," Pete The Crab continues. "Well, I'm still pissed about Dan Snyder, so I said to one of the high-ranking officials, 'How 'bout that Jeremiah Trotter?' He motions to be quiet. 'Shhhhh! I almost got fired because of him.' He said, 'Thank God I had medical backup when I got rid of him. I had doctors' testimony, MRI results, X-rays saying that he has no knees left and this guy's shouldn't be walking let alone playing football.'"

"Are you sure they were Jeremiah's?" Pete joked.

"The man didn't laugh." "He said," reports Pete, "believe me, I wouldn't be here tonight if they weren't his because I was called in about [Trotter] a couple of times and I had to produce the doctors' findings and the reasons we had to let him go."

So Pete The Crab and lovely Lisa left, and on the way out, the exit walkway under the dramatic awning was roped off, media and a crowd of onlookers on either side, limos waiting at the curb. So Pete The Crab played along. He waved and flashed that million dollar smile and did what he does best: Salutations.

Photographers snapped his picture like he was Hollywood, and the onlookers waved, thinking he was somebody more than just a celebrity saloonkeeper.

"Who are you?" one of the photographers finally asked.

"I'm Pete," he said.

4
SATURDAY

Will the circle be unbroken,
By and by, Lord, by and by?
There's a better home awaiting,
In the sky, Lord, in the sky.

Hundreds have assembled by the river's edge, most of them coming from great distances, willed by a wanting in their soul. The noise is like the stormy roar of the St. Johns, the throng of humanity becoming one whole quaking flesh, now moved to song, spontaneous song that sounds almost Elysian. Mind you, these are not, sans the priest and the nun that stand before me, choir people or professional church-goers with voices enhanced by angels. But there must be angels under this makeshift party tent.

Ecstasy pervades the room like a soothing mist.

What it feels like is what, according to *Church History Magazine*, the Rev. Moses Hoge described about another gathering by another river in another time, long ago: "The careless fall down, cry out, tremble, and not infrequently are affected with convulsive twitchings. Nothing that imagination can paint, can make a stronger impression upon the mind, than one of those scenes. Sinners dropping down on every hand, shrieking, groaning, crying for mercy, convulsed; people praying, agonizing, fainting, falling down in distress, for sinners or in raptures of joy! ...As to the work in general there can be no question but it is of God."

Where am I?

Surely what transpires before me is not born of a football game, some man-made pastime used to pass the time, a diversion to sweep us from our daily lives and their authentic meaning, empty or otherwise.

Can I get an amen?

Aw, hell, surely the convergence of all these souls is meant to lift us to another plane, not some capricious summit to revival root, root, root for the home team.

Surely this is another Great Awakening, taking all by surprise, just like the Second One that began in the summer of 1800 with Kentucky Presbyterian minister James McGreader's three small congregations in Muddy River, Red River and Gasper River. That area in southwest Kentucky was dubbed Rogues Harbor, since the majority of the people were refugees who fled from justice, mostly murderers, horse thieves, highway robbers and counterfeiters.

If everyone is right about these people before me, shouldn't this be Rogues Harbor revisited, dyed green? Just ask one Merrill Hoge, who is not a reverend but a former player turned Sunday pundit who became an enemy of these people for his weekly condemnations of their team. Today, he will sit on an open stage on the other side of the river taping a show for ESPN and he will be publicly chided and derided by some of these people, many of whom will brag to me about it later.

Hoge will be pelted with rotten eggs of words. Obscenities. Catcalls. Jeers.

"Hoge, you suffered too many concussions," they will say. "Hoge, you're a dope."

Merrill Hoge, who dons a fullback's square head and jutted jaw, who picked the Eagles to finish the season at 8-8 and stubbornly refused to change his stance when they were 8-0, who damned the team providential, unwitting winners, will later good-sport dine with three of these people at a sports bar.

Three absolute strangers.

Meanwhile, back at the turn of two centuries ago, convinced that

God was moving, McGready and his colleagues planned another camp meeting to be held in late July 1800 at Gasper River, the first of its kind where a continuous outdoor service was combined with camping out.

Or was it tailgating?

According to *Church History Magazine*, McGready recalled: "The power of God seemed to shake the whole assembly. Toward the close of the sermon, the cries of the distressed arose almost as loud as His voice. After the congregation was dismissed the solemnity increased, till the greater part of the multitude seemed engaged in the most solemn manner. No person seemed to wish to go home - hunger and sleep seemed to affect nobody - eternal things were the vast concern. Here awakening and converting work was to be found in every part of the multitude; and even some things strangely and wonderfully new to me."

Fly, Eagles fly
On the road to victory
Fight Eagles fight,
Score those touchdowns 1,2,3
Hit 'em low, Hit 'em high
And watch those Patriots cry
Fly, Eagles Fly
On the road...to...vic...tor...y
E-A-G-L-E-S, EAGLES!

FATHER JOE

"Unity is spirituality," says the Rev. Joe Campellone, OSFS. "Jesus spoke of the idea of unity. Jesus spoke of bringing people together. Following the NFC Championship, what a different city this was. It was neat. Everyone was together, black, white, Jewish, Catholic, united in the commonality of this team, united in goodness, the way Jesus had taught. It just so happened that the occasion of union was a football team."

Let us confess freely that Father Joe is a devout Eagles fan.

See, Father Joe, president of Father Judge High School in Northeast Philadelphia, the largest all-boys high school in Pennsylvania, will say Super Sunday Mass tomorrow and will wear a Brian Westbrook jersey beneath his vestments. The theme of his homily will be, yes, the unity of the community through the football team. How it's good to wear green today and hug thy neighbor. How Jesus called his flock to remember, celebrate and believe. How we remember today the genesis of the Eagles, the people who helped shape them, like Chuck Bednarik and Harold Carmichael and Mike Quick and Ron Jaworski. How we celebrate the happenings of today, the successes of this team, born of good people like Andy Reid and Donovan McNabb, and the joy it has brought us. How we believe that this team can win this game.

"A lot of remembrances, a lot of celebrating, a lot of belief in something," Father Joe will say. "This is something good. This is something pure! It takes people's minds off of so many things. However small, it gives us a little of what we are searching for to get us out of the bed in the morning. To let us view life a little differently. During the weeks, we've picked up so many others along the journey, even people who don't know much about the Eagles or the background of the team, and that's a wonderful thing."

After giving the final blessing to send those in attendance away in peace, Father Joe will strip off his vestments right there on the altar and hand them to one of the altar boys revealing his Westbrook jersey. He will walk down the aisle accompanied by the song: On Eagles Wings.

And this will upset the church's music director quite a bit.

Let us tell you a little about Father Joe, the urban throwback priest who reminds you of DeNiro's Father Bobby character in the movie "Sleepers." From a hardscrabble Philadelphia upbringing, Father Joe is forty-one years old, the youngest president in the diocese and a man's priest, which is to say he Fathers by way of real life, knowing and understanding that man is inherently flawed, offering redemption instead of condemnation.

Maybe it's because he knows a lot about redemption. Growing up, the neighborhood would have given you odds that he would have found prison before the priesthood. He spent his elementary school years at a school for those with severe learning disabilities and graduated to a reform school after that, and he'd tell you his turnaround was more inexplicable than Freddie Mitchell's Fourth-and-twenty-six catch that miraculously buoyed the Eagles to victory over the Packers two years ago.

Saved, he was.

Now he does the saving, more than his beloved Flyer goaltenders, mostly of the street urchins that remind him of himself. He tends to the high school and he works in rehab centers and supervises shelters for runaways. He started a "KO Drug Boxing Program" and he coaches youth hockey and he promotes unity rallies and anti-violence rallies. For those of us who were Catholic-school lifers, Father Joe is the kind of priest you always hoped for, caring and compassionate, versed in the language of teenagers, deeply into sports, dead freakin' cool. And though he Fathers without a scrap of sanctimony, he can see through you like a window without the newspaper coverings.

Since we all need our vices, Father Joe's is following sports, particularly the Eagles, particularly going to the games with his rowdy buddies on their bus, dubbed the Eagles Bus, an old school bus painted green and decorated with the team paraphernalia. He blessed the bus, you know, three years ago in the parking lot of Veterans Stadium.

I believe it was the same day he was thrown out of the stadium because some of rowdies brought beers into the game and someone knocked over the bottles so he saved them. He got caught by an usher and almost had to go in front of Judge Seamus in the old basement courtroom. He talked his way out of it, without playing the priest card, swearing that he wasn't drinking, and he watched the rest of the game at Chickie's and Pete's.

Father Joe probably could have finagled his way to Jacksonville. His boys made the trek in the bus. But he wanted to watch the Super Bowl with his four brothers, particularly Tim, who has season tickets to the Eagles and who has cancer. Tim has forged a relationship with Andy Reid, and so he was on the field for the Green Bay demolishing in November and then underwent major surgery. Tim healed enough to take Father Joe to the Minnesota playoff game and then the NFC Title Game.

So it was only fitting that Father Joe stay at home and watch the game with Tim and the other Campellone brothers, over at Michael's place, where the girls will be upstairs and the guys downstairs with wings and beer and their father's picture resting on the television. Dad died five years ago.

Before heading to Michael's, Father Joe will lead a rendition of "Fly, Eagles Fly" with the congregation following Mass, then head over to the bar to check on the pools. He calls me on the air to say the flavor of pregame Jacksonville is coming through his radio and he's stoked and he thinks the Eagles will win the game. Father Joe called the show yesterday, too, from the cafeteria at Father Judge with the students going wild, most of them wearing their Eagles garb, allowed to only if they donated two dollars to the tsunami victims.

Steve and I asked him to bless the tent.

He did.

Then he did an E-A-G-L-E-S chant.

"I want them to win for my brother and people like my brother," he said. "I want to see them win for these great fans. I want to see them win for Andy Reid, a compassionate man who does things that nobody will ever know of, a leader and a model even for me as a priest. And, yeah, I guess I want to see them win for me."

Back in the tent, in the middle of late Saturday afternoon delirium, where I can't hear myself talk, even with my headphones on, a nun stands before me. She must be close to eighty and she wears her habit with an Eagles' t-shirt overtop and dons green beads born of Bourbon Street around her neck. She smiles a creased, saintly smile and taps me on the shoulder during my commercial break and whispers in my ear with a sweet Irish brogue, "E-A-G-L-E-S, EAGLES!"

When we return to the air, Sol the Rabbi is the next caller.

I kid you not.

I thought it a sign, though I must admit I am overly sensitive to the underlying thread of the week and Sol calls the show all the time. He's a Philadelphia institution, a close friend to my next-door neighbor, Zion, who wrestled for his native Israel in the '60 Olympics and has kept his squat, well-muscled build through the years. He's become a great of fan of the Eagles since moving to this country, and every Sunday morning, he knocks on my door asking me if he should bet on them.

"Will the Eagle cover the eight points, my naayboor?" he'd say in his thick accent.

"Religion and football blended into one. That's the way it always felt to me," says Ray Didinger, who manned the WIP tent show with Professor Glen Macnow prior to ours. "It was Sunday Mass in the morning. Then after Mass, we'd drive straight to my grandfather's bar and go to the Eagles game. It was all one experience. I couldn't tell where religion left off and football began. It was one emotional cord throughout the day. My Sundays were structured that way: family, faith and football."

THE FIRST FAMILY OF FOOTBALL

Let us talk of Ray Didinger, one Benevolent Ray who has devoted his life to football as a member of a select order. Though he is enshrined in Canton in the writers' wing, after spending years covering the game for *The Philadelphia Daily News*, and now working as a producer for NFL Films and a radio and television analyst, Benevolent Ray should not be branded a media maven. To do that would be to diminish such devotion. For you can't categorize Ray Didinger's participation in football, somehow frame it to grasp it.

Benevolent Ray is a professional the way a priest is.

See, who really loves the game unconditionally, the way Benevolent Ray does? The fans cannot because they have a rooting interest, be it their team or their fantasy team, or perhaps the pointspread. Those involved in the game cannot because they have a vested interest. The media types, even the most ardent, cannot because they play the role of story hunters. This is not to say people don't adore this game, particularly now with its popularity at an all-time high, clearly overtaking baseball as the national pastime. After all, what other sport holds a seat at your table for the holidays?

I just say there are agendas everywhere, however valid, and those few like Benevolent Ray view it a tad differently, faithfully so. It's to the point, where the hallmarks of his life are forever tied to football, how he remembers birthdays and anniversaries and holidays; the day the Lions play early in Detroit and the Cowboys play late in Dallas would be Thanksgiving, yes, but it's deeper than that. "It's how I measure my life," he will say. "People would ask me, 'When is your daughter getting married?' And I'd say 'The day before the Steelers game.' I just couldn't say November 6. It used to piss her off in a bad way."

To explain further, we must travel back to Benevolent Ray's boyhood growing up in what could be Philadelphia's First Football Family, way back, to just after the second World War. Ray Didinger Sr., nicknamed Little Ray, although he stood six-foot-three, arrived home from flying B-24 bombers over the English Channel. Home was in hardscrabble Southwest Philadelphia, a small apartment above a shoe store, down the block from his father's tappy, where all the neighborhood men gathered to talk of what men talked of: politics, their wives' cooking and football.

Little Ray had married Marie, and they had a boy named Ray, whom everyone would call Young Ray, who would become Benevolent Ray, and how great was it to have a son to heap upon the family's one true passion. Little Ray first bought season tickets to the Eagles in '46, which made Ray's father, who was known as Big Ray, proud because Ray's father had been a fan of the ol' Frankford Yellow Jackets and he talked of watching Red Grange play halfback when the Bears came to town and he passed a love of professional football to his son with the reverence a man would a gold pocket watch.

Big Ray owned Ray's Tavern, right there on Woodland Avenue, and he began running bus trips to Eagles games in the early 40s. All the regulars in the bar were Eagles fans, and so one day Big Ray went to the Eagles' ticket office on 15th and Locust in Center City and bought a block of season tickets so they could all sit together. He put out all the money, for some 50 tickets, and the patrons would pay him off over the course of the season. Ray's father would charter a PTC (Philadelphia Transit Company) Bus to come to the bar for every home game, and they would all return there for a nightcap to talk about the day's events.

Ray's Tavern was one of the original sports bars, clunky black and white televisions on either end of a long oak bar cluttered by the Racing Form and Ballantine beer bottles and overflowing ashtrays. Wisps of cigar smoke would disappear into the air, like the arguments over Greasy Neale's playcalling.

As the years went on, Young Ray would often visit Big Ray in the bar, and all of the regulars got a kick of the boy, how he knew everything of the Eagles, all of the players by heart, down to the most obscure, their positions and jersey numbers. See, Little Ray would bring home the program from the game every Sunday and he'd leave it on the coffee table, and Young Ray, about five, would leaf through the magazine with wide eyes. Noticing this, Marie thought it a wonderful way to help teach her son to read and to use numbers through the programs. So she would sit him in her lap and flip through the pages each night, pointing to the head shots of each different player.

"Now who's that, honey?" she would ask.

"That's Steve Van Buren," the boy would reply. "Number 15."

"Very good, Young Ray!"

The boy became a sort of whiz. So when he'd tramp to the bar to drink Cokes and play shuffleboard, the men would plop him on a stool in the middle of the gang and make bets on whether or not they could stump him on Eagles numbers. They'd always start off with an easy one and gradually go tougher, the money growing to serious amounts the more obscure the player. "While other kids were reading 'Spot Chases Jane,' I'm reading the Eagles and Steelers lineup," the boy would recall as a man. "That's how I learned to read. Then I'd go to the bar and recite what I knew. I remember the guys all standing around me with money in their hands. They'd go wild when I reeled off each player and number, even the backup linemen. I knew them all!"

Is it a Philadelphia thing, the tappy thing? I can relate to the boy. I've always felt strangely sheltered in bars, taverns and corner joints, where the old ladies' entrances are now side entrances, sweating stale beer. I like the darkness and coolness that envelops you, and I know it's from those Sundays when I was ten and I would accompany my grandfather to his tappy. My grandfather, my Pop-Pop, would sling drinks at a place just like Ray's Tavern, the 12T Bar, on 12th and Tasker Streets in South Philadelphia. I, too, would sit at the bar with the customers and drink fountain Cokes with the gun powder syrup in tall, thin tumblers, and bestow my love of the Eagles, though my Norm Van Brocklin and Steve Van Buren were Ron Jaworski and Wilbert Montgomery.

My Pop-Pop, my father's father, Orazio Gargano, a robust man with sort of a bulldog face, heavy and worn by a life of intemperance, worked part-time in the rackets. He was this bear of a man, who, when I would visit overnight, used to wake me up with his bar breath, particularly scotch – though oddly it was not an unpleasant odor – at three in the morning to chat about football while he sat in the kitchen in his undershirt and boxers eating cold pasta and drinking Cutty Sark. Unlike some ten-year-olds when it comes to their male relatives, I never feared him. He appeared almost cuddly to me, and his unforced smile was a dead giveaway of his genuine nature and good soul. Once my cousin Joey made him a birthday card and taped a dime inside, and the man wept openly. Affable and happy-go-lucky is how everyone described him, which made him beloved to strangers and maddening to his wife.

It was there at the bar that he'd call my father and tell him of hot rims for his car and once of a hot chainsaw, and he'd hang with a guy called Shorty Days and argue over the Eagles.

Little Ray and Marie share an equal fidelity to the Eagles. Yes, Marie was every bit the fan her husband was, and so she eagerly complied that the family's vacation every summer would be football training camp for two weeks in Hershey, Pennsylvania. While the other families spent beach days at the Jersey Shore, the Didingers would drive to Hershey, before it became an attraction, before the amusement park, before the chocolate festivals, and watch the Eagles practice. They stayed at a hotel called the Cocoa Inn, down the street from the chocolate factory, and they would go out to the field twice a day and take in every second of each session. Then they would retire to the room, where Little Ray, the ol' war hero who flew those B-24 bombers in the same Eighth Squadron as another square-jawed young man who loved football by the name of Chuck Bednarik, would sit at the desk with his pen and the mimeograph copy of the roster, and pare down the squad. Through the years, Little Ray, who stayed active in the Air National Guard after World War II and would fly for another twenty-five years, so looked forward to that vacation with his family, with his life's passion. Little Ray worked long hours over at the plant on Water and McKean Streets, rising all the way to vice president of the Welded Tube Company of America. Imagine if Little Ray knew then what Young Ray would become, how he would achieve the unthinkable: Make your passion your life's vocation.

"Not a real surprise choosing the life I chose, huh?" Young Ray would say. "I wouldn't have had it any other way. I used to look at the kids going to Wildwood and feel sorry for them."

When the boy turned ten, he officially joined the club by attending his first game, something a man never forgets. The year was 1956, the home opener against the Washington Redskins, Connie Mack Stadium, Saturday night in a downpour.

Benevolent Ray closes his eyes.

"I remember riding up in the bus, and the excitement beginning to build. We get off and enter this stadium. We walk through the concourse. I hear the band playing on the field. I walk up the steps. It's dark. We get to our section and we walk up the ramp. We get halfway up the ramp and I see the glow of the lights. I see this big arc and the lights shining. I see the field. It was the first time in my life I saw a real football field. I'll never forget standing there, feeling my heart pound in my chest, to the point where it was hard for me to breathe. I never had that feeling before. I had been to sporting events before, but I never experienced anything like what I felt that day when I heard the band and saw the field. Standing there, my feet sort of planted to the ground, I couldn't get my next breath.

"I remember it vividly. I can see it right now. It was so different. I realized pro football for me was something I connected to."

He talks not being able to catch his breath, the feeling of rushing euphoria, a blast of the Holy Spirit, the bliss of love.

Benevolent Ray's eyes are still closed. He's remembering Hershey, the two-a-days on those muggy days when the air felt like paste, and he didn't want to leave. "They used to have Picture Day at camp," he will say. "I was maybe nine, ten. The players would come out in full uniforms. There were no ropes, no barriers, no security guards. You could walk right up to them. Talk to them. Pose for pictures with them. I must have met Chuck Bednarik twelve times, Tommy McDonald ten times, and he was my hero. The thing is, for a kid who loved football, they were so accessible to you in a way that they are not today. You were in a position to reach out and touch them all the time. They'd rub your head and sign your book. Take all the passion and love of today but combine it with the players being so accessible to you. It was like Wonderland."

Benevolent Ray is quite familiar with Canton, Ohio, a place of lore and past football lives. The building with its hallowed halls that houses the Hall of Fame is circular with a roof with a spouting middle, like a steeple but more stout, and it rests on well-manicured grounds, a tall pole brandishing the American flag near an entryway that features a quartet of bronzed football players plastered high above the glass doors.

It was here in '98, on the rising steps of the Hall looking out over the slope of the hill peppered with four thousand onlookers, including Gale Sayers, Bart Starr, Forrest Gregg, Lamar Hunt and Ray Nitchke, that Benevolent Ray played presenter for his idol Tommy McDonald for his induction ceremony. Tommy McDonald was the littlest guy who played with the greatest passion, Ray would say, who'd clap his hands after every play. He played the way you envisioned you'd play if you were on the field. He was the favorite player of all the kids Benevolent Ray's age. In youth football, they'd all want to pretend they were Tommy. When you're a child, you hope someday in your life you'd be lucky enough to meet your deity in the flesh, maybe get to shake his hands, have him smile upon you. You think that likely will never happen. Then you're the man he picks to ride in the parade with him, right there next to him in the slow-moving convertible, and you're the man standing on the steps of the Hall of Fame delivering his speech.

"Standing in the Hall itself, standing in line," the boy now a man, would recall, "Tommy put his hands on my shoulders before we went out and said, 'I can't thank you enough for what you did for me.' I said, 'Tommy I can't thank YOU enough.' We both had tears in our eyes. Then I'm out there before all of those people, those greats, and I never had a feeling like that before. I was never more nervous. I was never happier, an amazing confluence of emotion overwhelming me. My knees were shaking to the point where I thought I was going to collapse. I was sure my voice was quivering. Who would've thought? I remember screaming my lungs for Tommy and here I am his presenter for the Hall of Fame. What are the odds? How does that happen? To this day, I don't know!"

He had been there for that induction weekend before, you know, to receive his own honor of immortality. Little Ray and Marie were there that July 16, certainly, two weeks before their fiftieth wedding anniversary. The theme of Benevolent Ray's speech concerned Little Ray and Marie and his grandfather, Big Ray, and all of the patrons of Ray's Tavern, how they influenced him and how that influence guided him right to these steps. He described how the language at the dinner table wasn't English but football, how he was the only four-year-old who could pronounce and spell Alex Wojciechowicz, how he cherishes those weekends he shared with them. "I owe them so much," he said, upon introducing them to the crowd. "The fact that I'm here today is due to their love of football."

Little Ray is now eighty-two and Marie is 80. God bless them, they are in good health and they live in Florida, where they followed this season through newspaper clippings on the team that Benevolent Ray would mail and through the postgame shows on *Comcast SportsNet* that Benevolent Ray's wife would tape, featuring the governor of Pennsylvania (Ed Rendell) and the stylish ex-player (Vaughn Hebron) and the truly wonderful host (Michael Barkann) and their son, the expert. Sometimes in the offseason, like in this past middle of March, Little Ray will take a handful of tapes and retreat to his room by himself and study them, like he did the mimeographed roster way back at the Cocoa Inn in Hershey.

It's apparent why Benevolent Ray is the way he is, a member of that select order, foregoing that other calling: everyone at Saint James High thought Young Ray would enter the priesthood. I wonder what he felt during the Super Bowl, while he was in Jacksonville, manning the Comcast stage yesterday and the same seat in the WIP Tent that I did earlier on this glorious Saturday. Would he root for the Eagles?

"Know what I root for?" he will say. "I root for them to win to root for the city. I'm not necessarily for the team. I'm rooting for my parents, my grandfather, those guys that I rode with to the games on the bus. To me, they represent football in this city. When I think of Eagles football that's what I think of. The people in the neighborhood. The people sitting outside in the stands freezing their butts off. It's harder for me to root for the helmet because they changed it. My helmet was Kelly green with silver. The change of the uniform makes them just another team. I identify with the team I first saw."

Benevolent Ray has attended every Super Bowl since Super Bowl V, going on 34 in a row now, and he has never seen an outpour of emotion like this. "The closest thing to it was the first year the Steelers won in January of '75," he will say. "That was Super Bowl IX in New Orleans and everywhere you went you saw Black and Gold. Everybody from Pittsburgh, whether they could afford it or not went to New Orleans. Over the course of time, the game became more of a corporate event, the fan base more evenly split. This year was a real throwback. To see the number of Eagles fans that came to Jacksonville.

When I got down there, I couldn't believe my eyes. I guess I expected it to be that way a little bit. The fans in this city have waited so long, suffered so much. But wow. They were there in record numbers. It was totally a tribute of the way they feel about the Eagles."

In Jacksonville, Benevolent Ray would become wistful, traveling through his own annals, how he got here all the way from Woodland Avenue. How he arrived here with his son, David (there was "NO WAY" he would add to the confusion with another Ray), who is now thirty-two and just won his first Emmy Award as an NFL Films cameraman, proudly carrying on the family tradition.

"I thought back all the time," he would say. "That whole two weeks. From time the Eagles beat Atlanta, through Jacksonville, doing the tent show with all of those people, I relived my whole 50 years of following this team. I thought back on all of it. Back to '56 and riding the bus with all of the guys, walking up the steps to the stadium. I thought about that a lot. I really feel so lucky that I was able to spend my whole adult life writing, talking, making movies about this town's team that I love. You know, I used to go up to Hershey I would look over on side of the field and I would see [reporters] Bill Campbell and Hughie Brown, and I knew who they were. I'd see these guys standing watching practice. I thought, 'Boy what a great way to make a living. Football!' Here, I've had the opportunity, and there isn't a day in my life that at some moment I don't stop and think how lucky I am to do what I do. There isn't a single day that I've taken for granted. I consider it a blessing."

"You can tell the entire story of my life through this team," he would finish. "Some people would say that's not such a great thing to be proud of. For me, it is. I couldn't think of a better way to spend the last 50 years."

Football is our solace during depression and despair.

Football is an outlet for our cooked emotions, a superhighway for expression. Football connects us with our own history, specifically our youth, which we use as weaponry against mortality and gloom and anxiety and burnout and loneliness. Tragic or otherwise, exaggerated or not, football influences our self-esteem, however fleeting.

Football, most importantly, connects us with others. It provides bridges between generations and rekindles friendships. It bonds fathers and daughters and mothers and sons and every other familial combination, providing another vehicle for human relationships.

"Football can affect your life," Les from Ambler, a frequent caller, will tell me. "I got married the day of the Fog Bowl. I kept trying to find score updates during the ceremony. You can tell why I'm divorced now. The game I remember the most, though, was in '89 against San Francisco. It was the week my father was murdered. I watched the game and was able to escape for a few hours."

You have heard the psychobabble generalizations regarding sport and the masses: How sport enables people to unite, transcending race and social and economical standing. How the masses want to be attached to something successful. How in sport, it's not just one team against another team, but one city against another city, like the Olympics pit country and culture versus country and culture. How the masses personalize the team and the players. How the masses view athletes as representatives of their hometown.

Of course, most understand the stark reality of sport: that there is no lasting result to a team winning on a personal level. That it will not change people's lives on the surface a bit. It will not erase bills or heal sick friends or relatives or pave the way to self achievement or fulfillment.

Daniel Wann, a sports psychologist at Murray State University and author of *Sports Fan: The Psychology and Social Impact of Spectators*, says studies have shown about five percent of an individual's psychological well-being is attributable to an identification with a sports team. Religion, he says, accounts for a similar percentage.

"You know I do see the parallels between religion and football, I really do," Donovan McNabb said. "You know that is a really touchy subject with some people around here. When I look at the semantics of religion and football it's the spiritual aspect that as an athlete we praise the pigskin. I think spiritually we cherish. We admire the effort that people put forth to be the best at what they do. Obviously in religion you pray to one God and you admire and cherish Him up above.

Without Him being by our side and blessing us with the talent that we have we wouldn't be able to do what we do. I was in the Bahamas and a woman came up to me and she said, 'I just wanna thank you for everything that you have done, the season you had, and for giving us an opportunity as a family to come together on Sundays, and enjoy Eagle football games together.' You hear those things and you're left speechless. You don't think about it, but some people actually do get together as a family and sit back and watch Eagles games. People have certain rituals that they like the keep such as going to the same house every week, sitting in the same chairs, whatever they think they have to do think if they have to keep these rituals."

"You have to understand that everyone's watching. This is a big thing for kids. You know they aspire and dream to be just like me. You know I love to see the smiles on kids' faces when we're playing or when we're warming up. You know their parents are getting overly excited and the kids are just sitting there with their eyes wide open. That brings a smile to me. That's the spiritual nature of this game."

Columnist Tim Sullivan summed it perfectly in *The San Diego Union Tribune* when he wrote, "Beneath the tension lies a mutual dependency. The athlete needs his audience. The people need their circuses and their sense of community."

At the center of A Sunday Pilgrimage is community.

Community is the parking lots before a game, with those arriving hours before kickoff lugging their grills and lawn furniture and coolers and planting down their giant Eagles flag and doing what Father Joe says: Sharing remembrances and celebrating and believing.

There are 50,000 stories in the parking lot on a given Sunday, sometimes more. I know the group at the Artful Dodger tappy, led by Johnny Sar, will convene at the blacktop near the hotel and the food distribution center around eight for a one o'clock game, and most of them will leave to return to the bar by about a quarter to kickoff as to not miss a second.

I asked Johnny Sar once: Why do you tailgate if you don't have tickets to the game?

"I enjoy the atmosphere," he said. "I enjoy the revelry. Everyone just about knows everyone else, and it's like one giant party. There are good vibes in that parking lot."

Johnny Sar and the boys present an emperor's spread, the menu spanning a roasted pig to tender filets to shrimp cocktail, though that seems to be the direction of the new tailgate, the more elaborate the better. To hell with hamburgers and hot dogs, potato chips and a case of lite beer.

Chris Scarduzzio, executive chef at the exquisite Brassiere Perrier, is renown for his gourmet tailgates, down to matching wines with his dishes, a feast that would make the Last Supper look like a bedtime snack.

"I work long hours, and it's something that I look forward to each week," Scarduzzio says. "It's just the guys. It's our time, a break from the family and work. We get to catch up on life, and then root on our passion: the Eagles."

Some will even do themed fare, preparing the delicacies from the city of the Eagles' opponent, which could be Saints' gumbo or Ravens' crabs or Cowboys' barbeque. The setup is equally extravagant, with some building makeshift living rooms out on the parking lot, complete with leather chairs and a big screen television.

Community is what makes the highways and byways of Philadelphia dark on game day.

Community is in the homes, smelling of Sunday fare and life, nuclear families and extended families and the family friends huddled on the couch or the shaggy carpeted floor, under afghans and next to roaring fires, the Sunday *Inquirer* on the coffee table with the sports page fanning out, the television ablaze with the game.

"I've really thought about this the last year," Didinger says. "I began trying to understand what I've always taken for granted. The Eagles are family to people in this way that no other team is. You plan the whole week for the game and the tailgate. I'll get the charcoal. You get the hot dogs. It's something you share with people not just on that day but for the weeks leading up to it. It's a more involved commitment of time and emotion. And the game is the whole day. Talking about before, watching it, talking about what transpired. People are together for many hours because of it."

DAMN QUAKERS

In Philadelphia, we are more literal than literary. The profound nature that we prefer is served in a shot glass, bullish and harsh. It's out there, with no need of subjective meandering or hidden meaning. It's why Philadelphia is one of the rare old East Coast cities that connects more with football than baseball. There is nothing pastoral about football. There is no elegant metaphor for football. With football, the war homologies are patent and perceptible, the way we like our symbolism.

By comparison, New York purports regality, thus it chooses baseball and all of its historical grandeur.

In Boston, they boast of baseball as the "Thinking Man's Game," and wax poetically over its timelessness and storybook soul. In the haughty Hub, they equally can chant "Yankees Suck" at the Patriots' now annual parade and quote John Updike: "Fenway Park, in Boston, is a lyric little bandbox of a ballpark. Everything is painted green and seems in curiously sharp focus, like the inside of an old-fashioned peeping-type Easter egg."

Says Didinger: "Look at the heroes in other places: In Boston, you have the Splendid Splinter, and in New York, you have the Yankee Clipper, graceful stuff. Those people have an elegance about them, with DiMaggio almost being aristocratic. In Philadelphia? It's Concrete Charlie."

As people, we feel the need to invent a more interesting angle to explain our plight, a sort of cosmic consequence, because, let's face it, if everything is random in the universe, it makes for a boring afterlife and relegates our purpose to that of a squash. So Boston called upon its Curse for the failures of the Red Sox, which was such a great story, really, and the way it was lifted in epic manner, overcoming the evilest empire at the darkest moment. I mean, how could you not root for them? Even the most spurious sports fan, the banal troglodyte whose keen interest is confined to putting down others or betting a parlay, had to pull for the lovable "Saaawx." Meanwhile, in Philadelphia, we cannot refer to a curse. In Philadelphia, we feel damned. A curse can be lifted, but being damned is a sentence.

In recent years, the Eagles have become the embodiment of this town, the struggles, the anguish and the hardship. Three losses in three NFC Championship Games can be damn depressing. Think about it terms of life: failing at three marriages, or coming up short on that promotion three times. Three strikes and you're out. Three knock-downs and the fight's over. Sooner or later, you succumb.

In between potshots, Bernie Lincicome raised one interesting notion with his column: Does Philadelphia love itself? Is it so sub-merged in Quaker guilt and second city inadequacy — the town lost in the clustered Northeast between a world capital in New York City and a nation's capital in Washington D.C., without the Big Shoulders of mighty Chicago, the Hollywood glitz and seedy cool of LA, the beautiful aesthetics and Bohemian charm of San Francisco or the beaches and international flavor of Miami — that its denizens harvest self-worth through the fate of men in pads, knowing full well the frailty of men, particularly of those in pads? Knowing that in the end they will be let down? Deep down wanting to be let down?

Philadelphia can be a hard place to relocate to, with the insular mode of the live-here, die-here people when it comes to outsiders. It's an Old Soul, Old School City for a baby nation, steeped in its own ways. You might say about anything in Philadelphia that "it's done this way because it's always been done that way." Dissenters would be wise to keep mute, a sentiment that's partly due to the Delaware Valley's craving to be loved and any ill word to its ways suggests otherwise. This dives into the heart of the town's sports coterie, a notoriously fick-le bunch who in truth are easily deciphered and subsequently charmed by adhering to its one holy commandment: Appreciate playing for us.

By appreciate, they mean play like you care as much as them. An outward display of emotion usually helps, as histrionics provide tangi-ble evidence, like Vivacious Vai Sikahema furiously punching the goal-post padding as though it was a heavy bag, or Jeremiah Trotter drop-ping the axe, or Dooooce Staley emphatically pointing first down. Is it any wonder this town's historic favorites are usually the grunts, muttly types who get dirty? It likes the guy who shows up for work everyday. The town is suspicious of anything that draws a lot of attention, which would include its superstars, often loved at arm's length (witness what will be the Terrell Owens saga). It's more comfortable with mediocrity.

It likes the guy who shows up for work everyday. It's easy to like Michael Jordan, but it's hard to like the guy who rebounds.

While we speak of the inferiority complex, we must also speak of the ferocious pride Philadelphians take in being Philadelphian, a sentiment akin to ethnicity. They take it with them, sport it wherever they may go. New Yorkers, Bostonians and Chicagoans possess a similar kinship with their cities, but forgive my homerism ways: I do believe such sentiment is more acute in Philadelphia, primed that way from constantly having to defend its homeland.

Meanwhile, transplanted Philadelphians throughout the country enjoy this ride through phone calls home and internet visits. Sunday in Santa Monica, California, a huge crowd will pack The Shack, a sports bar with a strong Philly motif, down to the "Best of the West" cheesesteaks, with pregame people spilling onto Wilshire Boulevard amid continual renditions of "Fly, Eagles Fly."

Bedlam will ensue in Fort Lauderdale, Florida, where Eagles fans will pack The Parrot, a famed beach destination of Philly transplants, decorated with all sorts of Eagles trinkets and several back pages of *The Daily News*. During the Miami Monday night game, The Parrot played the natural hub, one night nearly five thousand fans lining the inside of the bar, the outdoor deck and the stairwell leading to the street, where a huge puddle of people stood and partied. You heard Eagle chants all the way to the pool at the Marriott Harbor Beach Hotel four blocks away.

Across the state, those expatriates have created a mythical place called TampaDelphia, with hundreds of members throughout the Gulf Coast of Florida.

When I lived in Chicago, we had this little clique, and when I traveled throughout the country or abroad and I met someone from Philadelphia, we had this little bond, partly due to being wistful of home, partly because the brotherhood is real. I do believe this city should truly be called: The City of the Brotherhood. Because while we are not more shove than love, we do present a lift the drawbridge, drop the fence sort of attitude toward outsiders, particularly parochial. Whether it's due to constantly being bedraggled that we retreat, recoil and then react, fighting the fight, not unlike a football team with that us-against-the-world mentality.

The quarters are tight here, even with many spilling out onto the small patch of blotched grass outside the back of the tent, where a grill is cooking burgers and hot dogs. People are mashed together, shoulder to shoulder. But there no malice here. There is only joy and song and intermittent chants, the way it was, I supposed, by the Gasper River, only the occupants all in green.

"From the other side of the river," a fan named Ed Minto will say, "I thought I was looking at Philadelphia."

By this point, Steve and I had given up on having any sort of serious discussion on the game. All week, we analyzed the game, autopsied it before birth: how the matchups broke down; how the Eagles could win; how Donovan had to run once or twice to loosen up the Patriots defense; how the Eagles had to pressure Brady the way the Steelers did in the regular season, perhaps forcing an errant throw; how it was almost mandatory that they score first and keep a lead, or risk Belichick the Brain devising a way to keep the ball and bleed the clock like he was ringing out a rag; how if T.O. was really able to play at a semblance of who he is, he had to make one monster play and enough little ones to create space for Brian Westbrook lined up on the outside. On and on, day by day, we went, since the Tuesday after the NFC Championship Game, some eleven days ago, repeating each point like the hot dog man at the stadium.

Now, here, it was about the revelry, about the celebration, even if it was similarly repetitive. I can't count the number of "Fly, Eagles Fly" renditions or those chants that will play over and over in Philadelphia's slumber.

By now, everyone just wanted to believe, hoot and holler belief. So many of them, so demonstrative, so passionate. I see Gary Smith from *Sports Illustrated*, a masterful writer and storyteller, whose words arrange to create life, right then and there, surrounding it with every smudge and ripple on the shirt, painting a scene with the detail of Degas. And like most proficient journalists, he bears the gift of perception, calculating the depth and meaning of what's before him, and he flashes me an appreciative smile over the scene beneath the tent by the river.

"I've never seen this before," he says. "Eagles fans have descended upon Jacksonville and brought a wider context to the Super Bowl. For the first time I can recall, the people took over this historically corporate event."

It continues back in Philadelphia, the mother hub, where 25,000 people yesterday bombarded the First Union Center at 5:30 in the morning. Some there all night, camped out in the mordant cold. They were there to witness Wing Bowl, the station's ballyhooed annual wing-eating contest, born of the minds of our morning men — over a decade ago out-of-the-annual failures of the football team — host Angelo Cataldi, the born soubrette, and witty sidekick Al Morganti.

Desperate for a Super Bowl, they created a Bowl of their own for the city to apprize, a sort of burlesque show, equally infamous and ineffable, featuring a band of mutant and heteroclite characters wrapped in elaborate motifs. Who among us in our youth didn't test the gormandizer of the group to see how much he can scarf of anything? I know my friend Bobby ate a dozen vanilla cream-filled doughnuts once and 15 Texas wieners another time to appease our pointless curiosity. Add in scantily clad strippers and strumpets, and you have a show of shows, one that has grown to preposterous proportions considering it began in the lobby of a hotel, moved to a nightclub, then to an arena, and I supposed if it didn't begin at dawn on the January or February Friday before the Super Bowl, it could fill a stadium.

Angelo Cataldi often wondered what it would be like if Wing Bowl coalesced with the Eagles in the Super Bowl.

The perfect storm. Pep rally for the ages, an arena packed for the wings and the Birds, typifying a city suddenly gone New Orleans celebratory over a football game.

"At the height of the insanity," Angelo Cataldi will say, "the fan passion was like nothing I had ever seen – and I was in Boston in '67, in New York in '76, and even in Seoul, South Korea for the Olympics of 1988. I walked the streets of Edmonton after Gretzky's first championship, I had blood splattered on my shirt during one of Marvin Hagler's championship fights, and I was there for the Larry Bird years at Boston Garden. Nothing came close to Philadelphia in 2004-05."

Angelo Cataldi, who discovered after a celebrated career as a journalist that he had the soul of a morning man, did something that few have ever done in this town: succeed as a stranger. Perhaps it's because he is extremely talented at what he does, a skill quite frankly that I do not possess, and his adoration for this city was sincere, and he accepted them first, and they liked that, and so they embraced him, Rhode Island accent and all.

He succeeded because, despite years of exposure to professional sports, including a stint covering the Eagles for the Philadelphia Inquirer, he actually roots for this team with sincerity, without self-interest, even if that comes by proxy. Perhaps it's because he had no real ties to anywhere, including his hometown, and he took the itinerant route that most newspapermen take, and decided this would be his land, and the Eagles symbolize the fealty he found in Philadelphia.

"On our show," Cataldi will say, "we had tickets to give away for the two rounds of playoff games. We asked a simple question of our callers: What would you do to go to the game? We had one well-nourished fan wearing only a coat of Eagle-green paint and a jockstrap, sprinting down the streets of Center City Philadelphia. He didn't win. A woman showed up one day with her Dad, who had been an Eagles fan for fifty years, but had missed their championship game in '60 and then missed again in their only Super Bowl appearance in 1981. She pleaded with me for tickets to the Super Bowl. She shed tears in the studio for the tickets. I didn't have any tickets, but an anonymous donor gave her the money [$4000] for two tickets, and they went. Both the woman and her Dad cried uncontrollably when we handed over the tickets."

"It was the craziest few weeks I have ever spent in Philadelphia. I loved every second of it."

Earlier this season, beneath another tent, they ate cockroaches for tickets.

Live cockroaches. Shipped in from Texas.

The other bookend of the station, Howard Eskin, the polemical afternoon host, predominant sports personality in this town for 25 years, offered tickets to the Dallas game if people ate the crawlers, a play off his labeling of local Cowboys fans as cockroaches because "they crawl out of the slimy ground when the team gets better after years of being garbage."

Eskin employed an exterminator to supply the largest ones he could find, some as large as three to four inches long, and even had a caterer bring chocolate sauce for dipping. Six creepy people volunteered to do so at the tent outside Lincoln Financial Field. "Only one guy ate them with chocolate," Eskin said. "Even after one guy won the tickets, two guys kept on eating them."

"These Eagles fans are sick!" he continued. "But it's a good thing. The things they do to get to a game never fails to amaze me, and if it's a playoff game they do anything. Every year they do more to win tickets. The women do outrageous things. They can get really wild, and they do have an advantage. For the first playoff game, I had one woman standing outside in twenty degree weather wearing almost nothing."

Howard Eskin, who spent the entire week leading up to the game in Jacksonville, covered the only other Super Bowl involving the Eagles, 24 years ago in New Orleans, and the difference was striking. "Yes, there were Eagles fans in New Orleans, but it wasn't even close to the incredible numbers that appeared in Jacksonville. New Orleans was just another Eagles road game. I think the fans in '80 were more baseball crazy. I don't think Jaworski and Carmichael could match the love the fans had for Pete Rose, Mike Schmidt and Larry Bowa. But it's clear Philadelphia treats football differently. It's bigger than anything in their lives. The fans here treat the Eagles as their property."

Which is why some fans were willing to risk their own property to journey to Jacksonville, why one of the big stories of the week is how fiscally irresponsible those people were in making the trip. To afford the Super Bowl packages that started at $4000, some maxed out credit cards while others borrowed against their homes.

Such deeds prompted Dayana Tochim to write on FOOL.com:

Forgive me, my head is racing. It's not often I hear about a financial move so monumentally stupid that I'm blitzed by potential story titles. But when the Associated Press reported that desperate Philadelphia Eagles fans were borrowing against their homes for game tickets, I struck headline gold:

> *Philly's Financial Idiocy*
> *Egad, Eagles Fans!*
> *Wining the Super Bowl of Stupidity*
> *Diehard Fans, Dunderheaded Finances*
> *Robbing Peter to Play Ball*
> *"Sometimes the cards are maxed out, and you gotta do what you gotta do," one fan said. "What we had to do was apply for a $4,000 home equity line of credit to pay for a Super Bowl package."*

How about this option: If you can't afford it, you don't gotta do it.

If you think I'm being overly harsh, let me remind you of something: Legend has it that these people once booed Santa Claus off the football field. If anyone can handle tough love, it's Philly fans. But don't expect bankers to dole out the tsk-tsks.

Try hosting a Super Bowl party from the trunk of your car.

Go ahead and lose your tempers, Philly fans. Boo Santa Claus, orphans, red shirts, puppies and your grandmother at the first sign of the New England Patriots. Bring it on. Just don't bet the house on your team.

PHIL FROM MOUNT AIRY

Here in the tent, I see Phil from Mount Airy. That's what he goes by when he calls the station, which is often since he's one of those people hooked on talk radio. He's utterly obsessed, yes, the radio playing always, in the background wherever he is, a constant like the hiss and caw of the jungle. For Phil, though I barely know him, I believe it's because he craves the energy of people, each voice that seeps from the radio another welcome companion. Blessed with intrinsic intellect, quick wit and an engaging way, Phil Allen, 43, a self-described speculator and self-employed entrepreneur, is a born showman.

Which makes him a caller.

Callers comprise less than one percent of the audience in talk radio, but they provide the lifeblood, particularly the good ones like

Phil from Mount Airy. My old boss, Tom Bigby, said they equal the records to a DJ. The good ones become as big a part of the show as the hosts, whether it's the bad guys (think pro wrestling): Cowboy Dave, fan of enemy Dallas, Jason, the resident gainsayer who adopted the name Hoge after Philadelphia archenemy Merrill Hoge, or machine gun e-mailer Steve Italiano, critic of all things Eagles, especially Andy Reid and Donovan McNabb.

Or the good guys: Joe, who watched the previous two championship games in a nursing home with his ailing father, and when the Eagles won this one, he looked skyward and said, "They finally did it, Dad. Love you." Or Jim and Avalon Brian and English Gary, a tough, rugby Brit and Manchester United soccer fan who's grown to fancy kindly this American football.

Or Phil, who just had to make the Pilgrimage, even if it was to Jacksonville, a terrible place for him. Phil didn't need to come back here and revisit that time in his life. Of all the Super Bowl towns, this is the one the Eagles choose? Seems so long ago now, so far removed. He's a family man. Kisses his wife goodnight every night. Coaches Little Phil's Little League team. Takes out the trash every week. He had almost forgotten what went down here. Anywhere would be better than Jacksonville, the scene of his crime.

It all began for Phil when was three, when his father disappeared. Actually, the man up and left his family, took off without a word or a wave goodbye. Typical "Hon, I'm goin' out for a pack of smokes and never comin' back" sort of deal, leaving Phil just another statistic, another boy in the 'hood without a pops. Just when he finally got used to it, the notion of a father, any father, so far removed from his thoughts, ten whole years removed, he had a chance encounter. He was in the supermarket one day with his mother pushing the cart. He liked to push the cart, popping wheelies, racing between patrons, making the sound of a car, until his mother invariably scolded him. Truthfully, he hated going to the supermarket. So he's there lost in a daydream, when who did they bump into in the freakin' frozen food aisle?

Yeah, Pops.

Following the reunion, Pops offered to land Phil a job at the Vet selling hot dogs. Now Phil didn't really want a job. He was barely in his teens. But he wanted a Pops, no matter if the Pops split for ten years. So he obliged, and every week after he finished selling that tray of dogs, he plopped down high up in the seven hundred level and watched the rest of the football game.

Talk about a life oasis.

He fell in love.

"Bad, bad Eagle teams," Phil from Mount Airy will say. "This was the McCormack era and I saw the Birds get destroyed by the Rams, crushed by Isaac Curtis and the Bengals, pretty much everybody, but I fell in love. And just when I'm getting to know the guy – yeah, MY FATHER – he goes and has a heart attack and he dies in bed. So the only time I ever spent with my pops was at the Vet."

So Phil, once again a fatherless boy, became an aimless boy, a restless boy with wanderlust, losing his way. At 16 and too smart for his own good, he doctored his birth certificate so he could run away and join the Navy.

Fast-forward two years: he is stationed in Jacksonville and running an office for the Navy.

Still cursed with a cunning way, the smarts of a scamp and that damn curiosity, Phil learns how to doctor the payroll. He cooks the books like one of those all-beef stadium franks, creating fake employees due real salary, and suddenly he's receiving twelve paychecks a month. He's another *Catch Me If You Can* kid who grew up without any concept of money because his mother didn't have any, and he's way, way out of control. He's gambling at the dog track and he's partying heavily on Jacksonville Beach, not far from where the Eagles will stay years later for the Super Bowl. He's buying drinks for all of the bums and he's flying home almost every weekend just to see the Eagles play live.

Hop a flight Saturday. Party Saturday night. Catch the game. Kiss Moms. Return Monday morning.

"This is the Vermeil time and things were getting better," he will say. "But for me they were the beginning of some tough times. My first was the Falcon playoff game when Mike Michel missed that chip shot field goal, and I was devastated. For me, the game represents my most painful loss of ALL TIME. I was watching the game at my girl's condo in Jacksonville Beach, right there on the tenth floor, oceanfront side. Michel misses the kick and her friends all start laughing at me – remember this was before the Jaguars, so the city mostly rooted for nearby Atlanta teams – and I snapped and I threw the television out of the window, ten floors to the beach. Needless to say, I spent that night in jail."

Many more nights like that one would follow.

Three months later, he's back at home again blowing the money, and his pockets fall empty and all he has left is one of those paychecks under a phony name. So he finds a check-cashing joint deep in the heart of West Philly, and that was all the Navy auditors needed to finger Phil Allen.

"I was the only one in the office from Philly, so it was like a flashing red light, saying 'Here he is, your culprit,'" he says. "The Feds charged me with 256 counts of stuff like wire fraud, mail fraud, forgery, you name it. You know how they do, get all carried away: The United States of America versus Phillip Allen. You kiddin' me?"

Phillip Allen cops to the crime and is shipped off to a federal penitentiary in Tallahassee. Eventually, he is transferred north to Allenwood Prison, Union County, Pennsylvania. He works in the furniture factory with the ABSCAM crooks and his foreman is former State Rep. Matthew Cianciulli, who had been sentenced to three years for his role in getting people who lived outside his district to register, including twenty who voted from his corner grocery store in South Philly.

"Matty Cianciulli, 6th and Reed's own, saved my life in prison," he says. "One night we're all watching the Eagles play the Giants in the dayroom when some call goes against us. I get pissed and throw my coffee mug through the screen. Well, there really is nowhere else to watch the game and these dudes decide I'd be the night's sporting event when Matty steps in. No more to be said. He gives me the lecture, bans me from the dayroom during football, and I had to watch the whole season through the glass, with no sound. But I didn't get hurt."

Phil from Mount Airy is black, of average height and build, with very little distinguishing characteristics, other than his face, though not the construction of the features on his face – which are ordinary and pleasant looking – but the perpetual glow upon it, augmented by a smile from the soul. There's a devilish innocence about him, that of a child caught with chocolates before supper.

Right now, just like the others, he wears the face of bliss, though his eyes are torch-fire orange, having slept very little after beginning this journey to Disney World with the family earlier in the week and then hopping a train to Jacksonville this morning. Very seldom does experience meet expectation, but he always thought it would be like this, way back, during those days selling hot dogs, all the way to the NFC Championship Game, from beforehand when he prepared himself for another great hurt to the final kneeldown and falling facedown on the carpet at his brother's house crying in jubilation.

"I never thought God wanted me to be this happy," he says. "Here I am, with my wife and my brother and I have a beer in my hand and I'm listening to people dedicating tomorrow's game to their family members. This is about the heart. It's just so real. All these people, we're one, together, like real brothers and sisters. Sometimes, I won't lie, you're aware of race at the stadium. It's not a big deal. It's only because you're such a minority at the game. I gotta tell you – listen, dude, this is real important – the only color that's here is Eagles green. Truthfully, dude. To be here in this tent right now, I'm thinking, Look at me, Ma – poor black kid from West Philly – I'm on top of the world."

Part of the reason behind Phil's dramatic soliloquy is that he's going to the game tomorrow, a perk for being part of a documentary on Eagles fans. He will sit with Evander Holyfield and Lebron James and Jim Harbaugh, about twelve rows from the field, and he will say right before kickoff that it is the greatest moment of his life.

The other part is that he will go to the game tomorrow here in Jacksonville, a place that no longer seems haunted by the past. Since Phil was last here, a city has sprung from the weeds. Look around. The Riverwalk. The skyline. The Super Bowl. Yes, Jacksonville has changed dramatically, but not more than Phil from Mount Airy, who is now the

Pops to his children that he always wanted. When he got here, he
opened his eyes. He looked for demons. He couldn't find any.

THE MIRACLE CHILD

He is here, too, I am told. Shall you see now, you shall see him for what
he is: a Child of Grace, the embodiment of innocence, beguiler of the
calloused, bestowing upon us the gift of context. So I am told, the
Miracle Child is here, somewhere beneath this tent wearing dark sunglasses that hide splintered eyes that hold no vision. Slinky even for
eleven and patently bony, which gives him an angular appearance, the
boy stands mashed against the hip of his father, easily lost in the deep
pocket of the throng.

Shall you see now, you shall see beyond the appearance of physical
frailty and see a boy who wields the will of a thousand men and the
valor of a thousand more. You shall see a boy's smile that could light a
candle.

The Miracle Child, who spent only twenty-six weeks in the womb,
weighing one pound and fifteen ounces at birth, less than a football,
and who spent his first days of life in incubation and his first four
months in the hospital, where he was diagnosed with two detached
retinas that rendered him blind and mild cerebral palsy, shouldn't be
here now. He shouldn't have been there two Sundays ago at Lincoln
Financial Field, singing the NFC Championship National Anthem
through the raking wind and brutal cold in front of all those people,
including those watching on national television, touching every one of
them.

The Miracle Child's name is Timmy Kelly, and how fitting is that?
Aren't all Timmys fine lads, freckled felicific souls? And *Timmy Kelly?*
A clean, virtuous name, summoning a vision of the Island with its
scrubbed hills glistening after a soft drizzle, devoid of any thought of
the troubles.

How properly fitting that there is a Timmy Kelly in this story.

How Timmy arrived here began when he was eight, shortly after becoming the first blind kindergarten child mainstreamed in a Philadelphia public school. A family friend told Eileen and Tim Kelly about open tryouts for potential Eagles anthem singers at Lehigh University. Timmy made the cut from five hundred to twenty-five finalists and was invited to Veterans Stadium, where he flustered during his second audition. "He started too high," father Tim recalled, "and so he had nothing left when he got to the high notes. He started crying and he was too embarrassed to finish and wasn't picked. We didn't encourage him to go back but he did and the same thing happened as he was picked to the final twenty-five. However, we were on vacation for the finals so he didn't compete and last year the same thing happened now at the Linc. So he's half-paying attention and suddenly they call his name, and he throws his boom box in the air and he's so excited. He's jumping up and down and going 'yeah' like 15 times."

So Timmy's first game was against the Saints in November 2004, and he sang their socks off. Two weeks later the Eagles' Denise Gallagher called with news that he had also swiped the heart of team president Joe Banner, who exhorted, "We just have to that kid back."

Never had the club received such a response over an anthem singer, the outpouring of letters and e-mails overwhelming. So there was Timmy before for the 49er game in December and before the first playoff game against the Packers, and because the league controls the anthem for the Title Games, there he was before the game belting out "God Bless America," and so many of the team had hugged him, from players to the office-worker bees, particularly the women, all of whom were hypnotized by the boy. "You're part of the family now," they told him.

They were true to their word, and so he tottered out on the field before the Baltimore game on Halloween, and how well he sang. How he loved the ovation, all those people hooting and hollering collective ly, making their own sort of music, a tribute to him.

But the story of how he came to be here in Jacksonville truly began two weeks ago, the Friday before the Title Game, when Denise called again with news, though she was quite furtive. It's a secret, she began.

"Could he be on call for Sunday?" Denise asked father Tim.

A massive snowstorm loomed and threatened the travel plans of the league-issued anthem singer, Fantasia Barrino, the *American Idol* winner, who was scheduled to fly in on a red-eye from California. Denise said the Eagles would give the Kellys three tickets to the game at the very least, in the event FOX's Fantasia could make it. So that Saturday, bunkered at his home in Huntingdon Valley, Timmy listened hard to the weather report on Channel 6 all day, and the snow fell like feathers from an exploding pillow. Timmy gave hourly updates: "Four inches, Dad. Seven inches. Eleven inches!" Finally, he came running from his room, knowing each step by heart, and he hollered, "Airport's closed! The airport's closed!" Two hours later, the Eagles called and confirmed that Timmy would be singing and asked if the family wanted to be picked up in a SUV.

In this town, we love a link to the past, and Timmy Kelly's story takes us to the last time the Eagles won the NFC Championship on a similarly cold day. A few years back, Timmy attended his first Broadway show, *Beauty and the Beast,* starring Philadelphia's Andrea McArdle. Following the show, he met McArdle backstage and he sang for her and she deemed him with talent and recommended that he take voice lessons from her coach. And he did, and now he would do what McArdle did: sing the national anthem in the game that boosted the Eagles to the Super Bowl.

The post-storm wind howled at 40 miles an hour on Sunday and the mighty cold's blast scorched the innards upon inhale. During the sound check, the wind took away the Miracle Child's breath and left him fighting his footing. Soon the Miracle Child, wearing an Eagles ski cap and heavy coat unbuttoned to show a Donovan McNabb jersey and those black sunglasses, leaned against his red-faced father on the frozen field, members of the Color Guard behind him in full salute, and began to sing for real. "When it came time to sing, the wind smacked him in the face and he pulled the mike back so you didn't really hear it," beamed father Tim, a grown-up, sturdy version of his son. "He struggled because of the wind but he did a bang-up job. When I hear him sing, I see this miracle unfolding before my eyes and I am somehow a part of it, aware of something special happening."

This was not an idolmaker afternoon suitable for performance appraisal. So Timmy Kelly noticeably fought through the elements, marshalling every bit of that will to get through the song as professionally as possible, and wasn't that the point of the day? The struggle? Surmounting it? Some said later they feared the crowd's response to the rendition, perhaps not knowing the backstory of the Miracle Child or not caring, That Reputation coming to roost. The stereotypers would have a field day: Gargoyles boo blind boy!

Alas, there was an ovation, a resounding one, tender and warm-hearted. And when Timmy Kelly finished, Chad Lewis, Jevon Kearse and Dhani Jones came to his side and they were especially affirming. "You did a great job," Chad Lewis said, and kissed him on his forehead.

Dhani Jones nodded hard. "Now that's the way to start a ball-game."

All the while, the crowd continue to stand and cheer, and Timmy Kelly beamed. "Yeah," he said, like fifteen more times.

The days following the NFL Title game, the Miracle Child still beamed. Just when he thought he had reached the pinnacle of his young life, he arrived at Murray Avenue Middle School to sing at a pep rally. Waiting for him a week ago Thursday was Action News (ABC-6) to present him with tickets to the Super Bowl, and the school district of Lower Moreland committed to paying for the Kelly's trip to Jacksonville with a campaign entitled, "Fly, Timmy Fly."

"The school picked up the tab for the trip right there on the air," father Tim would say later. "They had fundraisers to raise the money to put it back, and once they mentioned it over the air donations started pouring in. They had to stop it at some point. All we had to do was pack. A limo picked us up to take us to the airport and we were given the full works."

The Miracle Child would be a celebrity here in Jacksonville. He would meet people from Philadelphia and from New England and from California, Florida and Ohio, and they would stop him outside the hotel and he would pose for pictures with them and he would sign autographs for them and they would serenade him with the T.O. Song, substituting his name for Terrell Owens' intials: "Ti-meeee, Ti-me, Ti-me, Ti-meeeee...Tiiii-meeee, Tiiii-meee."

"The Eagles fans, everyone, celebrated Timmy and they did it in a profound way," father Tim Kelly would say. "They were so kind, so gracious and thoughtful. Their actions touched my wife and me in a very deep way and renewed our belief that people are basically good and sometimes they just need an opportunity to show it. For my family to be the recipient of all of this is just so overwhelming."

In the following weeks, I would stumble upon a website called 700LEVEL.com, where there would be a forum with those saluting the Miracle Child. And the father would be there, too, and he would express gratitude.

Tim Kelly wrote:

The community has rallied around our family because of Timmy. As his father I can tell you it is a deeply moving experience. Eileen and I will be forever grateful. More about Timmy: This is a boy who seems to take everything in stride. Imagine a day filled with a good amount of difficulty walking, a certain amount of pain, not being able to see where you are going and having to depend completely on others to safely direct you. Not an easy task. Timmy does this everyday and there is so much more that he just takes in stride. Despite these obstacles, Timmy is a very well-adjusted, happy child with a tremendous zest for life. He is very curious and inquisitive. His hearing is remarkable, and his ability to remember names with voices is just amazing. We got to meet Diane Sawyer and he asked her, "How do you move your notes when you are on the air?" Think about that question for a minute and think about Diane Sawyer. The next time you see her on "Good Morning America" watch what she does with her notes. Timmy could hear that and was interested in knowing what she does. Diane Sawyer was speechless.

I was reading Timmy a story written about him in a local magazine. The author said, "Timmy was one of the unlucky ones." She referred to his blindness and CP. Timmy stopped me and asked what she meant by that. I was in tears and struggled to answer and said, "Well Timmy, you are blind and you have CP. He said with authority, "Dad, I'm not one of the unlucky ones. It isn't so bad being blind and having CP." You tell me he is not a warrior with the heart filled love and the voice of an angel. Thanks,

Tim

THE RITUAL

Every city needs a thing. For better or worse, Philadelphia's is sport, which is not to neglect the obvious: the city's rich history and its standing in the birth of a nation, and that cobblestone charm which has been sustained, the lovely architecture and the vast array of arts and museums and cultural centers and fabulous restaurants and the livable nature of Center City, perhaps more manageable than any major downtown in the country. Truly, I adore the aesthetics of this city, from east Delancy Street in the Colonial thicket of Society Hill to west Delancy Street and its statuesque brownstones, just off posh Rittenhouse Square, to Delancy Street that runs through University City, not far from the campus of the University of Pennsylvania, where the romance of erudition is palpable beneath its ivy drapes. From City Hall to South Street to Old City to the surrounding neighborhoods, great pockets to the south and north and west, each with their own distinct ethnic feel and flavor. Magnify the entire area, from the Pennsylvania suburban sprawl to southern New Jersey to northern Delaware all the way to the shore, and you present a wonderful, unique living experience.

That said, the common thread through the Delaware Valley other than history is sport, perhaps because sport and history in a place like this is so intertwined. Philadelphia has cleaved to sport for its identity in recent years. We love basketball, both college and pro. We adore baseball, up through the pending ignominy of the first professional franchise to lose ten thousand games. We will be one of the few cities that embraces hockey when it returns. But in the end, it always goes back to football.

You can point to exactly when Philadelphia fell for the pro pigskin. It began when the Eagles moved from Shibe Park to the hallowed Franklin Field in 1958. Shibe Park was a much better baseball stadium than football venue, and so the move to Franklin Field – a classic football stadium with real tradition and wonderful sightlines – signified a step up in class, as though the team was moving uptown. Now that year, the Eagles also acquired Norm Van Brocklin, the club's first truly great quarterback, who had won a world championship. They were nicely positioned to capitalize on the momentum from NFL's first foray into network television, highlighted by the sudden death championship game between the Colts and the Giants.

Attendance steadily grew from the '58 season but the tipping point occurred on October 23, 1960, when the Eagles went into Cleveland to play a Browns team that had beaten them soundly in the opener. By this point of the season, fans knew the Eagles were a good team but still questioned whether they were of championship caliber. Capping one of the most dramatic games in team history, Bobby Walston kicked a 38 yard field goal into the wind literally at the final gun, and as Didinger tells it, "somebody set off a rocket Philadelphia."

The week before the Cleveland game, the Eagles drew a crowd of 38,000 for a visit by the Detroit Lions. The following week, with Pittsburgh in town, fans packed the stadium by the tune of over 58,000, mostly of a walk-up variety. "That was the detonation point," Didinger says. "It was palpable. Everybody had watched that game against Cleveland. From that point on you couldn't buy an Eagles' ticket. That was pro football's coming of age in Philadelphia."

A ritual was born that day.

"The difference between the Eagles and the other teams is like close relatives and extended family, relatives you may see once or twice a year," Didinger says. "You love them and they are your family but it's not same thing. Think about it. Nobody watches Eagles games alone. You experience them as a family. As a result they become your family.

"It's why I think people misjudge the booing. We all have relatives that are screw-ups, that cousin or uncle we get mad at. We love them and we want them to do well and when he screws up and he forgets to turn the lights out and kicks over the rotisserie, we get mad at him and holler at him and call him a dumbshit. But when it's all said and done, we still love him. We don't worry that he'll be all right because we believe he'll straighten up. And we still support him. We'll never turn our back on him because he's family. That doesn't mean you can't holler and say bad stuff to him. That defines how Eagles fans feel. They're part of who you are. They're not just somebody you root for. They're somebody you live with."

Sometimes it can be a culture shock for the players. "It's different in this city," Jon Runyan will say. "The Eagles are religion here. Coming here, it takes a year or two to get used to. Where I was before, in Tennessee, they were football fans. Here, it's all about the Eagles. Look at how they traveled. It felt like a home game at the Super Bowl. I couldn't believe it. I think it was good for the morale of the city. It's not the happiest place in the world to live. The Eagles give people something to look forward to."

Jeremiah Trotter will add: "Our fans have game faces. I have a game day mentality. There's me and a game day me, a.k.a., The Axeman. Our fans have the same thing. They get painted up. They got their green on. They've been in the parking lot getting prepared for the game with their tailgates. They're all lathered up. They got their beers in them, doc, and they're ready to cheer at the top of their lungs. The next day, they can't barely talk. They have just as much passion as me. They love the game. Because it's a tough game. Because it's down and dirty. They love down and dirty."

The person who illustrated this point best of all was portly James David Ryan, who to this day remains the great Buddy to the fans. Buddy Ryan embodied sports in Philadelphia better than a breathing boo wit'. Pudgy, garish, brash, loyal, wrapped in a cussing swagger, he loved a defense that gulped glass shards and bopped the beans out of players, particularly quarterbacks. Mean Crow Green he was, and he didn't care because he believed in sucker-punch football and so did Philadelphia. He believed football was a game without couth and so did Philadelphia. So the town loved the fact Ryan was the anti-Tom Landry, the coach who didn't wear a tweed fedora and speak softly and pander to the Redskins and exhibit respect for any of his opponents, but who did exhibit the class of a longshoreman.

The town with the patience of a candlewick adored Ryan even through zero playoff victories, a terrible fate for a team that was Super Bowl caliber. Even though they lost two of the playoff games, withering at home without a whimper against the Rams and Redskins, even after the team crumpled under the great expectations, the town hooted against his firing.

Part of the Buddy Phenomenon was the type of team he assembled, with an emphasis toward defense, a gambling defense that snorted and sent the house on a blitz and played with the edge of a leg-breaker. Consider, at the top of his game, following his appearance on the cover of *Sports Illustrated*, Randall Cunningham was more popular elsewhere. When he went into other cities, he was treated like a rock star. Meanwhile, Eagles fans preferred Reggie White and Jerome Brown and Seth Joyner, and those mean, hurt-you safeties, Wes Hopkins and Andre Waters.

"It's because they just loved that defense," says Didinger, who covered that team on a daily basis. "They just loved to see the Eagles bring it. I'm always struck by the perfect bottom line: If you go to somebody and ask what they remember about the Body Bag game, they say the eight Redskins carried off the field. Remember the score? No, don't remember the score. Who scored touchdowns? Nah. They say the eight Redskins and the fact that Brian Mitchell had to finish the game at quarterback. Here they know how many guys went for MRIs. Here, they count the concussions, the broken noses, how many times the ambulance backed up to the field. Here, they catalog the spilled blood."

Here, the memorable moments are the ones in which the Eagles bludgeoned the opponent:

Bednarik cleans Gifford's clock.

The House of Pain Game against the Houston Oilers, after which, Jerome Brown boomed, "You provide the house, we'll bring the pain."

The Bounty Bowl against the Cowboys.

Keith Byars' demolishing block of Pepper Johnson.

Load Left against the Cowboys, in which the Eagles stuffed Emmitt Smith on the same running play.

The goal line stand against the Cardinals. Eight tries from inside the two.

Any Andre Waters hit.

Any Wes Hopkins hit.

Brian Dawkins' bone-rattlin' hit against Ike Hilliard.

Brian Dawkins' bone-rattlin' hit against Amani Toomer.

Brian Dawkins' bone-rattlin' hit against Jeremy Shockey.

The smothering of Michael Vick led by Hugh Douglas.

The smothering of Michael Vick by Jeremiah Trotter.

Hollis Thomas' bop of Michael Vick at the 5-yard line in that same game.

That mindset continued through last year, even though the Eagles' offense was easily the most potent in the history of the club. Perhaps it's because the town wasn't used to such a devastating attack, particularly the seemingly effortless hook-ups down the field between Donovan McNabb and Terrell Owens or Brian Westbrook. I do not wish to diminish the adulation bestowed upon McNabb or Owens or Westbrook, but defense is forever the fans' darling here.

Just ask the Prodigal Son.

The Axeman.

PRODIGAL SON

The Night-Before Meeting has just concluded the way it always does, with Andy Reid offering to buy the players a cheeseburger, and so we are back in the yawning ballroom with the rows of long tables for that final snack before bed. The players are back in their same small clusters, and we zoom back in on the linebackers to the longtime friend sitting across from Ike Reese.

Jeremiah Trotter is carrying on as usual, bobbing his head, chewing hard on his food, laughing harder. By nature, he's a cheerful bloke, Jeremiah Trotter, a Jolly Cholly sort whose main goal in life is to eliminate static, anything oppressive, anything heavy, down to conversation. "You know me, doc," he says, "I just like to crack jokes. Just jokes, baby."

Even on the field, where he is a ferocious tackler, a middle linebacker born of Butkus, he is happy. He is the kind of football player who plays with personality, who jars the bejesus out of a ballcarrier with a smile and a cackle, and then his patented dropping of the axe, where he pretends to chop wood, thus his nickname: The axeman. There was a time earlier this season when he tackled a Giant a little too far out of bounds, in the heart of the New York sidelines, and when he looked up and saw where he was, he smiled and said, "Oh, Lord." Football being the ultimate macho game, members of the Giants took exception, and encircled the Axeman, pitching out their chests the way men do to intimidate other men. So he tip-toed and wiggled between the players in comedic fashion. Afterwards, while preparing for our radio show the following night with Ike Reese, he said, "I was all by my lonesome over there. Jevon [Kearse] was the only one who came over to help the Axeman."

To which Reese responded: "Man, I can't afford the fine to go save your ass."

"Man, Ike, I see how you roll," Trotter cracked.

By the way, the Giants already had their issues with Jeremiah Trotter after the first game between the teams, in which he drilled their punter with one of those brutal blocks that prompt a cringe and an ooh. Since it sort of offended the unwritten code that protects kickers, New York special teamers were out to get him the rest of the game, prompting this from Trotter, "The cat wears a helmet, don't he?"

Of course, the Axeman is carrying on right now. Life is the way it should be, damn near perfect. He is where he should be, playing for the Eagles, starting for the Eagles, right there in the middle, and he's at the Super Bowl, too, after playing the game of a linebacker's life against Michael Vick and the Falcons in the championship game. He was on the cover of *Sports Illustrated* two weeks ago. Tam is pregnant. The car wash – the Trot Spot, over in Jersey – is bustling, and last month he broke ground on another in the city. The Axeman T-shirts are selling like popcorn at the movies. It's all finally fallen into place for him, even if the knees inside look like the frayed top of an old shoelace.

Really. How unlikely was this story? How is Jeremiah Trotter back here after what happened? After how he left the first time, storming into Andy Reid's office that day that spring 2002, a madman over his contract predicament? He'll tell you. He was out of control and out of line, the way he went about it. In the middle of the contentious meeting, Andy Reid summoned Jim Johnson to his office, thinking maybe the presence of the beloved defensive coordinator would calm Trotter some.

The Axeman wielded a nasty edge that day, all the way out the door.

Torched the village, he did.

Within minutes after Trotter huffed away that day, Reid took off the franchise tag that would have assured his return the following season. So the Redskins swooped in and signed the 25-year-old Trotter for the big money he sought, to the amount of 36 million dollars, including seven million up front, and you know the trappings of big money.

Neal Peart of Rush wrote the words:

Big money pull a million strings
Big money hold the prize
Big money weave a mighty web
Big money draw the flies

Big money goes around the world
Big money take a cruise
Big money leave a mighty wake
Big money leave a bruise

Big money got a heavy hand
Big money take control
Big money got a mean streak
Big money got no soul…

So there he was in Washington, pockets full, feeling strong. Yeah, he'd show Philadelphia. Let him walk like that. Believe that? Ain't right, man. Just ain't right. Here in D.C. he had new coach Steve Spurrier, mastermind of offense, architect of the Florida Gators' Fun and Gun. He had Spurrier's inventive equal coaching the defense, Marvin Lewis, and LaVar Arrington, another beast, playing alongside him. Best linebacker tandem in the league, everybody said. He'd show Philly, and he'd show 'em right quick. The two teams were scheduled to play in the second game of the season, a much-hyped Monday nighter at FedEx Field.

Meanwhile, the Redskins had won their season opener in impressive fashion over the Giants, and the Eagles had lost theirs, a tough one in Tennessee.

Entering the game, the prevailing notion, even in Philadelphia, was that of a possible power shift in the NFC East, starring spendthrift owner Daniel Snyder's Redskins. The oddsmakers also thought so, installing Washington as a field goal favorite over the Eagles. I recall doing the show the day of the game, and one of the topics was a straw poll featuring the question: Who would you rather have as coach right now, this second, Steve Spurrier or Andy Reid?

After five hours and countless calls, even though Spurrier had coached exactly one game in the NFL, Reid won by only one vote.

That night, Reid's team won the game by 30.

The Eagles scored touchdowns on each their first two possessions with astonishing ease, quickly beating the life out of the Washington crowd and the new Redskins. Led by Donovan McNabb, the Eagles racked up 451 yards against Jeremiah Trotter's defense, scored seven times, punted only four times, and won the game 37-7.

The loss sent the 'Skins spiraling. It was a miserable year for Washington and Trotter, who hurt that knee on Thanksgiving and never returned.

It didn't get any better in 2003, the Skins equally miserable, Spurrier proving a terrible bust in the NFL, the players suddenly squawking about how he would beat them off the practice field, jogging by them to make his tee time.

Meanwhile, Jeremiah Trotter, took his share of criticism because he was another of Daniel Snyder's disappointing big money free agent signings. When Joe Gibbs returned to coach Washington, Trotter was among the first cap casualties. "I learned a lot over that time," he nods. "Such a trying time in my life. The money was great, but I wasn't happy."

So now Jeremiah Trotter is free again, but it's not a good free, not with serious questions surrounding his health. The knee, man. Football is hell on the knees. He prayed about it. He talked to his pastor, a good man who was always his sounding board in Philadelphia. He thought about New York. But the Giants failed him on his physical. Then he had a dream.

True story, he swears.

In the dream, he is playing for the Eagles again. He makes a big play on special teams. Forces a fumble on the kickoff. Falls on the ball to win the game. Then he's in the locker room, and he's with all of the guys, his old friends. There's Brian Dawkins, and B Dawk is joking on him because he has an Afro. It's a big Afro, and everybody begins teasing him. And he's happy. He's the old Trot again. The Axeman.

The next morning he woke up, and strained to recall the details of the dream. "Man, I thought," he says, "what does this mean? I wasn't going to say anything about it. But I keep thinking about the dream. So I actually tried to call the front office myself. I was told, 'Coach is out of town on vacation.' I talked with my agent, and he told me, 'Listen, Trot, I can get you Andy's number if you want it.' I said, 'Get it'"

So Jeremiah Trotter called Andy Reid the next day. Now they had talked once since that spring day in Reid's office. When Trotter got hurt in Dallas on Thanksgiving, Reid was watching. So the next day, Reid called Trotter at home in the morning. "I was sleeping," Trotter says. "But as soon as I heard his voice, I knew right away who it was. He told me, 'Hang in there, Trot. I want to see you back on the field soon. You're a great competitor.' You don't know how much that phone call meant to me."

The day Jeremiah Trotter called Andy Reid, the coach was fishing on a boat in the middle of a lake deep in the Midwest, and he had remarked earlier how he couldn't get any reception on his cell phone. But Trotter's call went right through, and he told his former coach about the dream he had and how he'd like to explore the possibility of returning. Andy Reid welcomed the notion.

It made sense for the Eagles to see how much game remained in Jeremiah Trotter. The team never did replace him. In 2002, the Eagles went with a combination of lumbering Levon Kirkland and backup Barry Gardner in the middle, and the position patchwork didn't work. In the end, in fact, in the one true NFC Championship Game that got away, it proved disastrous, with Kirkland huffing way behind Tampa Bay's Joe Jurevicius on a catch and the 71 yard run that breathed life into the Buccaneers. The Eagles led 7-3 with momentum whirling their way in the first quarter and had Tampa pinned deep in its own territory when Jurevicius broke loose slanting over the middle on the third-down play, setting up a go-ahead touchdown plunge by Mike Alstott.

"Oh, yeah, I would have made that play," Jeremiah Trotter said when I asked him about it once.

The following year, once again the middle linebacker spot came back to haunt the Eagles in the Title Game. In the offseason, the team signed Mark Simoneau, a speedy but light linebacker, away from the Falcons and manned him in the middle. While there were stretches where Simoneau played well, winning the Defensive Player of the Month honors for October, he wore down as the season wore on. With injuries decimating the line and tackle support for Simoneau, the Eagles' rushing defense leaked mightily. In the first playoff game, the

Packers pounded the ball with much success, but astonishingly drifted away from the run and allowed the Eagles life and overtime. Even in the extra period, the Packers opted to pass instead of giving the ball to Ahman Green, and Brett Favre threw a terrible interception that left the Eagles survivors.

The Birds would have no such luck against Carolina the following week, as the Panthers learned from the Packers and stuck to their strategy of hammering the ball with Stephen Davis and DeShaun Foster and shortening the game. Carolina quarterback Jake Delhomme, who would have a career day in the Super Bowl against New England, completed only nine passes in 14 attempts the entire game for 101 yards. Meanwhile, the bruised Davis, coming off a quadriceps injury, rushed for 76 yards and Foster another 60, including the game-sealing touchdown in which Simoneau pinballed off him at the goal line.

Meanwhile, the fans howled, particularly since Trotter was a fan favorite in the first place and most never wanted him to leave. Philadelphia could take losing the war but not the battle. Aesthetics are important here, particularly on defense, where the fans don't take kindly to the Bend But Don't Break kind. Just ask Marion Campbell, the old Swampfox who succeeded Dick Vermeil in 1983 and played that style of defense and lasted only three seasons, leaving under a firestorm of Marion jokes.

This is why Buddy Ryan held such a stature in this town without a playoff victory and why Bud Carson and Jim Johnson became celebrity coordinators. It's also why east of Chicago, nobody appreciates a middle linebacker like Philadelphia, even if Bergey, B&E Evans and Trotter aren't quite Butkus, Singletary and Urlacher.

So when Trotter's name hit the waiver wire, the fans, in full snarl over Simoneau, clamored for his return. On the surface, the possibility appeared a pipe dream, and it might have been had Trotter not made the phone call. I recall talking to Andy Reid on the phone the day he made the announcement and expressing my pleasant surprise, and he said, "I've never been one to hold grudges. I'm not about that stuff. You separate the business side from the personal side. I think that's very important, especially if you're the head coach and have that tag as the general manager. I know Jeremiah is a good person.

Whatever was said by both sides – he said some things, I said some things – we meant from a business standpoint, not a personal one. We were both able to throw those things out of the window and come together as mature human beings."

Reid made it clear that The Axeman would be coming in strictly as a situational linebacker, playing mostly on special teams, and that Simoneau would keep his starting job. For the first half of the season, Trotter's role was exactly that, seeing the bulk of his playing on short yardage and goal line situations, even though he often stood next to Johnson on the sidelines during the game and begged him to let him get in there.

Much to Trotter's credit, he never made a wave, even if he felt he was better suited to start in the middle, even when the public clamored for him to replace Simoneau. He praised Simoneau publicly, kept silent on the rest and played hard on special teams, a difficult assignment for a player who had started his whole life. His teammates welcomed him back like a lost brother, the affable Axeman who always exudes energy, down to Jon Runyan. The two came to blows once during training camp in what turned out to be a legendary bout. "Yeah, that was a classic," Runyan recalled with a smile while he sat in with Trotter during a Monday night show, looking back almost fondly. "My first year here. I took out [someone on the line] and you know I was coming in with that reputation. So Trot went to help and came running from my backside and took me low. Next you know we were going at it pretty good."

"Big Jon and I were dancin'," Trotter giggled.

Fast-forward to Week Eight of the season, the Eagles having entered Pittsburgh the last undefeated team in the NFL. "I remember thinking during pregame warm-ups, this is going to be a tough one," Ike Reese told me the following the day. "The crowd was really, really pumped, waving their towels. There was electricity in the air. I didn't feel good about the game. I thought we were prepared. We had a decent week of practice, even though the media kept talking about going undefeated. But I could tell when I got on the field we just weren't at the same emotional pitch as the Steelers. Football is a game that is so dependent upon emotion. A lot of times it can mean the difference in a game, especially now with so much parity in the league."

Reese was right. Buoyed by that emotion, buoyed from knocking off the previously undefeated Patriots the previous week, the Steelers overwhelmed the Eagles from the start, scoring touchdowns on their first two drives of the game. Even without the injured Duce Staley, the bitter Doooce who had pined to play against his former team, Pittsburgh buffeted away at the interior of the Eagles defense. Behind the old, bruising Bus, Jerome Bettis, the Steelers gained 252 yards on the ground, and held the ball for nearly 42 minutes en route to a 27-3 romp.

Andy Reid and Jim Johnson had seen enough, especially after how the defense played when Trotter, with Simoneau injured on the sidelines, manned the middle against Cleveland two weeks prior, collecting 16 tackles. So Simoneau moved to the outside, where he was better suited with his speed, and Jeremiah Trotter became a starter again.

With Trotter in the middle, the defense, which already featured hard hitters like Brian Dawkins, Michael Lewis and Jevon Kearse, seemed to have more teeth. Trotter is a very emotional player, very vocal and dynamic, and the results were palpable. Prior to Trotter, the unit ranked twenty-fourth in the league and twenty-seventh against the rush. In the following six games, the defense allowed an average of just 70 yards on the ground, 227 total yards and less than eleven points, helping the Eagles give up the fewest points in the NFC for the season.

"You're talking about our defensive MVP," said Lewis, the whack-em safety. "He gave us the presence that we needed."

So despite his short season as a starter, Jeremiah Trotter made the Pro Bowl for the third time. But he saved his best game for the NFC Championship Game. The days leading up to the game, the hype centered on Michael Vick, who runs from the quarterback position like no other before him, turning into a phantom when you try to tackle him. In this thrice bitten city, fans couldn't stop obsessing over whether the Eagles could stop Vick and a mighty Falcons' rushing attack that rolled through the St. Louis Rams the week before.

Led by Trotter, the Eagles held Vick to just 26 yards, half of them on one play in the first half, and completely stifled Atlanta backs

Warrick Dunn and TJ Duckett. Dunn, who gained 142 yards against the Rams, was held to 59.

Trotter's success prompted Gibbs to say, "Right now watching him play, he'd fit into anybody's plans. Sometimes you make decisions, sometimes they're good, sometimes they're bad. I'd say we came in making evaluations off of what we thought, watching films, the availability of free agency, and sometimes you make bad decisions. In this case, we made a bad one."

Trotter will sit back and reflect on what transpired over the past few years, and he will never say never again. "Man, I'm still having trouble now believing what happened," he will say. "I went from my lowest point ever to my highest point ever. Lower than my rookie year. I mean, I was just Jeremiah Trotter then. I wasn't The Axeman. Nobody expected me to be great. But now I was going from the Pro Bowl to special teams, from being The Axeman to my lowest point. It was a humbling process. Took a lot of praying. Now I'm at my highest point, professionally and spiritually. Going through that allowed me to get closer to God and be a better family man.

"Made me step back and appreciate playing football. Only a small percentage of people play the greatest game in this country at this level. I spent all that time [after being released] working out, not even knowing if I was going to play football, if I was going to get another chance to be on a team. Made me dig down deep."

The Axeman will soon be free. Again.

His contract will expire after Jacksonville, after completing Redemption Season, after The Education of Jeremiah Trotter. After everything, what will he have learned? He will have another choice, quite possibly between the place he swears he never should have left and the wink and wiles of Big Money.

Though the Eagles will offer him a contract, he will do the smart thing, and provide himself options. No one should ever begrudge a man for seeking options. It's what he does upon weighing them that is up for scrutiny.

So Jeremiah Trotter will go on tour with prospective employers, with scheduled stops in Kansas City and Cincinnati and perhaps Chicago, the teams that will display the greatest interest. So he will go to Kansas City on a March day to meet with Dick Vermeil who desperately needs to fix his defense and he will spend all day with him. They will talk football philosophy and of life. He will have his knees prodded and probed. He will be booked on a flight leaving for Cincinnati at six o'clock. But Vermeil will stall. When a team is hot after a player, it will try to prevent him from leaving town. Keep him local until you can sign him, killing any last-minute courting by somebody else.

Vermeil will tell Trotter to hang tight, that he's finalizing an offer to his agent. Meanwhile, Trotter will miss his flight to Cincinnati and the next one and the one after that, until finally it got so late his agent will tell the Chiefs, "Take Jeremiah to a hotel. Let him stay there and we'll give you an answer tomorrow."

In his hotel room, Jeremiah will get nervous and begin to agonize over his pending decision. See, deep down, he really will prefer to stay with the Eagles, but the Chiefs will be hot to Trot.

About eleven o'clock that night, I will be out for a late dinner with Butchy at Bomb-Bombs, a tiny tasty little corner joint in South Philadelphia that got its name because it was bombed twice back in the fifties, and I will see a missed call on my cell. It will be Jeremiah. Just as I show Butchy who it was, his cell phone will ring, and Jeremiah's name will surface on the caller ID. He will give me his phone to answer and Jeremiah will say, "Who's this? Cuz? I was just trying to reach you. You have Andy's cell phone number?"

I will give him the number, and he will call back a moment later and tell Butchy, "No answer. I need Andy's home number. It's really important."

Andy will just be getting home after spending the day in Kansas City delivering a speech, having flown there in the morning on the same flight with Chiefs president Carl Peterson. The two would sit next to one another. Trotter will tell Reid, "Listen, my agent has to get in touch with Joe [Banner]. These cats are putting pressure on me. They're not letting me out of town without a deal."

"Hey, man, let me call, Joe," Reid will tell Trotter, and then will call him back promptly, and say, "Be cool. We'll get this done first thing in the morning."

The next morning, Trotter will depart for Cincinnati to keep his date with Marvin Lewis, now the head coach of the Bengals. He will arrive at the gate at the airport in Kansas City and overhear a woman in line bemoaning the fact that she got bumped out of first class. "I heard it's over Carl Peterson," she will say. "Better not be. If they bumped us out of first class for him, he better be going to get us some defensive players."

Trotter, with his first-class ticket in hand, will walk through the jetway and enter the cabin and the first person he will see is Peterson. "Out of all the flights in America," Trotter will say. "[Peterson] asks to switch seats so he could sit next me, and the first thing he says is, 'So you're going to Cincinnati, huh?' Now I'm supposed to be back at the hotel. I told him, You know, I gave Marvin Lewis my word I was coming to town, and my dad told me never to break word. He had no choice but to respect that.

"[Peterson] spent the next hour trying to recruit me. He said, 'The way you play, with your leadership, with your big play ability and your ability to get players around you to a play a level above what they can, that's what we're looking for here.' I told him I'd give him a decision later on today."

Trotter will arrive in Cincinnati and he will tell Marvin Lewis, "Don't bother have me go through some exhaustive medical examination. If you want to take an X-ray, fine, but no two-hour MRIs. I haven't passed a physical since I started playing in the NFL. All you gotta do is pop that tape in and make your decision. They say fine, and the doctor says the knee doesn't look good. But the cat doesn't miss practice. We don't know everything. Sometimes there are things you can't explain."

While Trotter will undergo X-rays, he will have an epiphany, and he will act on it after the Bengals made their proposal. "I didn't want to leave Philly," he will say. "I called my pastor. Then I called my agent and told him to do the deal with the Eagles, even though those cats didn't budge off their original offer. I calculated the numbers over three years. The offers weren't that far apart. My agent told me, 'Trot,

I think you're making the right decision.'

"I figured this is going to be my last deal. I don't want to play until I can hardly walk. I don't want to be one of those dude, some of those cats, who can't play catch with my son. So if this is it, I want to play where I want to be, regardless of the money.

"The moment I realized I made the right decision," Jeremiah Trotter will continue, "is when I got off the plane and there was a crowd waiting and news cameras waiting. Butchy and a police officer were waiting for me in the jetway to escort me through. I thought that was cool. People were clapping and clapping, and saying, 'The Axeman is back! The Axeman is back!' Almost brought tears to my eyes. God puts us in certain places for certain reasons. I'm just glad nobody offered me six or seven million more, I might have done something stupid."

TRAITORS AND BRAGGARTS, SELLOUTS AND SYCOPHANTS

Here in the tent, I see Ringo, a caller to my Monday night radio show with Jeremiah Trotter. He is Mike Ring from Havertown, maybe in his late twenties, and he's wearing the Trotter jersey he so cherishes. See, one night in December, Ringo called the show and asked to come clean to Jeremiah.

"You were my all-time, all-time favorite Eagle," he said. "But when you left, I hated you. I taped an A and I over your name on the back so it spelled TRAITER [traitor]."

Trotter laughs.

"Dude, I need a favor?" Ringo said.

"You said you hated me and you want a favor?" Trotter said. "Uh, all right. What's up?"

"I'm a season ticket holder and I sit right near the tunnel where you guys come out of. If you win, I want you to come over to my seat and rip off the A and the I from your name."

"You got it, doc."

So moments after the Eagles won the game, Jeremiah Trotter

walked smiling toward the tunnel and there was Ringo gesturing, waving the jersey at him. So Trotter smiled over and ripped off the two taped letters, scrunching them up into a ball in his hand and flinging it to the ground.

Following the show, in search of the rest of The Caravan, I am inside the lobby of the Radisson Hotel by the river, crammed equally by the prominent and the parvenu. There are familiar faces everywhere, smiling faces that connote being at an event like the Super Bowl.

I see the prodigious, mustachioed Garry Cobb, a local television and radio celebrity and former linebacker for the Eagles, Lions and Cowboys in a healthy NFL career that spanned 11 years. I've always been fascinated by the game of football, particularly its strategic element, so intricate and detailed, from the fat binders of formations to the chalkboard and the coach's chart to its execution by those men in pads and how to get those men in pads prepared mentally and emotionally. So I've always enjoyed my long conversations concerning football philosophy with Garry Cobb, who bears a great wisdom of the game. I must say that of all the athletes, football players understand the complexities of their game most, a fact probably due the hours of film study, dating back through college.

G Cobb, from Stamford, Connecticut, was a gifted baseball player who rebuffed contract offers from the Cubs and Angels to choose football and Southern Cal over a hundred other colleges. This father of three now resides in Jersey, is an active church member and preacher of values who bears a great wisdom of life. But I tell you about G Cobb because he bears a great wisdom of this weekend.

Especially for the legion of players who never got here.

There aren't any lights that shine any brighter than the Super Bowl lights, he will say. You know you're going to see the best of everything at the Super Bowl. All of the stars, from music and film, business and journalism, everyone who's anyone, descend upon the Super Bowl. But to the players, it's all about being able to walk into the lobby of the hotel, or at a restaurant, or at the stadium, or at any of the parties or events, and catch the eye of somebody you played against and know that you've got a ring.

For a while, at least one year, you ruled.

Many times it's unspoken, but it's always there, hovering in the air. Those who bear rings love the Super Bowl because they can laugh a little louder than everyone else. They walk a little more upright, their chest flared out, their strut more pronounced. Their grin is wider. Their steaks are more saporous, the wine with it more divine.

"Nothing bothers me more than to hear Joe Theisman talking incessantly at a bar, restaurant or golf course," G Cobb will say. "It's the penalty you must endure when you don't have a ring. Players will give up everything else for that. Players never stop jabbing each other verbally and talking smack regardless of how old they are. Winning a ring gives you the chance to always end the conversation with the upper hand."

Talk to the ring.

G Cobb is wistful, and he will make that "so-close" face, and he will say, "Over the years, when I've seen Seth Joyner, Reggie White, Randall Cunningham, Byron Evans, Andre Waters, Eric Allen and all of those guys from our team, there's always that unspoken absence that we all endure. Some of the guys got to the Super Bowl and won rings but we never did it as a group. It hurt, especially when we kicked the butts of championship teams during the years they won it. You see, because everybody on that team cut their teeth as an Eagle and that team was close, everyone sees the Eagles as their number one team.

"Things have changed in the NFL because guys are making so much more money and free agency has had such an impact. But that Eagles team was the closest I've ever played on, because we went through a bitter strike and we grew close and we got deep into each other's personal lives and we loved each other."

We survey the room buzzing with people, some who bear rings. They have all come here to Jacksonville for tomorrow, for what is a celebration of competition and excellence and victory wrapped in a football game. Reward to the winner is one of those rings you get to bear, and ultimately to end any hospitality bar debate.

I see it in his face. I know what G is thinking right now.

"Boy, I wish could experienced this when I was playing. It's the stuff you dream about when you start playing on the playground as a kid. Everybody wants to be on Center Stage when the bright lights are shining. There are none brighter than that of the Super Bowl."

The Caravan of Destiny is on foot now. We are walking among the crowd, a great crowd that seems to stretch from the Jacksonville city limits to the beaches, dipping into the St. Johns River, home to the many private yachts and sailboat sleepers, and enormous cruise ships that were brought in to compensate for the town's lack of hotel rooms.

Flesh following flesh.

To nowhere in particular, just trudging along, from our tent on the grounds of the Radisson Hotel along the riverbank, from the lobby of the hotel that felt like the floor of a rock concert, scores of people having spilled out of the Lobby Bar to the center of the large room, milling around the portable bars, basically kiosks with booze, sitting on the sides of potted plants and ledges and steps, down the Riverwalk and up the winding the steps to the foot of the bridge that leads to the other side of the St. Johns.

The bridge reminds me of the traffic we would face to cross the one entering Wildwood on the last Sunday morning in July every year, only with people. Frankly, I felt claustrophobic, especially after manning the tent, where we were stationed along a side nook, only a flimsy nightclub rope and yellow police tape separating us from the massive crowd. We nudged along, as though the Gates of Heaven were there to greet us on the other side.

Away from the concentration of Eagles fans, this is truly the Super Bowl. A throng of people, wearing football jerseys and event T-shirts and all of the peddlers' gear. The street opens up on the other side of the bridge, cut off from the moving traffic, with Super Bowl trinket shops and food stands and more makeshift bars that sell sixteen ounce beers in plastic cups for eight-fifty. The guy with the beach ball beer belly in front of me slobbers over a fried turkey leg on a stick that would make a king jealous.

American gluttony on spectacle.

I should say that we picked up a late-arriving member of the Caravan who flew in this afternoon, one Tim Chambers, Hollywood Tim who's only Hollywood because producing film and television shows is his profession. His real nickname is Uncle Dirt, which aptly suits him. Tim is the antithesis of that three-finger, look the other way handshake town, raised in real world, Delaware County, part of a large Irish family, 12 kids in all, nine boys, three girls, two crackerjack parents, regular people with strong values, noble people, backbone kind of people. Though I met him late in life, Tim is the kind of guy you've known forever, the buddy across the street growing up, always ready to play ball.

He's everyone's kind of people.

The kind who can attend a swanky premiere of his movie *Miracle* – the story of the U.S. hockey team's gold medal run in 1980 – and sleep on the floor of a shabby motel room between Vinny and me and empty beer bottles at the Super Bowl.

Like the rest of us, he grew up a raging Eagles fan, but there's another story behind Uncle Dirt and this team. Back in the day, Uncle Dirt was a real player, a standout defensive back for the University of Pennsylvania, helping the Quakers win three Ivy League titles, earning Penn's first ever Ivy League's Player of the Year Award in '84 and twice being named on the all-Ivy League team. He still holds the Quakers' career interception record with Chuck Bednarik.

"Fourteen," he will say, the way men talk about their youthful exploits with women or athletics.

"Have everyone on tape back at home," he will kid. "Wanna see?"

Upon graduation, the Eagles invited him to camp as an undrafted free agent, the kind of player who fills out rosters, whom teams might later deem themselves geniuses for plucking. One late afternoon, during a voluntary workout at the Vet prior to camp, assistant coach Fred Bruney asked Timmy to work out with Ron Jaworski and Mike Quick, who were running patterns. Now Timmy had worked in the weight room earlier in the day, concentrating on lower body, and it felt like someone shot him in the leg when his hamstring pulled and squealed. "I didn't know veterans were going to be running patterns later in the day, but when they asked me to run with those guys, I couldn't refuse.

What free agent would? I idolized those guys," he would say. "I was never the same. Two tenths of a second is the difference between being on television and being in front of your television."

He performed well enough to make it to the final cuts, where he lost out to another safety by the name of Andre Waters. The following July, he hooked up for camp with the Indianapolis Colts. As the older Catholic women say to ease the pain of disappointment, it was not meant to be.

So Uncle Dirt took his finance degree from Penn, put on his one good suit with the power tie he just bought and went to work as a stockbroker for an investment company in the city. The job paid extremely well, and he thought such is life: you work in an office, put some money away, meet a nice girl, get married, move to the suburbs, have kids and retire at 55 to somewhere warm. All and all, the perfect American existence, the reason his parents pushed him to Penn in the first place, another of their children they could check off from the worry list.

Tim Chambers' life was laid out like an interstate. All he had to do was drive.

But it wasn't him. He enjoyed the weekends too much, when he worked as a color analyst for Penn football games.

"You're going where?" his sweet mother asked him incredulously, the day he told the family he was quitting his six-figure job and moving to Los Angeles to pursue a television career.

He did it without knowing a soul out west, armed with only the Penn directory and the hope that an alum or two could lead him in the right direction.

So Tim Chambers got an apartment in West Hollywood and started taking classes when a casting director visited the school looking for a "sportscaster" to act in the soap opera *Santa Barbara*. Uncle Dirt got the part, and parlayed that into a few national beer commercials, one for Miller Lite, with Hacksaw Reynolds and Bob Ueker, and another for Old Milwaukee. With help from a Penn classmate, he worked as an unpaid intern for Hollywood parapets Stuart Benjamin and Taylor Hackford, who had reached acclaim with *An Officer and a Gentleman* and later *Everybody's All-American*. He read scripts and answered phones and soon drew a paycheck, and when the partners split, he followed Benjamin.

For Uncle Dirt, it was the real life version of *Swimming with Sharks*, without the total dehumanization of the assistant.

"Stuart liked that I could seamlessly repair the drywall in his office," Uncle Dirt recalls. "He was known to put things through walls – ashtrays, paperweights, his fist."

Uncle Dirt was also part of the development team that worked on the movie *Ray*, the biopic about Ray Charles. It took Benjamin and Hackford fifteen years to make that film.

You reflect about life during benchmark events like the Super Bowl, and so Uncle Dirt will say, "I thought about my football career down there, and what if? Especially because it was my team, my Eagles. That's the worst part about playing football. There is no afterlife. Basketball players have the YMCA and pickup games. Baseball players have men's hardball and softball leagues. Football? There's nothing. It just ends. Over. A love affair that starts when you're eight and ends when you're 22. Alas, she turns into a mistress, trading up for someone bigger, faster, stronger. That bitch leaves you at the altar.

"There are times I still think about the game or dream about it at night. My therapist said that's normal. That's the way things are when you grow up in Philly."

We would wander about for the better part of the night before attempting to attend the Maxim Party. I knew somebody and Tim knew somebody else, and we were going to wriggle our way in, partly for grins, partly to give Nick an even better story when he went back to school. So we stand outside a reception tent in a long line manned by young women with clipboards and a party list and well-muscled, beefy types with ear-pieces and walkie-talkies. We watch the pinups parade by with their phony designer bags, noses pointing toward the crescent moon over Jacksonville, their hands clasped hard by their escort, usually a garishly-dressed man staring hard back at the men staring at his date.

The entire tableau is absurd, yet rather entertaining if you are a people watcher. I've been to many of these types of parties in the past, and everybody is a somebody, even if they are a nobody, your typical tawdry types, posers and pretenders who wear too much jewelry and butcher French proper names, fakers and fools, sellouts and syco-phants, namedroppers and social climbers, as shallow as a shot glass. Like many of its brethren this week, including the Playboy Party, the Maxim Party, though not without its harlot appeal, is a wannabe won-derland, where the B-celebrity is potentate.

"Now you know what it's like to be at a Hollywood party, only sometimes the names are bigger," Uncle Dirt says.

After several references to the list, we're finally led into the party by our contact, when he frantically stops half of our party. "I can't let all of these people in," he shrieks, nervously, "only you guys here."

"My man, you've got to be kidding?"

Now the first commandment of friendship among men is never leave anyone in the group behind, especially for the frippery of a Super Bowl party. Otherwise, you're one of THEM.

So, yes, we sally forth, bushwhacking the scene on the way out. We pass a limo driver who was passing out free drink cards to one of the strip clubs, and another huckstering his car for two hundred. "Fellas," he catcalls, "you can style and profile and find hoochies to join you in less than a mile."

We sit in snarled traffic on the way out of the city, retire back to skid row motel, order a pizza and drink beer on the balcony deep into the night, dissecting the Eagles' chances tomorrow, the faithful way to spend the Saturday night before the Super Bowl.

5
SUNDAY

The morning brings forth luminous sunshine and a succoring breeze, easily the best weather of the week, the reason why the winter worn flock to Florida in February. What a quixotic morning! So utterly Sunday morning. The soul is nourished on Sunday mornings.

I've always monitored the stark difference, though only a piddling of time, between Saturday night and Sunday morning. It's rather pronounced where I live in the city, not far from South Street, which can appear as a road to perdition on weekend nights, and suddenly hark halcyon at daybreak. It's true what they say happens at night, though I freely admit to being a creature of it. It's true how they describe the night, particularly in the city, festooned in fear and transgressions. How it's forbidding. How those born to it and who lurk in it are prone to iniquity. It's equally true what they say of the morning, particularly Sunday morning. How it washes away the night, purges its sins and invokes rebirth. How supernal you feel upon harvesting the day's first rays, the light of the sun magically medicinal.

Those in the Caravan arise early on this day, though there is another reason behind this fact.

It's Game Day.

Oh, how I love the morning of Game day. The exhilaration. The anticipation. The morning of Game day is why football reigns supreme. Why it's the perfect game, played weekly, just the right amount of spacing, enough to have you panting in between. It's the only sport where you miss it during the season. Thus, it can never grow desultory in the dog days of the season, like the other team sports, because there are no dog days. Each week as one, each Sunday slate of games, through Sunday night and Monday night, represents an event.

I love the morning of Game day because I prefer pregame to postgame. Because, to me, there's nothing better than a cup of coffee, the Sunday *Inquirer* and ESPN Game day. It's been that way since I was ten, when it was the Sunday *Inquirer* and the Sunday *Bulletin* and the NFL Today on CBS, with Brent Musberger, Irv Cross and Phyllis George, and Musberger cooing over the liveshot, "You are looking LII-IIVE at a soooold-out Vet...erans Stadium in SOUTH Philadelphia, where...in just minutes, folks, the Eagles will battle the Dal...las Cowboys for the lead in the 'ollll...ways tough NFC East Division."

Imagine it is your team, the one since your were ten, the morning of Game day, the game now the Super Bowl, and being on site to revel in the hype. I've covered countless Super Bowls in my career, and while I've always embraced the rush of Game day, none has engendered this sort of sensation. I hadn't counted hours since Christmas Day 1980, and I see it with the others. They all don something Eagles, Vinny, Boo, Bubba, Timmy, Steve, Nick, Dave, Brian Robbins, another of our fine producers, even my cousin Joey, who hasn't worn a jersey since the Keith Byars' one I bought him for his birthday in the eighties. There he is entering my room, looking spry and effusive, in a green T.O. game jersey.

I think it appropriate to reflect back.

BETHLEHEM - BIRTH OF A SEASON

Let us begin not long ago, in August, up in the Lehigh Valley, the foothill town of Bethlehem, where the Eagles train, that day when this part of the Pilgrimage took place in the form of the physical. That day, the first Friday of camp, where practice really is in its infant stages, the players just beginning to settle in, we were supposed to broadcast live from the sidelines and the furthest we got was a mile outside of the field, stuck in traffic, the type you endure on an LA freeway in morning drive, from eight a.m. to a little before noon, the one-lane access road intersecting Bethlehem choked by gridlock.

For on a resplendid summer day with low humidity and a cool mountain breeze, ensorcelled by the new-look Eagles, adding headliners Terrell Owens and Jevon Kearse, 25,000 people descended upon Bethlehem.

"It was like *Field of Dreams*," Andy Reid said.

I talked to Butchy on the phone that morning, and he said he needed to put his old police flasher atop his SUV to negotiate the traffic and deliver Coach Andy to practice on time. Later, he would order a police escort to deliver him to the dorms.

The attendance was easily a league record for any training camp, however unofficial the tabulations. Two days earlier, for the first day of two-a-days, a little more than ten thousand fans show up, hundreds lining up the night before, camping out for camp.

For camp.

Players don't even like camp.

"There were more people here today for training camp than we had for some games in Arizona," remarked Darwin Walker, briefly a Cardinal.

For the record, we never did make it to the broadcast, partly because our equipment was stuck a half-mile behind us. Finally, under orders, we turned around, passed the fans who had left their cars on the side of the road and decided to hoof it, and returned to Philadelphia, agog that twenty-five thousand people willed to attend training camp.

I used to make the rounds every midsummer to NFL training camps around the country, sometimes hitting upwards to twenty of them, and I had never seen anything close to that Friday in Lehigh. A good team usually generates a couple thousand onlookers, the bad ones a couple hundred. The flock flocked in great numbers for the entire three weeks the Eagles were there, anticipation mounting for the season opener against the Giants at the Linc.

The Eagles fell behind 7-0 in that game, then scored 24 unanswered points, with Donovan McNabb and Owens combining for a touchdown on the first drive of the season, the first of their three for the day. The offense portended a potency unrivaled by any other in this team's history, shredding the Giant defense for 454 yards.

The following Monday night featured a matchup of hyped hookups, McNabb and Owens against Minnesota's Daunte Culpepper and Randy Moss. The Vikings played the Eagles tough, but it was another long strike from McNabb to Owens that finally sealed a 27-16 victory. The story of the game, however, was the play of the young cornerbacks, Lito Sheppard and Sheldon Brown, who combined with their safety support to corral Moss, allowing him only 69 yards, limiting him to only underneath receptions. Even when the Eagles vacated their two-deep zone for the blitz, leaving Sheppard singled up on Moss, the explosive wideout never broke free downfield for his patented home run ball.

Lito and Sheldon. Sheldon and Lito.

Side by side in the secondary. Drafted the same year. Together replacing mainstays Bobby Taylor and Troy Vincent. Integral part of Andy Reid's architecture.

"We're like brothers out there," Brown said.

How they perfectly compliment one another, Lito, the fleet one, the super cover stick 'em who had five picks over the course of the season, Sheldon, the physical one, a tad taller, the bump and runner whom Jim Johnson likes to unleash on his corner blitzes.

Oh, the worry they engendered from the flock, however understandable since they were replacing the popular veterans Vincent and Taylor this season. Too small, the flock fretted, comparing their size against the taller Taylor and Vincent. Who's going to man those big receivers? Receivers like Randy Moss? What about experience? Both played some of the past two years due to injuries, Lito more than Sheldon, but this would be their first full season as starters, with no safety net that wasn't a safety behind them.

How silly the worry. Lito Decorian Sheppard, who, like Harold Carmichael and Brian Dawkins, is from here in Jacksonville, having attended Dawkins' Raines High, made the Pro Bowl and became the first Eagle to return two interceptions for touchdowns since super corner Eric Allen. Meanwhile, Sheldon Dion Brown had two picks and three sacks, and prompted Johnson to say, "Those guys are probably the best cover corners that we've had. I don't stay awake at night worrying about them."

Lito and Sheldon. Sheldon and Lito.

They embody the philosophy of Andy Reid. The coach and general manager of this team follows the Shell Principle: spending your resources – salary cap room and high draft choices – on corners, safeties and ends on defense. "The rest are interchangeable," he says. "This is how it's done today. Teams pass 60 percent of the time. If your tackles up front can give you a push, that'll make a run support manageable."

Meanwhile, on offense you build your team around the tackles and the quarterback. Look at Reid's first two big moves: he drafted McNabb with second over pick in 1999 and he spent a fortune on free agent Jon Runyan to man the right tackle spot, having already inherited Tra Thomas on the left side of the line. He had his franchise quarterback and his bookends locked up.

Fast forward to this season: While Terrell Owens got all of the free agent play, equally important was the signing of Jevon Kearse. Knowing Tennessee was cap strapped, the Eagles had quietly targeted Kearse a possibility, especially with the defense struggling to generate an organic pass rush from the end spot. "We were wondering if Tennessee would tag him [as the franchise player] or not," Heckert said. "They had been losing so many players, and they had a little player revolt happening. When they didn't tag him, Joe got on the phone fairly quickly. The injury deal we covered right away. Once we got his physical, we had no problems."

Kearse, hampered by injuries the past couple of seasons, returned to his '99 form, when he was named Defensive Rookie of the Year. He recorded seven and a half sacks and twenty-one hurries against constant double teams, and sprung Derrick Burgess free on the opposite side.

Lito and Sheldon. Sheldon and Lito.

They embody how this team has been able to sustain during an era depicted by much dramatic movement in the standings from year to year. Behind Reid, Joe Banner, sultan of the salary cap and personnel director, the Eagles have accomplished staggering consistency: five straight playoff berths, four NFC Title appearances, four NFC crowns, five seasons of double digit victories, three straight of 12 or more wins.

For the antithesis, look no further than the Redskins, whose impatient owner succumbs to whims, forcing his football people to overpay for name players, usually on the backside of their career.

"The trick is drafting well and staying away from those big name guys who are going to cost you a lot in signing bonuses," Heckert says. "That's how you get hamstrung by the cap."

Andy Reid has thick black binder on his desk. On a spring day, he flips through the pages to those with the names of his players, broken down year by year, with their contract status and position on the depth chart highlighted. He fingers the page to 2007, where names are already in place at certain positions, quarterback being one, cornerback another. He squirrels away draft choices, often flipping current selections for future ones, stockpiling them for maneuverability, the way he does cap space, hoarding it so that if a Terrell Owens and a Jevon Kearse become available he can "attack." Right now, heading into 2005, he knows that the free agent market will be brimming with backs, so while he certainly would like to sign Brian Westbrook to a long-term deal, he does have options if that does not happen.

"What we've done best on our end to sustain this thing is communicate," Reid says. "If you look at modern day football there are a couple of different ways to go about it. The best way I believe is if the front office and coaches are all on the same page. Joe, Tom and myself are on the same page."

The cornerback position highlights this, beginning with the 2002 draft. Both Vincent and Taylor were going to be over 30 when their contracts expired, so even though they were solidified at the position in the present, the Eagles spent a first-round pick on Sheppard and the second of their two second-round picks on Brown.

Sheppard and Brown spent two years learning under Vincent and Taylor, and so a painless transition took place this season. Of course, this was done at the expense of two very popular veterans, both leaving town unhappy, and making the flock furious.

It's hard for a fan to understand. They fall in love with a player. They buy his jersey and chant his name – "Dooooooce" – and then they must say goodbye to him, a cap casualty of the current economical landscape in the NFL. It's even harder for the players. Duce Staley left town completely resentful.

"You don't like it," Ike Reese will say, who will be one of those players forced to sign elsewhere (Atlanta). "I would have preferred to finish my career in Philadelphia. You gotta give the Eagles credit. They're never over the cap, like some teams. Look at Carolina. They had to cut Mushin Muhammad, their leading receiver. The Eagles' theory is to play to win today AND tomorrow, not putting all of their eggs in one basket. They're going to keep knocking on the door until one day that door opens. They pay players on what they project they will do instead of what they've done in the past. It's an ingenious business practice if you're on that side. If you're on the other side, well, it's tough. I swore I wouldn't be bitter. Duce is bitter. It's a shame. You just have to learn how to accept what it is."

Runyan will add, "That's part of the business. You can't take it personally. Sooner or later, it's going to happen to you. You just better be prepared for it to happen. You have to separate yourself and not let it affect you. Management wants to win as much as you do, as much as they want to pad their pocketbook. They're not stupid. They're trying to make an effort to make a team."

PROMINENT MAN, INNOMINATE MAN

This is a story of faith, healing and resurrection.

It is the story of a prominent man who defied medical syllogism to perform on America's grandest stage and the innominate man who helped him do so.

It might be the greatest football story ever told.

Terrell Owens hurriedly hopped up and down on one foot to the sidelines, telling himself it was just a normal sprain. Okay, maybe it wasn't a normal one. The pain was excruciating, and it shot high up on the ankle. Not a good sign. But T.O. had resilient body parts. T.O. had missed only seven games in nine years in the NFL. The tendons and the ligaments would surely snap back in place. Nobody existed on this earth in better physical condition. Maybe the same as him. But not better. Hell, no. T.O. treated his body the way most men treat their cars.

Not now. Why now? One more touchdown and the beefy coach has to wear spandex. What a year it's been. All those catches and yards and touchdowns, and the dances after the touchdowns, making more headlines than any of them, Manning, Moss, Pitt, Cruise. Everybody loves T.O. Men, women, children, desperate football fans, desperate housewives.

Maybe it'll just be a couple of weeks. So what? Miss the rest of the season. The rest of the season doesn't matter much anyway. Because T.O. made that so. But T.O. has to be ready for the playoffs and the Super Bowl. All those spectacular years, and T.O. has never played in the Super Bowl. The Super Bowl and all of its grandeur and holy hype was designed for T.O.

Who's kidding whom? This is bad. Really bad.

T.O. needs God's help on this one.

The Eagles entered a December 19 rematch against the Cowboys at 12-1, with all but three of their victories coming by double digits. However lulled into waiting for the playoffs to arrive, they were feeling good, if not indomitable. So there was little panic when they came out uncharacteristically flat in the first half and trailed Dallas 7-6 at halftime.

That would all change dramatically two plays into the third quarter, after Terrell Owens caught a pass 20 yards downfield on a seemingly innocent enough play.

Owens crumbled to the ground awkwardly after he was tackled by Dallas safety Roy Williams from behind. Williams employed his infamous Horse-collar Tackle, where he grabs the inside back of the ball carrier's shoulder pads and yanks him to the ground from behind. That technique, which would be outlawed by the NFL Rules Committee after the season, seriously injured six players in 2004, four by

Williams, most notably Terrell Owens.

Owens' right leg had bent backwards and he immediately grabbed for it.

Severe high ankle sprain. Fractured fibula.

Surgery. Out for the year. Seventy-seven catches, twelve hundred yards, 14 touchdown gone with a wince.

Andy Reid immediately began working on contingency plans for the offense. He had the cushion of an entire month to figure it out. Losing T.O. was a terrible setback. But this team had come too far. He dealt with crippling injuries before. He wasn't losing the NFC Championship Game this year. No way.

"The next day, that Monday," Ike Reese would say. "I was one of the guys over at the NovaCare Center. T.O. had just come out of the MRI/X-ray room. He was talking about how his ankle was broke. That he needed surgery and needed screws put in. I'm thinking, 'His season's over, man.'"

Everyone thought so. Except T.O. Terrell Owens had one final missive to Ike Reese and the handful of other players in the trainer's room:

"Get me to the Super Bowl, and I'll win it."

The prominent man's arrival to the stadium engenders a stir: crackling exchanges on security walkie-talkies and ripples from the "It's him" crowd that has gathered on the stadium's veranda high above the parking lot. It's him, of course. The out-of-state license plates of the BMW 745 with the crunk rims that hypnotize howls it: EIGHTONE.

The prominent man parks on the outside, the first spot next to the tunnel opening, next to the emergency vehicle. He's much thinner up close, especially in the legs. They look like chopsticks. He's also rather muted for a guy who goes by initials, down to his very collegiate dress: checkered shirt under a burgundy sweater, collar out, jeans, electric white sneakers, throwback baseball cap backwards. He wheels a piece of luggage behind him the way a flight attendant does and heads to the locker room, where he'll sit by himself draped in his own aura, offering little interaction with the room, and later with the field, where he'll stand on the outskirts of the pregame makeshift mosh pit comprised of his new mates, absorbing the scene, detached from the group the way the elite always are.

You know the prominent man. Sort of, which is to say you know of him, though he'll say that you only know of his portrayal. "You'd think I was a felon the way they talk about me," he told me one day. THEY talk about the incidents that accompany his mad skills. It's never an occurrence or happening with the man but always an incident, which is a dirty word to begin with: the Sharpie, stompin' on the star at Texas Stadium, the public display of insubordination with his coaches in San Francisco, verbal jousting in the press with his former quarterback in San Francisco, calling him gay. He'll feign a deaf ear, pondering of his infamy, "Only got my family and a few friends, and that's all who matters in this world."

What do you expect him to say? The prominent man, however surprisingly cloistered, is driven by self. Pride, along with Andy Reid, brought Terrell Eldorado Owens to Philadelphia.

Out in San Francisco, Owens' storied eight-year career with the 49ers had reached the point of irreconcilable differences. Owens beefed in the papers with quarterback Jeff Garcia and out in the open of the sidelines with the coaching staff. A looming free agent, Owens bemoaned the bedraggled state of the team, damned by the salary cap and a blundering blueprint.

The Eagles madly needed a playmaker, the playmaker needed a home. While the fit seemed obvious, conventional wisdom deemed the marriage a long shot for two dominant reasons: Owens, and his ostentatious ways, supposedly belied the ways of Andy Reid, and the 49ers charged that Owens' agent at the time, David Josephs, had failed to file his client's paperwork by the necessary timetable, thus forfeiting his right to free agency and making him property of San Francisco.

Unbeknownst to all, the Eagles had targeted Owens for the latter part of last season, following closely his decaying situation in San Francisco. "I was curious to see how it would all play out," Reid said. "If it worked out, we were going to make a play for him."

"We identified him last year," added Tom Heckert. "We didn't know if they were going to franchise him or not. There was so much bad blood and the tag cap number was so big and we knew they were in a little cap trouble."

Shortly after the Super Bowl, the Eagles began their due diligence on Owens, beginning with assistant head coach Marty Mornhinweg, the offensive coordinator in San Francisco from '97 to '00 who championed the idea. "Andy and I talked to everybody in the world about him," Heckert said. "You couldn't find anybody to say a bad word about the guy. They all said the same thing: 'Great player, works his butt off. Not a problem in the locker room.' We knew he had a little bit of groin problem last year. He missed a couple of games. But he still was really, really good."

Things heated up in Hawaii at the Pro Bowl, where Reid, McNabb and Owens converged. McNabb and Owens had become friends, and the quarterback, begging for a hook-up, began his own courtship. So the story goes, McNabb and Baltimore's Ray Lewis were at the hotel pool in Hawaii, each trying to convince Owens to come to their squad. Meanwhile, offensive coordinator Brad Childress, a rising star in this league, interviewed for the vacant Niner job and struck up a friendship with Owens. "I knew for sure after Hawaii," Reid said. "I got to know T.O. a little bit there. We didn't know each other at all before. But Marty was very close to T.O. and I trust Marty's word. Then Brad and he got together. I knew Donovan and him were best buddies. I trust Donovan. We needed some help there. It all made sense."

With Owens' status as a free agent apparently nil, the Eagles began trade discussions with San Francisco and thought they had come to terms on March 4, the day they introduced their other marquee signing, Jevon Kearse. "That was a complete fiasco," Heckert said. "They gave us a list of four players, including Brandon [Whiting], and wanted a fourth-rounder. Thought it was done. They gave us permission to talk to [Owens' agent] and we worked out a deal. There was apparently an understanding between [49ers GM Terry Donahue] and T.O.'s agent that they would get to work out a contract before he was traded. So we go down for a press conference for Kearse and we find out they traded him to Baltimore. They tried to screw him. We called Baltimore right away but they didn't want to make a trade."

Owens immediately protested the trade, failing to show up for a physical and vowing to play only for the Eagles. The Ravens had a press conference without him, even making up a jersey for him. Meanwhile, the union filed a grievance on behalf of Owens to make him a free agent, and the league set up an arbitration hearing.

However, on a murky Tuesday in March, a settlement was reached before "special master" Stephen Burbank, a University of Pennsylvania professor, would issue his ruling. The Eagles sent a fifth-round draft pick to Baltimore and Whiting to San Francisco, and the Ravens received back the second round pick they traded for Owens. Speculation afterwards was that Burbank was going to rule him a free agent.

Owens wasted no time making an impact. He caught three touchdowns in the season opener against the Giants and never looked back, providing McNabb with his first true impact partner and the Eagles with their most lethal offense in the history of the franchise.

He also provided their most controversial player ever.

For Terrell Owens is part Narcissus come to life, part Leon from the Bud commercials. During the good times here, for much of last season, the Eagles believed Owens was either completely changed or some of those stories were exaggerated.

"When T.O. was in San Francisco, I thought he was an asshole," former Eagle great Harold Carmichael told me in October. "Then you get to know him, he's not. He's just one of those guys you hate playing against. I did the same stuff he does when I played. Back then we only had one camera. Now I understand him, and I think it's good to have a swagger."

Owens contended that day, "I'm here because of Andy Reid. He did his homework on me. He knew what kind of player and person he was getting. He wanted me. I'm not gonna change. Why should I change? I'm the same guy. I'll always be that guy."

Owens' notorious ways went beyond the towel-dropping promo of *Desperate Housewives* on Monday Night Football, an episode completely blown out of proportion, or the celebrations after touchdowns or the public admonishment of McNabb. He was just so very different for this Eagles team, a wild, unpredictable soul, prone to outrageous whims, like the contract embroilment that would ensue long after the season's end and Jacksonville's heroic showing. That would threaten his future with the Eagles, after just one season and a vow that he wouldn't be divisive and a vow of forever loyalty to Reid, McNabb and this team.

That is entirely another story, one right now without an ending.

The problem for Terrell Owens was that he tore the deltoid ligament that holds the tibia and fibula together. The fractured fibula, believe it or not, was not troublesome. Owens underwent surgery that Wednesday in Baltimore, three days before Christmas. Renowned orthopedic surgeon Mark Myerson performed the procedure, inserting two 2 1/3-inch screws along with a plate. Myerson did so with the extremely remote possibility in mind that Owens might return for the Super Bowl, setting the screws a little longer.

Following the surgery, Owens swore he'd return and immediately went to work on his rehab under the watchful eye of Eagles trainer Rick Burkholder, one of the best in the league. Burkholder was one of the pioneers in helping players recover from Lisfranc sprains, a potential debilitating injury to the bones and ligaments that join the forefoot and midfoot, named for Jacques Lisfranc, a French field surgeon in Napoleon's army who first noted the injury after seeing it occur to soldiers who fell from their horses without their feet releasing from the stirrups. Burkholder helped save Duce Staley's career.

Myerson estimated a conservative recovery time of eight to ten weeks, which would have taken Owens well past the Super Bowl. In his research into the injury and how he would approach the rehab process, Burkholder found one NFL player who played the same position who incurred a high ankle sprain and had a fracture up high during training camp and played at a high level on opening week, a span of six weeks. An optimistic Burkholder made Owens' return goal the NFC Championship Game, barely four weeks after the surgery.

"I'm a pretty good healer, believe me," Owens said. "I've already moved my hyperbaric [oxygen] chamber down to my living room. I'll be in that day and night."

Burkholder monitored Owens' rehab closely and charted his progress, while in constant contact with Myerson. Burkholder was amazed at how he improved almost daily, the results tangible. Suddenly, he began to believe what Owens believed.

Fast-forward to the Tuesday morning before the championship game. With Owens having made great strides, Burkholder asked Myerson: "Doc, if he breaks the screws or suffers the exact same injury, what happens? I want to be sure. Our biggest concern is T.O.'s future well-being. I don't want him risking his career. So…what happens?"

"I'd fix him," Myerson said.

"The same way?"

"Same way. Good as new."

But Myerson knew what Burkholder was getting at. Under pressure from Owens' attorneys, fearing a malpractice claim, Myerson said there was no way he would clear him to play against the Falcons.

"He was actually ready to play in that game," Burkholder said.

Tuesday night, Andy Reid stopped in to see Burkholder.

"What's the deal with T.O.?" he asked.

"Myerson won't let him play," Burkholder said.

"Why not?"

"Doctor's being stubborn. The attorneys are getting to him."

"We'll be fine without him," Reid said resolutely. "We're gonna win this week. Try to get him ready for the Super Bowl."

"Well, I gotta work some magic. To me, Myerson is taking the emotional component out of it. Myerson doesn't understand the component. I want to take him to the game Sunday. Get him to see it first-hand."

"Go all out with him," Reid said.

So trainer Rick Burkholder went all out seeking Dr. Mark Myerson's medical clearance of Terrell Owens. For the championship game, the Eagles brought Myerson up from Baltimore, set up a lunch with owner Jeffrey Lurie, issued a pregame locker room pass and brought him into the training room, got him really good seats, gave him a field pass and had him celebrating with the team on the sidelines upon winning the NFC crown. During the game, Myerson sat next to another surgeon, Dr. Craig Morgan, who had previously operated on Hugh Douglas' shoulder.

Early that week, Burkholder called Morgan.

"Doc, what's Myerson's mood?" Burkholder asked.

"You're not going to get him to budge," Morgan responded. "He's so afraid of the liability."

That Tuesday, Burkholder and Owens drove to Baltimore for a visit with Myerson, armed with a portable DVD player and a video montage of the player's rehab. "We're gonna make him see how good you're doing and hard you're working," Burkholder told Owens. "We're gonna guilt him into letting you do it. I don't know, though. I don't think he's going to let you play."

"I'm about to fire him as my doctor," Owens cracked.

In the office, Burkholder asked Myerson again, "What happens if he injures the ankle the same exact way? Tears up everything. What happens?"

"I fix him," Myerson said.

"Guaranteed fix?"

"One hundred percent. It's just all lost rehab time."

"Let's go," Owens interjected. "We got our answer. We're outta here."

"Hey, Terrell," Myerson called out, "you're an adult. You're going to do what you see fit. But I'm advising you NOT to play."

Myerson could not let himself be swayed by the emotional component. It is a doctor's duty to eliminate such factors from the equation, assessing the situation strictly from a patient's medical condition. Was he being overly cautious? Yes. Was he fearful of a malpractice suit? Certainly, and who wouldn't be in these litigious times? But in the end, Myerson could not offer his clearance if he had an iota of belief that

Owens was pushing it too soon.

But Terrell Owens had already made up his mind to play. He had done so that Monday, five days after Christmas, the moment he walked out of the MRI room back at NovaCare, and told Ike Reese and those guys to get him to the Super Bowl and he'd be there. Meanwhile, Burkholder had never been one to press forth with an injured player without a doctor's clearance. But, secure in knowing Owens wasn't risking his career or substantial long term damage, he relented. He knew the only reason the doctor didn't clear him was out of fear of a lawsuit. So he was on board. He would advise Reid that the star wideout should play in the Super Bowl in lieu of any setbacks, thus putting his reputation on the line.

"I respect Dr. Meyerson and his decision to not medically clear me, but prior to going down to see him for that last visit I can honestly say God had already cleared me," Owens would say. "It really doesn't matter what the doctor says. I've got the best doctor of all, and that's God."

Later that night, Burkholder had Owens running on the treadmill. Owens reached 11 mph before he stopped him, though Burkholder believed he could have gone even faster, perhaps 13 or 14 mph. Burkholder had him working out all week and running at full speed. That Friday, he brought Owens into the practice bubble at the NovaCare Center to perform skill work. Former practice squad quarterback Andy Hall was throwing passes to him, when Reese and some of the other special teams players entered the bubble and went wild at what they witnessed.

"I got chills," Reese would say. "I felt like a little schoolgirl. It was the first time I had seen him run in six weeks. The whole time I'm thinking, 'He ain't playin'. This cat can't play. No way. He ain't gonna be able to run.' Then I saw him running those routes. I was like, 'This is crazy! He's playin'!'"

"Our Dog's gonna play," another player shouted out.

"The more they hooted and hollered," Burkholder said, "the better he did."

Owens flew to Atlanta that night to see his chiropractor in the morning, an act to prepare the rest of his body for game action. A terrible ice storm hit the city over that weekend, and Owens nearly got stuck. He barely made it back in time Sunday to fly with the team to the Super Bowl.

THE HEALER

Rick Burkholder is not overly large. Under six feet, he is sturdy-trim, what you would call fit, built with knowledge of the body, the nutrients and exercise that it craves to run well. However boyish looking, with sunken eyes under a pronounced brow that forms a natural stare, he looks like a football trainer, as opposed to, say, a personal trainer, usually hulking and overly muscled.

Rick Burkholder hails from near Pittsburgh. He attended Pitt and his first NFL job was with the Steelers. And this is important to the story because Pittsburgh people are hearty folk. There's no pretense in Pittsburgh people, regardless of social status, whether steeped in old mountain money or dirt from the earth's belly, those mill workers with knobby, black fingers. They are barstool people who like Friday night football as much as Sunday afternoon football. You don't have dote on Pittsburgh people. In fact, Pittsburgh people usually make the best doters.

Pleasant, patient and typically Pittsburgh, Rick Burkholder was born to be an athletic trainer, just like his father, Richard Burkholder, was. Richard Burkholder, still at western Pennsylvania's Carlisle High after some 45 years and a member of the Athletic Trainers Hall of Fame, is a forefather in the field, when it was an obscure field, before the boom, before it became chic and became Sports Medicine.

So Rick Burkholder was born to play the innominate man in the greatest football story ever told.

Let us travel back to early 1999, when Andy Reid first came to Philadelphia, and he was building a staff, handpicking lieutenants for the massive rehab job ahead, one in every facet of football ops. The right trainer is crucial to a team's success. See trainers in any professional sport, particularly those in football, are more than body people armed with scissors and tape and a handgrip that detects pulls and strains and muscle cramps. They play an integral part in a team's core, "playing" part den mother, part school nurse, part valet, part priest to the players. They are a liaison between the player and coach and provide, however fine the line, a trusted ear to both parties.

"When I got here, they had the worst stadium, Ray (Rhodes) was on the way out, and the team had finished 3-13," Burkholder said. "It was just a mess. Now remember, I was coming from a storied franchise, one that was very much family. There are only 80 full-time employees for the Steelers other than players. At my going away party at a bar in Pittsburgh, a buddy of mine who worked for the team said, 'I hate to see you do this. I think you're making a huge mistake. I'm afraid you're going to fail and fall on your face. I don't want that to happen. You're a part of us.'

"Nobody thought we could do it. The whole league didn't think so. The Vet, as bad as it was, was twice as bad on the Eagles' end. When I came in for the interview, I was like, 'Oh, my God! This is horrible!' I talked to Andy and Jeffrey and Joe about that during the interview. They said, 'We're going to change that. We're going to change the image of the Eagles and the image of the players to the city and to the NFL. We will get to the Super Bowl and we want you to be apart of it.' They had a vision and I believed in their vision."

More than six years later, on that Sunday night of the NFC Championship Game, smack in the middle of the Terrell Owens saga, Rick Burkholder cried. "Real tears," he said. "So much of it was the journey. That night, I can't describe the feeling. I had visions of my 12 seasons in football. I was all bundled up, Gatorade down the side of me because I was standing next to Andy when he got hit. I hugged and kissed everybody. I turned to my assistants, Sugs [Eric Sugarman] and Chris [Perduzzi], and said, 'We did it!'

"I cried and I laughed. I hugged every player. Guys like Trot and Ike. I thanked those guys for being there. The week before the Super Bowl, I called Troy and Carlos [Emmons], guys that helped build this thing. The emotion of getting to the Super Bowl was so much for me. But I had to calm down and realize why we're down in Jacksonville now. To win it."

Burkholder's job: to get T.O. ready.

And while doing so, he was suddenly thrust onto center stage of America's grandest stage, a profound moment for someone confined to and contented with the background, to a mere prop in the play.

"I was nervous," he said. "I didn't want to do anything wrong. You know, some of the other trainers in the league were pissed because I went against the doctor's call. But they didn't know the whole story. I like to carry the banner for Athletic Training. I'd do anything for this profession, and this was the first time in a Super Bowl that an athletic trainer really had such a big part in it. I wanted to make sure that when I took that stage, I represented my profession well.

I'll tell you a story of how big a pilgrimage it was for me. Two of them."

They happened on the same night. Wednesday night. Burkholder and Tom Heckert went out for the night in Jacksonville Beach. They met some of Burkholder's old Pittsburgh buddies and they were standing at a crowded bar, when they overhear a loud debate between an Eagles' fan and a Pats' fan. Said Burkholder, "The guy from Philly is obnoxious – got his faced painted and his jersey on, you gotta love him – and he has no idea we're behind him. So the guy is arguing. 'Donovan is a better quarterback than Brady. Our receivers are better. Our defense is better. And we've got a better TRAINER than you have.' My guys from Pittsburgh went wild. 'You're famous!' they said."

Burkholder and Heckert then decided to go across the street to another bar, a hot one that's entirely packed. Some 50 people are waiting in line to get in. Word is Michael Strahan is inside, and Burkholder had met Strahan at the Pro Bowl and wanted to say hello. Burkholder spotted a sidedoor manned by a typically beefy bouncer.

"We're not standing in this line," Burkholder told Heckert. "Watch me. I'm going to BS that guy."

"Can I help you?" asked the bouncer, eyebrows raised.

"If I told you we work for one of the teams in the Super Bowl, would you let us in?" Burkholder asked.

The bouncer immediately let his guard down. "Dude," he said, "you're the trainer for the Eagles. Come on in!"

"I can't believe this," Heckert joked. "This is absolute bullshit. I put this roster together and you're the damn trainer, and you're getting me into bars."

"Shut up and drink!" Burkholder said.

Terrell Owens and Quinn Burkholder had it all prearranged. If Owens scored a touchdown, he would celebrate with the dance that the adorable little four-year-old girl taught him.

Rick Burkholder started taking his daughter with him to Terrell Owens' house because he was so busy during the intense rehab that he spent precious little time at home and thought at least he'd have the car ride through South Jersey with her.

He didn't know T.O. would fall in love with her. In fact, Owens and his girlfriend, Felecia, looked so forward to seeing Quinn that he requested Burkholder bring her over, even during days he hadn't planned to do so.

"They were big-time buddies," Burkholder said. "She idolizes him."

One day, Owens told Quinn, "Teach me a dance, sweetheart."

She taught him the Hoky Poky. So it was all set. If he scored, he was going to honor Quinn with a notable touchdown celebration by doing the Hoky Poky, putting his right ankle in first, of course. FOX, which broadcast the Super Bowl, was in on it. If Owens reached the end zone, it would show him doing the dance and have Quinn tell the story of it.

"Everybody was dying for him to score a touchdown," Burkholder said. "We wanted him to do the Hoky Poky."

Everyday in Jacksonville was trial and error. Burkholder said, "You know how T.O. was saying he was Smarty Jones? It wasn't a lie. You know how horses are real sensitive. We had to balance knowledge and how he was feeling to get it right. The synergy of rehab and treatment came together."

Meanwhile, Owens spent every spare moment in the hyperbaric chamber, believing in the healing powers of oxygen. "He told me guys were coming up from Alabama to deliver it to his room at the hotel," Butch said. "I told the people at the hotel, 'Let 'em up there.' I had to go in his room for something early in the morning one day. So I'm knocking, 'Yo, wake up! KNOCK. KNOCK. KNOCK. Yo, get up!' I walk in with the key, and he says in that way of his, 'Good morning, Anthony.' He's the only one on the team that calls me Anthony. Hell, only my mother called me Anthony. My mother and T.O. Anyway, he pokes his head out of that thing. Like he's stuck in a suitcase. He was sleeping in that thing."

Did you ever see a huge duffle bag? One of those hockey duffle bags, long and wide? That's what the hyperbaric chamber looked like.

"He had that chamber," Reese said. "I walk in his room and saw this cat really is sleepin' in that little chamber. I'm like, 'This guy is weird.' He sleeps in a tube. He takes naps in there. He stayed in there. In that tube. The cat's got a tube! The cat's crazy!"

By midweek, Andy Reid hadn't written up any plays for him in the game plan. "I don't want to get Don and Pinky ready for him if he can't go," Reid said. "He's got to prove to me that he can practice."

Burkholder said, "One time Andy came up to me said, 'I don't think I'm going to use him. He's not good enough yet.' I think he was just doing that to piss me off."

Owens subsequently practiced and looked impressive.

As a precautionary measure, Burkholder and Reid held Owens out of practice on Saturday. The national media took it as Owens had suffered a setback, when in reality it was going to be a light 45 minute practice and they had decided to totally rest him and have him ready for the game.

The morning of the Super Bowl, Burkholder was frantic with worry. He must have checked on Owens every 15 minutes. "I wasn't nervous that he would hurt the ankle," he said. "I was nervous for him. I didn't want him to perform badly. I remember seeing Jimmy Johnson, a guy who I really respect, say, 'I'll tell you right now, T.O. will not be a factor in this game.' You know how sweet that was? Even the experts didn't expect him to do what he did."

The experts expected Owens to play as a decoy, if he at played at all.

Wrote veteran football writer and broadcaster John Clayton on ESPN.com: "Ultimately, Owens' chance of playing are a long shot. It's worth the try, but don't count on him."

Even those inside the Eagles' locker room were astonished by Owens' performance. Sport is fertile ground for miraculous feats of the physical, those that defy logic and belie mortal beings, where myth and materiality intersect on the corner of Lore. I was in the arena the night Michael Jordan fought through a raging fever and flu to score 38 points in 45 minutes against the Jazz in Game Five of the '97 Finals, the series tied 2-2. I recall the account of Brett Favre overcoming a terribly sprained ankle that kept him off his feet the entire week leading up to a game against the Bears, and he threw five touchdown passes, noticeably hobbling up and down the field. I know the legend of Jack Youngblood snapping his left leg in the second quarter of the Rams' playoff tilt against Dallas in 1979, but finishing the game, and then playing two more after that, including the Super Bowl.

How Owens came back coupled with how he played rivals any feat that sounds like a fable. It was like Willis Reed actually playing in the game and scoring 40.

Owens immediately showed he offered more than just his presence on the field. On the second play of Super Bowl XXXIX, he went into motion and rolled to his right in perfect stride, catching a seven-yard pass before being pushed out of bounds. Throughout the game, he made several acrobatic catches, and was easily the team's best offensive performer. He finished with nine receptions for 122 yards, including a 36 yarder.

Astonishingly, Owens might have done even more.

"A couple of times," Burkholder said, "I was like, 'Why isn't T.O. in the game?' Andy held him back some. He didn't know his conditioning. He didn't have a breaking period. If Andy had known better, if T.O. was able to play in the NFC Championship Game and Andy had a semblance of a barometer, I think he would have given him even more plays. He would have turned him loose even more. There were some plays in crucial moments where it was Pinky, Freddie and Greg

Lewis on the field, and it was because I couldn't totally get him ready quick enough. You know, his best day in the whole rehab process was Sunday. Super Bowl Sunday."

During the game, Reese theatrically fisted his eyes in disbelief at how Owens was performing. "I was like, 'Get the hell out of here with this.' That's one of the most miraculous things I've EVER seen. When he broke his ankle, I thought it would take a miracle for him to come back. Literally, a medical miracle. We're on the sidelines and we're talking amongst ourselves on the defense, sayin', 'You believe what this guy is doin'? Throw him the ball! Give him the ball! He's killin' these guys. Give him the ball anyway you can!'"

"The game was sweet and sour," Burkholder said. "The sour was we lost, the sweet was we played it absolutely perfect with T.O. You know, it's ultimate story if we win. If we win, he's the MVP."

And the innominate man would be by his side, forever forsaking obscurity.

The morning of the Super Bowl, Butch had told Burkholder, "Hey, man, if we win, you're going to get your own damn car for the parade."

"Everybody had their own little story down there," Burkholder said. "Mine was attached to biggest ego in the game. Here's a guy who doesn't like anybody but he and I were cool. He's standing in front of the media and saying, 'That's my boy Rick. He got me ready.' Here's a guy who thanks nobody but himself. And here is telling the world about me.

"In my career, no player now will ever question whether I try to do the right thing. They'll be like, 'Man, he got T.O. ready to play at that level. It was more than a Super Bowl experience. It was like an out-of-the-NFL experience. It was a life experience."

Terrell Owens did everything in the Super Bowl but score. In fact, on the Eagles' first touchdown of the game, the play was designed to go to Owens. But Owens was mugged at the line of scrimmage, thrown to the ground without penalty, and McNabb checked off and found tight end LJ Smith for a six-yard scoring pass.

Around one in the morning the night of the game, with Quinn not feeling well, the day too long, the phone rang in the Burkholders' room. It was Owens, who was downstairs at a postgame reception.

"You coming to the party?" he asked.

Oh, no, Burkholder thought. The ankle swelled.

"What's up?" he said. "You hurting?"

"No," he said, "I just want to see Quinn. I'm leaving for Hawaii tomorrow with Felecia and we're not going to have a chance to see her."

Burkholder would say later, "Here, this guy just played in the biggest game in the world and he wants to see my daughter."

Months later, embroiled in his contract holdout, Terrell Owens would text message Rick Burkholder:

"Tell Quinn, Don't worry, I'm an Eagle forever, until they cut me. Tell her I miss her."

THE RAVING RODOMONT

It was a fitful month for the flock. With the Eagles having clinched home field throughout the playoffs, Andy Reid opted to rest his starters for the final two games of the season. While the move seemed a prudent one, especially after the Eagles lost Westbrook in the final game of the season last year, the flock howled about rust, though I believe most of the flak was residue over missing Owens. With him, the offense was so potent, and the flock wouldn't get a chance to see what it looked like without him entering a playoff season that was Super Bowl or suicide.

The Eagles, after clinching the first-round bye, wouldn't play a truly meaningful game for 28 days. In this town, it felt like an eternity.

So the holidays came and went, the flock growing restless, particularly after enduring desultory football over the final two games, losses to St. Louis and Cincinnati at home in the season finale.

Paranoia gripped the town over potential first-round foes, the flock first obsessing over the Carolina Panthers ("John Fox knows how to beat us!"), who got hot down the stretch, but missed the playoffs on the final week of the season. Then it was the Packers, fearful of a sudden rebirth by Brett Favre, and the Rams, due to their always explosive offense.

It turned out to be the Minnesota Vikings.

Now the Vikings instilled little trepidation entering the first playoff game, especially with Randy Moss coming up lame the following week in Green Bay and again creating turmoil. They were a mess, with embattled coach Mike Tice, golf pencil behind his ear, desperately trying to keep a team together that had such high expectations earlier in the year. Meanwhile, under Andy Reid, the Eagles destroyed teams like Minnesota, those built with flimsy foundations along the interior of both sides of the ball, those with dramatic offenses and irresolute defenses.

The Eagles dominated the game from the opening kickoff, and the outcome was never in doubt, thanks to a dominating defensive performance, led by Trotter, Reese and Kearse. The defense pressured Culpepper into costly mistakes, and once again, behind Lito and Sheldon, shut down Moss. Meanwhile, Freddie Mitchell had the big game on offense with five receptions and two touchdowns, one after recovering a fumble by LJ Smith in the end zone.

Ah, Freddie Mitchell. Where to begin with self-aggrandizing Freddie Mitchell?

Every story needs a raving rodomont.

At first, Freddie Mitchell's freewheeling discourses were charming, innocent idiocies that jazzed up a sometimes homogenized group. He played college ball for UCLA, so he liked to LA name-drop and play the Hollywood persona. Even when he gave himself nicknames – Fred-X, First-Down Freddie, Fourth-Down Freddie, The People's Champ – you laughed. They were clever, a play on words, a play on the miraculous Fourth-and-26 conversion reception that saved the playoffs against the Packers last year.

But the acquisition of Terrell Owens and subsequent relegation of

Freddie Mitchell to specialty receiver, where his talents suggest he reside in this league, turned him positively prehensile over the lack of attention he now received. Prior to Owens' arrival, he chastised those who suggested the receiving corps needed to upgrade. But Mitchell, a former first round pick, never distinguished himself as anything more than a role player with a propensity to promulgate. While he could make tough catches over the middle, he didn't have the speed to play on the outside nor the size to dominant. By receiver standpoint, he hovered around average.

And it ate him up.

Worse, however, was the space that Owens commanded off the field, leaving little spotlight for anyone else, let alone a hollow talker like Mitchell. See, Owens represented all that Mitchell aimed to be, but he had the skills to execute it. So as the T.O. phenomenon raged both locally and nationally, Mitchell grew more discontented and petulant. He lashed out in little ways. At the end of the Carolina game, Mitchell, a member of the hands team, recovered an onside kick against the Panthers. As he neared the sidelines with his teammates applauding, Mitchell rapaciously barked in the name of Keyshawn Johnson, "Now throw me the damn ball!"

It happened overtly again, during the Eagles' destruction of the Packers. With the Eagles leading big in the second half and driving again, Mitchell waved his arms frantically in the end zone, only to see McNabb complete a pass to someone else. Well, Mitchell gestured wildly at McNabb and pouted afterwards, even though his team had won its biggest game of the season in a most impressive fashion. He made no secret how unhappy he was, suggesting to someone close to the team that me might go over Andy Reid's head to make himself a bigger part of the offense.

When Owens got hurt, you could hear the delight in his voice. The morning after Owens suffered the injury, Mitchell, according to one eyewitness, entered the training room, mocking the fans' T.O. chant, snickering, *"TOoooo, TO, TO, TOoooo, OH, NOOOO, TO. Oh, noooo, oh, no, oh no, oh, no, OH, NOOOO, TOOOO."*

Mitchell, who entered the Vikings game with 22 catches on the season, including six in the scrub game against the Bengals, and 90 total in his four years with the Eagles, reveled in his game against the Vikings. Following his touchdown reception, he mocked Moss' post-touchdown mooning of the Green Bay fans a week earlier by pretending to pull his pants up.

After the game, Mitchell said, "I'm a special player. I want to thank my hands for being so great."

The following week, Mitchell showed at the stadium wearing a fur coat and an outrageous hairdo, blending cornrows and a Mohawk.

The Cornhawk.

He caught two passes for twenty yards in the victory.

Freddie Mitchell morphed further into character. Life imitating art is one thing, but life imitating a beer commercial? Self-expression can be a wonderful thing, but Mitchell's was as fake as a ROLECKS.

Mitchell's troubles escalated earlier this week, coincidentally after it became apparent to the team that Owens would play. The morning of the Super Bowl's annual Media Day on Wednesday, Andy Reid held a team meeting, reminding his players not to say anything inflammatory. An hour later, Mitchell, upset that he wasn't one of the featured players with his own kiosk but was relegated to everyone else's status on the team, took a verbal swipe at the Patriots, saying he didn't know the names of the New England secondary and adding he "has something for" Pro Bowl safety Rodney Harrison.

The Patriots didn't take kindly to Mitchell's barbs. Said linebacker Willie McGinnest, "All I can say is, Rodney Harrison is the wrong guy to mention, especially if you're a receiver. [Mitchell] is not humble. He hasn't done enough in this league to be on TV talking about that. Philly has a lot more class than that. It's just one guy."

The Patriots weren't the only ones who took exception to Mitchell's outburst. His own teammates denounced him, deeming his insults to New England strictly as a way to gain notoriety.

"Freddie alienated a lot of people," Ike Reese would say. "Guys didn't like him stepping outside our team box. There was already one guy pretty much with a free passage that people have to deal with in T.O. We didn't need another guy trying to be T.O. It was brought up in the morning meeting, and the first camera opportunity it was said. Big Red was pissed. I know Andy thought about sending him home right there, but that would have been probably even more of a distraction.

"To us, it was like, if Donovan can adhere to the rules, who are you to defy the coach? And do it with that me-first attitude? Guys didn't like that. Being the type of players we were, we didn't want to make it a bigger distraction. You know how you choose to ignore something? Not acknowledge it? I talked to Freddie. I told Freddie to his face. He was in denial that what he said or what he did was wrong. I told him, 'You said it. I heard it. You said it, man.' I said, 'You should stand up and apologize to Big Red. Call him. Apologize to the team. You got guys on this team who you're on their bad side. It would go a long way to mending the few relationships that you do have.' But he didn't want any part of that. He said they can think what they want to think. He wasn't having that with the players. He didn't see fit to do it."

While Mitchell called Reid to apologize, he never addressed his teammates.

"Shoot," Reese would continue, "Freddie didn't care. He was like, 'I'm going to do what I want to do.' Guys were tired of him. They were like, 'You want out of here so bad, go. Go to another team. Get the hell out of here. I wish you'd go to another team.' It was crazy. The worst thing that happened was the game he had against Minnesota. He came back the next week with that ridiculous hairdo. Now he's a rock star. It was like, c'mon, you look like a cartoon character. He had a good game, no doubt, but it wasn't exactly against a great secondary."

Meanwhile, Harrison would have another career game in the Super Bowl, picking off two passes and recording seven tackles, including a sack. Mitchell would finish with one catch.

"Of course it (provided motivation)," Harrison would say. "You make them go out there and know your name. I bet you he knows our names now."

Patriots coach Bill Belichick would be more blunt. "All he does is talk," he told *Sports Illustrated*. "He's terrible, and you can print that. I was happy when he was in the game."

Following the Super Bowl, Mitchell would grease his way out of town by making several swinish statements about his team, obviously to force his release. He launched several attacks at McNabb, some profanity-laced.

When asked about Mitchell's assault, McNabb would just roll his eyes. "I don't get involved in stuff like that," he would say.

Another player would tell me, "Why would anybody pay attention to anything Freddie Mitchell has to say? Freddie's a clown."

Suddenly, the clever nicknames he gave himself were being cleverly edited by his former teammates.

The People's Chump. Fifteen Minutes of Fame Freddie. Fraud-X. Me-First Down Freddie.

Freddie Mitchell would receive his release from the Eagles in the spring. He drifted without a team for weeks before finally hooking up with the Kansas City Chiefs for a minimal salary. He vowed to talk less.

A SNOWSTORM, FATALISM, AND THE MYSTIC

Oh, but there was deep dread in town the minute the Vikings game ended and thoughts whirled right to the Championship Game. Three times bitten will transform even the eternal optimist into a fretful fingernail biter and handwringer, no matter if the Eagles were immediately installed as a healthy favorite by the sapient oddsmakers.

Rationally, logically, intellectually, sensibly, there was very little reason for over-agonizing. The Eagles were clearly a better team than the upstart Falcons, with or without Terrell Owens, deeper and well-rounded, with a dramatic edge in experience. The game was to be played in Philadelphia, anyway, in front of that frothing crowd and in the deep freeze, sure to doom the domed Falcons, even it did not the balmy Buccaneers two years prior.

Michael Vick, however dynamic a player, paled in comparison to McNabb as complete quarterback, a one-dimensional wonder still learning how to throw and when to throw in the NFL. God, you couldn't escape Michael Vick that week. Everywhere you turned, you saw his face, usually grinning, you know, that shark-eating grin, talking about the Michael Vick Experience, brandishing a pair of bright white Nikes that can't dull that grin. Let's preface a rant's rant by saying Mike Vick should be a wonderful quarterback in this league, but the ballyhooing over him that ensued was way, way out of control.

Funny, the castigation of the system by the It Was Better Back In The Day crowd usually prompts a shrug with me. I hear the line – "It's all that's wrong with sports" – tossed around as often a Vick overthrow. Alas, they had a point there. I don't want my MTV with my sports, and the MTV mantra of sell before substance, prostitute before proficiency, BMW before seventeen and Crystal before eight in the morning, has poisoned society, let alone sports.

Seriously, pop culture has no class, anymore. It's loud and obnoxious and stupid and selfish and crippled by ADD. It's just a lot of noise. It's Paris Hilton and American Idol and Michael Jackson Again and Hummers and hogging a spotlight that needs to last a lot less than fifteen minutes. It's just a turnoff. And it's permeated sport, as least the huckstering of it.

Mike Vick can help revitalize a dead franchise and pitch shoes and French fries, but he couldn't pitch the ball a lick against the Eagles, so I professed, pointing to the two others times he played Jim Johnson's spying, mush-rush defense and was completely encircled, trapped in a goldfish bowl, nowhere to mad dash.

But three times bitten? The mind plays tricks on you. You analyze the game long enough and you see ghosts. Those of the other three games. You say you were equally confident before, if not entering the one in St. Louis, then certainly against Tampa Bay and Carolina.

The worm of doubt…

You wonder. It's one thing to beat the Vikings without Owens. The Falcons defense is clearly better than Minnesota's, and the Falcons' running game did look daunting against the Rams and perhaps all Vick has to do is make one big play which he can certainly do, and they have a pretty good returner in ol' Allen Rossum, the former Eagle, and what if he takes one to the house like he did last week? You know how a play like that skews a game, messing with the momentum. And damn, what about the poisonous parallel? Tampa and Carolina and Atlanta are all from the same division

What really sent the flock into a dither that Tuesday of Title Tilt

IV was news that an impending noreaster was projected to rock Philadelphia the day of the game, producing gale force winds and upwards to a foot or more of snow.

Snowstorm.

Panic swept through the city. In football, inclement weather always favors the underdog. It's the great evener, friend of fat chance and the fluke play and otherworldly occurrences. It stunts the strengths of the better team, and usually forces the clock into a mad sprint. It's even more pronounced in a matchup such as this one, with the Falcons relying heavily on pounding the football with the rush. Worse than the potential footing for the pass-happy Eagles would be the high winds, taking McNabb's throws where they want, especially the deep ones, which became a huge part of the offense this season.

So the flock wailed at the notion of this looming storm of epic proportions, suddenly feeling forsaken by the fates of football. "Makes you wonder if the gods really don't want us to win," Ralph on the mobile bemoaned.

Someone who goes by Phantom on the message board at 700Level.com wrote, "It's official. God hates the Eagles. Bad wind and a snowstorm were the only two things that could have kept this game close. Look like we're getting both."

Desperate, we were willed to witchcraft – again. Prior to the playoffs, the town T.O.-less wary, we had Bubba cold-call psychics from the phone book to hold a supernatural sports summit on the air. Four showed up at the studio: a woman named Vivian with a faux English accent who read tarot cards; another woman who scolded that she was not a psychic but a spiritual adviser; Carol, the most normal of the lot, very sweet, who seemed rather authentic, claiming her "gift" provided certain perceptions into life and that she didn't have a crystal ball; and a man in a black cape who referred to himself as "Mystic."

Tall and thin, with a large nose and an ashen face hidden by long slatternly hair, a cross between Howard Stern and any metal band member, the Mystic talked of his third eye, the mind's eye, and claimed to have presaged many disasters, including the recent deadly tsunami that rocked the Pacific Rim. His website that he often plugged blazoned:

"Even in ancient Biblical times, 'Seers' of what is to come have been used by Kings and Leaders in every corner of the globe. These "Seers" offer their help in healing and spiritual advice. Some were given their own realms to live and rule. During the years of progression, their numbers fell to a new industrial age. What few 'Seers' remained carried on in secret, and soon themselves fell into legend … 'Til now… One 'Seer' has been born unto this earth to fulfill ancient tasks, here in the 21st Century…THE MYSTIC."

"I'm seeing…," he began, eyes closed, when asked the question whether the Eagles would make it to the Super Bowl. "I'm seeing…American symbols…yes…an eagle…and…the flag…colors of the flag."

Mystic – whom Steve called "Mis" – swore little knowledge of football, and that became apparent upon our conversation, but he correctly picked each round of the playoffs, down to Eagles versus the Patriots. We put his final pick of the Super Bowl in a sealed envelope.

(For the record, Mystic predicted the Patriots would win by the odd, non-football score of 18-11)

So we called the Mystic that Wednesday, and said, "Hey, Mis, sure that bird wasn't a Falcon?"

"No," he replied, "it was definitely an Eagle."

Meanwhile, local weather forecasters tracking the storm gave hourly updates during the entire week.

"You gotta understand," Butchy would say, "they were going to play that game no matter what, if there was a monsoon, typhoon or tornado. No matter if it snowed ten feet."

By Friday morning, the storm had picked up its pace and was now scheduled to hit Saturday, breathing guarded optimism into the flock that maybe, just maybe, it would be out to sea by three o'clock. Meanwhile, that sensation of snow before a storm beetled in the air, as scores of people braved a benumbing cold for the high noon pep rally at Love Park in the shadow of City Hall. I don't know why it surprised me, after the endless displays of devotion, how the single-game tickets for the playoffs vanished in fewer than five minutes, potential purchasers calling ticket outlets all over the United States, wheedling the attendant to stay on the line until the clock struck 10 and the tickets were released to the computer.

I've seen the ingenuity of these people in search of seats evolve from mass dialing the local ticket offices, using laptops and elaborate tagteams, to discovering that you could call any outlet in the country as soon as the team released the tickets, bypassing the busy signal. Some called El Paso, Texas, others Des Moines, Iowa, staying away from major cities that others might try. The trick is keeping the attendant on the phone long enough to ask about the availability of Eagles tickets the very moment they are released. If you ask prior to 10, the attendant will say they are not available and hang up on you. Thus most feigned interest in other invents, concerts and the like, and struck up "where ya from?" small talk, inveigling their way to a pair.

Bundled in their Eagles parkas and jerseys over thermal underwear, they chanted and cheered and donned homemade signs, and sang the Eagles Fight Song until the cold blistered the throat. We broadcasted live that day from next to the stage, and witnessed the park slowly fill around 11, swelling to thousands by the start of the pep rally, the flock emerging out of office buildings and buses and taxi cabs, others traipsing on foot from God knows where.

A pep rally is so, well, collegiate, antithetical to a major city like Philadelphia. Yet, perhaps because of the town's parochial temperament, it somehow fits here amid the mild irony of the setting. Love Park, a concrete commons with sparse green that sits at the eastern end of the Benjamin Franklin Parkway, the yawning thoroughfare modeled after Paris' Champs-Elysee, used to be JFK Plaza. The name change occurred because of Robert Indiana's LOVE statue, one of the most recognizable works in America art, loaned to the city for the Bicentennial Celebration in 1976. It left two years later and ultimately returned after it was purchased by Fitz Dixon, Jr., then chairman of the Philadelphia Art Commission. The LOVE sculpture features four stacked letters with a tilted O, described by Indiana to the *Indianapolis News* in '95 as "concrete poetry – a poem in one word."

Indeed, love imbued the chilled air.

Snow began to fall by 10 Saturday morning. The first flakes were waffle-sized, before settling into a normal, steady stream. The city was on high alert, dispatching an army of salt trucks, according to Nick

Martino, Philadelphia County Maintenance Manager for PennDOT, with a heavy concentration on the roads surrounding Lincoln Financial Field. Stadium workers arrived at the Linc by mid-afternoon to begin preparing for the great dig out.

"I left for the hotel hours before I usually do," Ike Reese said. "I didn't want to get stuck."

The airport closed by early evening. Across the country, 3,000 flights were cancelled, stranding about 800 passengers in the city, without a single hotel room available.

By evening, the city was caked in snow, ten inches having already fallen. A snowstorm hushes a city, especially at night. A snowstorm freezes an entire city into a single snapshot, one of splendor with the snow still glossy white, virginal for that moment, unaware it will soon turn gray and repulsive. Through my window, I like to watch the snow fall amid the glow of a streetlamp, the only movement of the night, the demons driven into slumber.

Over at the stadium, they worked feverishly in their brightly colored jumpsuits, layered clothing underneath, clearing the snow as it fell, inch by inch. Martino, who is in charge of all interstate highways in Philadelphia County, had begun work at eleven on Friday night. Martino, I should tell you, is a boyhood friend of Joey's, which makes him a boyhood friend of mine, since I was the little guy tailing along, four years younger than the rest. He is Nicky Martino to us, a bear of a man like he was a bear of a boy, a wonderful athlete and always affable, a trait that has remained strong over the years, as has a fierce devotion to the football team. So Nicky begun work Friday night at eleven and didn't finish until eleven in the morning on Sunday, after which he promptly went right to the parking lot to tailgate. His wife, Danielle, knew better than to expect him home. Nicky is a season ticket holder, and so he went from work to the parking lot to his seat in the stadium, where, upon arrival, his entire section gave him a standing ovation. Following the game, invigorated and imbibed by the outcome, he stopped across the street at McFadden's Pub inside the Phillies' lovely new stadium for a toddy, then went home and watched the postgame coverage on Comcast. "I finally crashed at one in the morning," he will say. "I was up for a total of 51 straight hours."

The weekend was filled by stories like Nicky's, the city workers and stadium crew toiling through the sleepless hours to get the Linc and its surrounding area in operating condition. Inside the stadium, there wasn't a flake of snow on the heated field or on the seats.

After dumping fifteen inches, the storm finally departed by mid-morning on Sunday, angling up the coast to New York and New England, giving way to dazzling sunshine, but leaving behind arctic winds and blasts of Canadian air.

Four-wheel drive vehicles, covered with ice and snow and Eagles flags and banners, began arriving the stadium at 8 in the morning and became a steady stream as gametime approached. The temperature at kickoff was seventeen degrees, with winds from the northwest at twenty-six miles per hour, with gusts reaching 45 miles per hour. The windchill recorded at five below zero.

"You had real fans at the Championship Game," Jeremiah Trotter said. "Those were real Eagles fans in the stands going for broke. It's not about hype or money with those people. They're ready to punch somebody. They'd start shooting if they could get a gun in the stadium. The long wait. Three years of losing that game. All those years before that. Harold Carmichael told me there's nothing like winning the Championship Game at home. You get chills, he said. He was right on. I feed off the energy of the crowd, and that Championship Game was the most energy I've ever felt in my life."

...AND FIVE WILL LEAD THE FRANCHISE

Let us travel back to Tuesday, to a shopping mall in Jacksonville, one that can be found amid any cluster of population in this country. Yes, typically American, this shopping mall, with four department stores and a movie theater anchoring the array of stores, several for women's fashions, a few mall-trendy, unisex clothing spots for the younger people, hip-hop and dance music pounding away, the checkout desk manned by the cute teenage girl with the bare midriff and belly button ring, the electronics shop, the overpriced jewelry store and the bookstore. Over there in the nook is the spot Santa Claus recently vacated, and if you walk further along in the cool, processed air, just around the corner is the food court, with the pizza place and Smoothies stand and the sandwich shop and the fast-food burger joint and the Chinese food kiosk that sells basically four things: egg rolls, fried rice, barbecued spare ribs and General Tso's chicken.

Walk past the food court and the escalators, and you'll see them entering a sneaker store. Foot Locker. They appear just a tad different than the rest of the shoppers, a little bigger and definitely more prince-ly, a dashing quality about them, down to their accessories, fine time-pieces and designer belts and perfectly polished shoes.

You can always tell a professional athlete, even if you do not rec-ognize him, the way you can always tell a plutocrat. It's how they pur-port themselves, an ever subtle promenade for a walk, with a certain flare, one born of confidence and wealth.

For a good portion of their shopping, a pleasant enough way to kill most of a free day, they went about their business unnoticed. Invariably, though, the recognition would come, partly because they are six men (except for the wide receiver), of similar builds and that same developed neck, and partly because they are six black men bear-ing similar panache. Mostly, however, it is because He is in the middle of that group. It's all of those commercials He does. Pitching the soup and the satellite television and the video games.

Happens all the time. Usually it goes something like this:

"Aren't you?"

"Yes," he replies, "I'm Donovan McNabb."

Donovan McNabb grins widely, indulges in a moment of small talk, then maybe signs his name on something and departs, still grin-ning.

Tuesday, a man in his late twenties, was the first to identify him, as the crowd of mostly kids and teenagers bulged as word spread of their presence. But instead of the usual puffery, the young man pro-ceeded to angle between Ike Reese and Jeremiah Trotter, Nate Wayne, Todd Pinkston and Michael Lewis, right up to McNabb and tell him, "It's important for us here in Jacksonville that you win the game. It's important for us that a black quarterback win the Super Bowl in this city."

The man went on to speak of a racial tension hidden beneath the glow of the Super Bowl, and how a victory by Donovan McNabb provided a victory for the black people of Jacksonville. "It wasn't the usual sort of thing," Ike Reese recalled. "He had this straight, serious face. His eyes welled with tears. I could see them watering. None of us knew what to say. It kind of took Don by surprise."

"We'll do our best," Don said to the man.

The players left the store and exited the mall, an awkward silence hovering over them.

Reese said, "We were like, What was THAT all about? Sometimes the game seems bigger to some people than it is to us. I should say it takes on a bigger meaning to some people than just a football game, even if it is the Super Bowl. We were kind of speechless. You wanna say, we'll try to deliver a win for him because it meant so much to him. It was like a guy on his death bed asking for one last wish. Pretty heavy stuff."

"We were kind of shocked," McNabb would say. "We just wanted to walk around the mall and see everything."

Now add racial strife in Jacksonville to a protracted list of why Donovan McNabb must succeed.

The road to NFL stardom has been an odd journey for Donovan McNabb. It began with the draft-day booing that, while context suggested otherwise, was nonetheless wounding to him, and continued with the championship losses that were heaped upon his shoulders, the criticism offered by Rush Limbaugh, and a vagarious relationship with Terrell Owens, and eventually the last five minutes, forty seconds of the Super Bowl.

For someone most comfortable in normalcy, who prefers to be as benign as warm milk and consciously shapes his public persona that way, who relishes playing the role of the Good Son because that's truly him, he has a knack, however unwitting and unwanted, for finding situations.

"Sometimes he's like a billboard for criticism," Reese said. "He's a walking target."

A portion of it is due to the landscape of playing the glory position in the most celebrated sport, but the quagmires McNabb has faced exceed that very fact, beginning with the curtain of boos that greeted him at the draft and lingered throughout the years. As misdirected and misunderstood as they were, meant as an editorial statement of the Eagles' strategy and a want for Ricky Williams, they became ingrained as part of his story.

So, too, was Limbaugh's puerile commentary of his struggles during the early part of the 2003 season, that McNabb was only being exalted by the media because of his race. Meanwhile, race had already been a backstory in Philadelphia, with many believing that his unwillingness to run was due to his desire not to be typecast as a running quarterback, a.k.a., a *black* quarterback. Suddenly, McNabb was thrust to the center of a raging national polemic that subsequently was followed with Limbaugh's dismissal from ESPN's pregame show, and greatly improved play on the field by him.

When asked to reflect on the ordeal a year later, as he got off to his best start yet earlier this season, he said, "It was kind of a motivational push for me. But as of right now, I haven't even thought about it. My focus – as it was last year – is to continue to do the right things. There are better things to think about [than Limbaugh's comments]."

This illustrates McNabb's appetite to just be left alone to play football. Truly, he rebuffs the notion that he plays football for some grandiose purpose. He does not bestow great complexity to what he does or who he is. He just is.

Despite all of the past acclaim, and the intense notoriety of Super Bowl week, Donovan McNabb remains endearingly simple and grounded. It's just that simple. What allegorizes the point is that here in Jacksonville he has a roommate, linebacker Nate Wayne, a defensive player on top of that. See, professional athletes of McNabb's stature don't have roommates on the road. In fact, in baseball and basketball, no players have roommates. Terrell Owens doesn't have a roommate.

Michael Jordan sometimes enjoyed his own floor of a hotel.

McNabb embraces being part of the group, in his case, the team, the anti-Owens who rebuffs the estrangement that often comes with status like his. I swear, you know Donovan McNabb. He is the best athlete from your middle class neighborhood, from your street, just like he was on leafy Diekman Court in suburban Chicago. He is the kid who played everything and excelled, who all scholastic coaches liked because he was trouble-free, who did the sort of things every other kid did, from video games to rooting for the Bulls, who just happened to make it in big in the NFL.

I swear, he is your father's quarterback, consumed by the electric bill and leaving the bathroom light on, mindful of every acorn. Right after his rookie season, we hooked up one happy hour at what used to be a Friday's just off South Street, and I nodded toward his car, a burgundy Chrysler, a dealer's car, and he sprang to defend it, "What did you expect? A Benz? I like this car. It's a nice car." I shrugged. I had also thought it to be a nice car.

That day we hung at a back table, along with former Eagles tight end Luther Broughton and a female friend, and had a bar food feast — buffalo wings, chicken fingers, potato skins, mozzarella sticks. He wildly dipped everything in Ranch dressing, and anointed it, "The bomb, especially when you run out of mayonnaise." It was so college, so twenty-something, and on another similar day years later at a finer restaurant, he leaned over to me after we ordered a cold appetizer of fresh prosciutto and buffalo mozzarella drizzled with olive oil and asked, "They have mozzarella sticks?" I swore then he didn't change a lick from the first time I sat down with him for more than a postgame Syracuse quote, right there in the family room of his parents split-level home on Diekman Court, the smell of Wilma McNabb's hotcakes wafting in the summer morning.

I found him to be unsullied then and attributed it to upbringing and playing his college ball at Syracuse, way up north, imprisoned by the murky Finger Lakes and a dreary, endless winter, but close enough to swill Canadian perspective. Truthfully, I figured fame would deflower him, if only because I've seen it countless times — apple-cheeked, aw-shucks sort takes one bite of the big-time and forever loses his soul under the thick, fatted layers of ego. But it never happened, McNabb remaining as together as mashed potatoes, as grounded as the curb, even if should we fast-forward to a recent morning in May, Jacksonville a far away memory inside the cafeteria at the NoveCare Center, the players in town for a voluntary camp.

Next season comes with such damn precipitancy. So little time for reflective regalement. It's time for breakfast, anyway. Tray in hand, sliding it along the rail, Donovan McNabb reaches for the oatmeal and green grapes.

"You know," he said, "you can't forget what happened last season and you have to remember what happened last season, and all you can do is get ready for next season. If we keep doing what we've been going on offense and click on all cylinders no one will be able to stop us. You know, we CAN get back!"

The fans want to hear that, I replied. You're learning.

He laughs.

Yes, the fans. Part of the peculiarity over the years is his relationship with them, which isn't to say it's been strained. It's just been, well, different. You might think the Good Son would be the Favorite Son. After all, in this Era of Estrangement in sport, where the divide between athlete and fan has become great, the source salary and the mercenary movement via free agency, McNabb has been a staple in this town, the way they used to be back in the day, the heroes of Philadelphia past like Mike Schmidt and Julius Erving and Bob Clarke and Ron Jaworski. He is the franchise player, the one who has grown into a star before this town's very eyes, who will likely stay here throughout his entire career, who plays the glory position, who is the face of this football team.

Entering this season, it wasn't like that. It was admiration, without unabashed adoration. Speaking in generalities, it seemed McNabb and the fans were still suspicious of each other after five years, an arm's length between them, partly because I believe the flock felt it had to share him. Due to his national stature, he wasn't solely theirs, a product of Chicago first, the NFL second and the Philadelphia Eagles third.

For example, while McNabb lives in Arizona during the off-season,

Allen Iverson, despite his travels, resides fulltime in Villanova, and despite his flawed past, they see him around town, however shady some of the places.

The relationship, however, changed over the season, certainly because the Eagles were so dominant and he had a career year and he finally delivered a Super Bowl, no matter how it ended. In this town, to be enshrined in the heart, you must win like the heroes of Philadelphia Past.

Meanwhile, for the first time in his tenure here, McNabb bathed in unadulterated applause, and who doesn't like to bathe in that? He didn't hear the groaning of the underbelly, no matter how shallow the pool. He didn't hear the nitpicking of his game, how he needs to run more and throw with more accuracy, and there were no distant calls for A.J. Feeley or Koy Detmer. It was him and them, for better or even better. For the first time, he felt truly loved by these hypercritical people.

"What a better place to be able to celebrate it than Philadelphia," he said. "It really touched me. One way of looking at it for us was that we were there three times in a row and the experience just continued growing every year. So then it was kind of like the weight is off of our back, and the fan support and the people of Philadelphia are going out in the city and acting crazy and excited, and deservingly so. They had a great time with the whole deal and we had a great time with the whole deal. They were like, Welcome with open arms. It seemed like every time you talked to someone about football, they had an uproar. It seemed like every time you turned the radio on, football came up. It's just the excitement that builds up around me the whole time that I love.

"You see the commercials with the Boston Red Sox fans and what their talking about. Well, here they're taking out second mortgages. They're putting their marriages up; I swear, they'll get rid of their wife! You know stuff like that entices us."

He talked further of the pilgrimage, how astonishing it was. So, I said, do you understand these people yet?

"Out here in Philly? Yes. Yes," he replied. "I mean, I'm from Chicago so I had the Bears. At that time you know the Bears were winning. You know, you had the best defense and offensively you had Walter Payton and Jim McMahon. When we went to the Super Bowl and won it, that was the start of something special. Because the Bulls started winning, and baseball was doing so-so and the Blackhawk's had made the playoffs. The fans were really similar in some aspects. But when you come to Philly there is extra love here.

"We know they're always going to be there, no matter win, lose, or draw. When we were down two years ago you know everyone had their opinion. But they went down there and packed a stadium. They are the same fans who boo and throw things, and at the same time they are the same fans who cheer for us and pat us on the back. There are always a small percentage of fans who boo you. But for the most part, these people are true fans who are always going to be there."

Five minutes and forty seconds.

Your average wait at the bus stop or the dry cleaners or the fast-food burger joint. Your average time it takes to shave. The average length of the coming attractions before the movie begins. He will not be haunted by five minutes and forty seconds.

For the last time, he will say.

He didn't get sick. He didn't get exhausted. He didn't get hurt. He didn't panic.

The story is, there is no story.

Trailing by ten to the Patriots, following a 50-yard punt by Josh Miller, the Eagles received the ball with five minutes and forty seconds remaining in Super Bowl XXXIX. They needed to score and score fast. Score and use their two remaining timeouts on defense, utilize the two minute warning as a safety net third one, and hopefully have a full two minutes for a possession to tie the game and force overtime.

The offense moved the ball, but it looked painfully torpid doing so, lacking the frenetic approach of a typical hurry-up situation. The offense appeared in half-hurry-up, with McNabb heading to the line like a heavyweight brawler in the fifteenth round. The Patriots defense, which, in successive weeks of the playoffs, had grounded the dynamic

Colts' attack led by touchdown king Peyton Manning, and harried Pittsburgh rookie sensation Ben Roethlisberger into several mistakes, took away the deep strike and the middle deep strike. The Patriots forced the play underneath, in front of the linebackers, safeties and corners, allowing the would-be tacklers a direct line to the ball.

Beginning at his own twenty-one, McNabb took the short stuff. Tight LJ Smith for four. Greg Lewis in a reversed call for four. T.O. for five. Fullback Josh Parry for two. Under pressure, he tried to break a run up the middle, but was stopped for no gain. Meanwhile, the clock dissolved, and each time McNabb motioned for the team to huddle up, fans from Philadelphia to Jacksonville, groaned.

The Eagles eventually scored on the drive, as McNabb angled a lovely throw to Greg Lewis for a 30 yard touchdown pass. But it occurred on the wrong side of the two minute warning. The Eagles couldn't convert the onside kick, and squeezed the ball back. But seconds remained at their own four, and McNabb was intercepted again to end the game. In the end, he put up numbers, but he did not play well. He did play what the Eagles call Five Football (after his jersey number). Too many mistakes. Too few Five plays.

The following night, center Hank Fraley and tackle Jon Runyan appeared on Comcast SportsNet's *Angelo Cataldi Show* and claimed McNabb fell ill during the drive. While trying to give his quarterback credit, Fraley initiated a raging controversy by saying, "He fought to the end. He gave it his all. He could hardly call the plays – that's how exhausted he was trying to give it his all. If you remember back when we played Jacksonville two years ago and Donovan ended up puking, it was close to that scene. He exhausted everything he had."

Fraley added, "He didn't get a play call in one time. He mumbled and Freddie Mitchell yelled out the play we were trying to bring in. He was puking at the same time, trying to hold it in."

Mitchell, speaking in a local television interview, said, "[McNabb] couldn't get it out so I just had to finish the play up. It was my first time being the quarterback in the NFL. It was hard. He kind of tried to get the hand signals to the team, but I knew what he was thinking. I just finished the play up."

Two days later, McNabb, while in Hawaii for his fifth Pro Bowl in six seasons, dismissed the allegations as nonsense. "If people want to use that as an excuse for why we lost – that's not the way it was – but I'll put it on my shoulders," he countered. "I'll take the blame. I know I'm quarterback. It's my job to take the blame."

He also scoffed at the notion that he couldn't get the play out and Mitchell had to relay it to the rest of the team. "No," he said, "Freddie didn't call a play. I get the plays in my helmet, so he couldn't call a play."

On the radio station, Five Minutes and Forty Seconds raged on for weeks. It seemed as though everyone in town offered a theory on what happened to Donovan McNabb.

Vomiting is a symptom of a panic attack. Yes, he had a panic attack.

He was sick. He had a cold earlier in the week. The weather was crappy all week, and it got chilly during the game and he was feeling the remnants of the cold.

He took two big hits earlier in the half, and they made him woozy.

He was flat-out gassed. Totally spent. He's a big man. Carries a lot of weight. He was exhausted.

He underwent a dramatic adrenalin rush to start the game. He wasn't used to the extended halftime of the Super Bowl, which threw off his body clock. By the end of the game, he was completely enervated.

While bemoaning his contract situation, Terrell Owens would also take a swipe at McNabb's performance, saying, "I wasn't the one who got tired in the Super Bowl." Owens was upset that McNabb didn't publicly support him in his demands, and insinuated to Stephen A. Smith of the *Philadelphia Inquirer* that McNabb was a "company man."

Well into the off-season, Reese, now a Falcon, would come to McNabb's defense. He would say, "It's infuriating some of the things some of the guys said about him. To give of his body like he did in that game and all season long, it's just wrong. Bottom line, he came up short. It happens. Take it for what it is."

Over breakfast that May day, Donovan McNabb would reiterate that there was no great mystery behind Five Minutes and Forty Seconds: "What happened, happened. We scored, didn't we? You have to really understand how big it really is. When things are really going good for you, your expectations get higher and higher. Obviously, we've reached the particular point where now you have to win the Super Bowl. And when we didn't win, it was like what happened? Everybody has their own critiques. We had some turnovers and things didn't work out as well as we wanted them too."

In a general statement, he would also address cutting remarks by Owens and the parting shots by Mitchell, who cursed the quarterback during a visit to the Harvard Business School, saying McNabb's personal feeling toward him was the primary reason he didn't get the ball. He told *Sports Illustrated's* Peter King of Five Minutes and Forty Seconds, in which McNabb threw to him twice, completing one, "The way we approached that long drive, the sense of urgency wasn't there. Maybe, if anything, Donovan should have run off and let [backup] Koy Detmer come in."

"One thing people don't realize about this team is that the quarterback is like the head coach," McNabb would say. "If the team can see that you want to burst out and show a side that no one's really seen, then your respect value really goes up. Personally people know me as a calm and collected guy, who understands what goes on, and realizes what my job is and what I need to do in order to get where we wanna go. You know I can't really let any person that I talk to, or what people on TV are saying, bother me at all. It's not like if you have something bad to say about me we can't go to war. But if I have nothing to do with what you are talking about then don't talk about me. If there is something that you need to say then we can talk, I'm here. You know where I'm at."

We would joke about the quote McNabb said at a news conference addressing the Owens flap. I used to joke with him about being a terrible quote. Bland as bran, you are, offering those scripted answers meant to offend no one.

"Eeeeeeh, yeahhh,"McNabb stammered when I asked if he purposely opted for the colorless demeanor and boundless clichés to the media. "Yeah, it varies," he said. "I just like to have fun, you know? I don't need to cause no havoc. Don't need to try to get anybody in a bad spot where you gotta make a decision or somebody might get yelled at. I try to be smart with everything."

Pushed into a corner by Owens, he said, "Just keep my name out your mouth."

"Like that one?" he would laugh. "Seriously, you know me. I like everything to be smooth. You never heard me throw anyone under the bus, even though there were times when I could have. I try to handle things like a man."

Let us not allow Five Minutes and Forty Seconds and the aftermath of the Super Bowl begrime what was a bewitching season for the franchise quarterback.

Let us travel back to happier times, beginning at Week Five, before the Eagles would extract revenge that middle October day against the Carolina Panthers:

The room is the size of an airplane hangar, though more lounge than locker room. There is carpeting and wood finish on the stalls, which provide ample space, even for the extra large men who dress here. Yet it feels rather close with the noise. Yes, the noise was what we noticed before anything else an hour before this rematch of the NFC Championship Game, the hollering and the music. There was Hugh Douglas perambulating, what he does best off the field. Old-school Rick James bleated, the "Best of CD," and Douglas wailed:

"What else can I say, baby, sexy, sexy, sexy
Cold. blood-ed
Holy smokes and gee whiz…"

In the middle of the song, he suddenly stopped singing along and began to talk of this game that followed a bye week.

"Gotta shake that rust off," he brayed to no one in particular. "Choo-choo! Gotta catch that train to work! Choo-choo, c'mon, catch that train. Ya'll runnin' 'round the city tellin' everybody you play for the Philadelphia Eagles. Tellin' them ho's that you love 'em. C'mon now, let's go to work. You, too, T.O., be ready."

Terrell Owens was dressing, and didn't stir. He was always the storyline now, and for that one it was over Panthers cornerback Ricky

Manning Jr., who ragdolled Eagles receivers in the Title Game and whom Owens targeted in the days leading up to the game. "That young boy wants a piece of you, T.O.," Douglas continues. "Be ready now."

Douglas began singing again, as the players waited for Butch Jr. to signal the two minute warning. The room turned serious then, and they filed out of the double doors, wound down the other end of the tunnel that led to the field and into the blowup helmet for pregame introductions.

Donovan McNabb noted of the locker room, "All that's missing are cocktail waitresses."

A moment ago, McNabb bumped butts with ample defensive tackle Hollis Thomas. It's not atypical to see him as loose as an old table leg before a game, but he's scaled a new level of comfort during it.

"The main reason I really wanted to come here was to be with the caliber of quarterback like McNabb," Owens said that day. "[Jerry] Rice had Steve Young and those guys. I left a lot of plays on the field. I wanted to see how good I could be."

McNabb and Owens started off hot together, before their February fallout. Fast friends they were, from that first preseason game with the long pass, faster dance partners, developing a connection that borders on telepathy. Trainer Rick Burkholder even noted a brotherly respect at that time, saying: "Donny can throw one in practice that jams T.O.'s finger and T.O. can say, 'Throw it right' or 'I'm open, Donny, I'm open, throw me the ball.' They can get pissed at each other and get along real well. Part of it is Donny gives him the time and deals with him when he's got a problem or when's he's open and doesn't get the ball."

"I think being around Donovan has been good for T.O.," Reese had said. "He rubs off on him. Like the other day, those two cats are runnin' around with fake snakes. They got Michael Lewis. T.O. had it in a towel. Threw it on Michael. He squirmed like a schoolgirl.

"The thing I was worried about most coming into this season was the chemistry, that there were so many different personalities. But here we are, all the new guys settled in, and nobody's a big-timer. Everybody fits."

So the Eagles beat Carolina on the kind of Sunday afternoon we imagine in northern autumn, though to a man they rebuked the notion of revenge. And though this was their fifth straight victory by double digits to open the season, there was little merriment.

Andy Reid walked to the center of the locker room and rasped, "All right, bring it up."

Some players dawdled, including Terrell Owens, and Reid's voice deepened and grew louder. "Let's go. Let's go. C'mon. T.O., bring it over here."

Reid winked at Owens. There was a movement through the thicket of weary men, and then Reid addressed the group.

"How 'bout Lito Sheppard out there?" he said.

The team hooted for the young corner who wrote in his journal the day before he'd snare the first interception of his career. He had two.

Reid beamed. Like McNabb, Sheppard is his guy.

"There are no empty wins," he said. "They're all good. See you Wednesday. Now let's pray."

The players dropped to one knee and clasped their neighbor's hand and recited the Lord's Prayer in unison.

The team that prays together...

Kept winning.

McNabb kept cataloging gaudy numbers, even through the mild dustup with Owens during the team's first defeat of the season in Pittsburgh, where cameras zoomed in on the Eagles' sidelines and captured the receiver vituperating the quarterback, gesturing wildly. Afterwards, both downplayed the incident, with Owens saying that he was just trying to instill some life into a sagging McNabb.

The following week in Dallas for Monday Night Football, the two would recreate the scene, play-acting it out during a rout of the Cowboys. McNabb was splendid in the game, leading the Eagles to five touchdown drives in the first half, including four in the second quarter, and another in the third, set up by one of the most spectacular plays of his career. Under a blitz, McNabb dashed from sideline to sideline, avoiding tacklers with an array of jukes and sidesteps, some just falling off him. He held the ball for 14 seconds, an eternity for a quarterback, before unleashing a money ball 60 yards downfield to a streaking Mitchell. He threw for 345 yards in all, with four touchdowns and zero interceptions.

McNabb enjoyed a similarly flawless, incandescent performance three weeks later against the Packers in a game then touted as a matchup for the NFC regular season crown. In that one, he threw a whopping 43 times and completed 32 of them for a franchise-record 464 yards and five touchdowns, all in the first half, as the Eagles steamrolled out to a 35-3 lead at intermission. McNabb shredded a confused Packers defense with ease, at times looking like he was playing catch, mostly with Owens and Brian Westbrook out of the backfield, a duo that seemed impossible to defend.

The spacing the two created brought Andy Reid's offense to life, forcing defenses to abandon the blitz early for fear of getting burned and allowing McNabb several options, including the now overlooked bit players on offenses: Todd Pinkston streaking deep and LJ Smith or Chad Lewis deep over the middle.

"We try to put guys in different positions so we can create mismatches, and we're the guys to do that," McNabb would say. "You know, as you can see, teams fear Westbrook. You know, he is the secret weapon. Are you going to double team him or T.O.? If you do that then LJ is going to be open or Todd going to be open. We even have Josh Parry and Jon Ritchie coming out of the backfield. See, that's what makes it exciting for me as a quarterback. It even makes my role as a quarterback limited. It makes it so that I am not a running quarterback. I'm not running for that anymore, I can give it to those guys and let them have their own fun."

For the first time in his career, unsaddled by plebeian targets, the likes of James Thrash, Torrance Small, Charles Johnson and Na Brown, McNabb felt as though he didn't have to make everything happen on offense. What happened? He set a team record with nearly thirty-nine hundred passing yards and became the first quarterback in NFL history to throw more than thirty touchdowns [thirty-one] and fewer than ten interceptions [eight].

"I was one of the guys that felt we would never win a title here unless we had a topnotch wide receiver on this team," Ike Reese said.

"Someone Donovan had as a go-to guy. Nothing against those other guys, but I often thought, How much could Donovan do if he had a Torry Holt or a Marvin Harrison or a T.O.?"

Reese recalled an encounter he had with McNabb following a game last season at the Meadowlands during the height of the quarterback's struggles, in which the Eagles beat the Giants solely on defense and a punt return for a touchdown by Westbrook. McNabb was feeling quite low, half wondering if maybe Rush Limbaugh was right, at least about him being overrated.

"I stink," he told Reese that day.

"He was really down on himself," Reese said. "We struggled on offense and his numbers weren't great. He threw for like fifty-something yards. The receivers had a tough game. He had some tough throws. I said, 'Listen, man, I don't think we'll ever win a championship unless you have some help at the wide receivers position.' We needed a star. We needed someone who the defense says, We have to stop THAT GUY.

"You know, on defense, we never talk about the opposing quarterback. We talk about who the quarterback is getting the ball to. When the Rams had that great offense, we talked about Marshall Faulk or Holt or Isaac Bruce. We never talked about Kurt Warner. You need playmakers, guys who get the ball. If a defense doesn't respect your playmakers, they're gonna take you out of the game. That's the way Tampa beat us. They played a hard Cover 2, got physical with the receivers at the line and took Donovan out of the game. Same thing with Carolina. Don broke his rib but was willing to stay out there, and balls were being dropped, routes being cut off. It was tough for him, and he stayed out there through the whole third quarter."

McNabb easily played the best quarterback of his pro career during the season. Gone were the worm balls, the erratic throws and the indecision, replaced by precision and intuition, which can be attributed partly to the addition of an honest to goodness target in Owens, and partly to professional growth. A recent first-time father, he even looked recast, sporting presence with his new braids. Someone within the team suggested that in addition to the added arsenal it was because Troy Vincent had left for Buffalo and "it's absolutely Donovan's team.

He rules the locker room. There's no doubt about it.'"

"In past years, Don was a little self-conscious," Runyan said. "This season he took on that leadership role. He made it clear that we're going to go as far as he takes us. Him stepping up made you feel good. That he was in control and he knew what he was doing. He proved that the whole season. He was just so much more assertive in the huddle. Before he was like, 'C'mon, guys, we can do this. We're all right.' This past year, he flared, 'Let's get this shit straight. We're not losing this fucking game.'"

Another point of growth came after Owens injured his ankle in Week 14 against Dallas. With the city drowning in misery, feeling forsaken yet again, McNabb came out publicly and said, "T.O. is not our whole team. We can go to the Super Bowl without him."

So they did. In the playoff opener, the Vikings' permissive defense proved little challenge for McNabb, whose only mistake the entire game was having the clock expire on him at halftime with the Eagles in the shadow of the Minnesota goal line.

He nodded as he jogged into the tunnel: Poor time management. My bad. Can't leave points on the field.

The second half was a breeze. McNabb threw for 286 six yards and two touchdowns, with his main target none other than Freddie Mitchell, who caught five of his 21 completions.

Then came the Title Game. Yes, yes, that game. Such a hurdle for him, beginning with the one in St. Louis, where he put forth a fine enough performance, sans the fumble on the first possession in the face of mad-rushing Leonard Little, and the interception on that last-chance, fourth-down play, the Eagles fifty-two yards from the Super Bowl. It should be noted that Freddie Mitchell turned the wrong way, cutting his route off on the play.

So close, the underdog Eagles were, leading at halftime on the road, nearly able to surprise the Rams the way the others would surprise them in that same game. At the conclusion, McNabb stayed on the field to watch the celebrating Rams, a covetous voyeur, wanting to feel what those players felt.

He thought he would the following year against Tampa. Like everyone else he thought it to be kismet, especially after he rehabbed so hard to recover from the broken ankle and make it back for the playoffs. It was apparent in the playoff opener against Atlanta that McNabb suffered lingering affects from the injury, but they were exacerbated by the Bucs' swarming defense, like just before halftime, when he drove the Eagles to the Tampa twenty-four but couldn't elude a scuttling Simeon Rice and his old high school buddy knocked the ball loose from him for a fumble. He endured more fits in the second half, the offense grounded like peppercorns, before Rhonde Barber delivered the deathknell with his now infamous interception.

So then it was Carolina, the Panthers, with their fearsome front four and clawing defense, and McNabb felt terribly isolated out there on the field. He had lost his only game breaker in Brian Westbrook that fateful Saturday night in D.C., freak injury in the last game of the season, not even touched by a Redskin. Of all the luck. He had a rock in Duce Staley, and he was a wonderful safety valve, duke of the dinks and dunks, but he needed the speedy Westbrook for the passing game to work down the field, as exemplified on a fly play Reid usually ran for Westbrook that just went off the fingertips of Staley.

Without Westbrook, he had to rely on the outside guys, a middling bunch consisting of Pinkston, Thrash and Mitchell, and they played awful. Pinkston directly caused two interceptions, one a killer deep in Carolina territory after he ran the wrong route, prompting the usually reserved McNabb to bark at him as they left the field. Thrash caused a third, again thwarting an Eagle drive, when a catchable pass bounced off his shoulder pads and into the awaiting arms of Ricky Manning, Jr.

Manning Jr., a puny toughman, had three picks, and manhandled Pinkston and Thrash all game long.

With the Panthers playing ultraconservatively, often running the ball on third and long, to avoid any mistakes against the gluttonous Eagle defense, McNabb's team was in it nearly the entire game, even if he finally had to leave it in the final quarter, finally succumbing to the separated rib cartilage he suffered in the first half. He finished the game only ten for 22 for 100 yards and zero touchdowns.

So here he was for the fatal fourth try, the wind howling in his face, along with one of the best defenses in the NFC, the Dirty Birds reborn.

McNabb threw darts through that wind, and he also ran the ball, appeasing the flock ten times, for thirty-two yards. He played it smart, riding his defense, making only one errant throw the entire game, a force to Westbrook with the safety bleeding in that was intercepted and dropped late in the third quarter. Without Owens, he completed passes to eight different receivers, including two touchdown throws, with Chad Lewis, McNabb's longtime companion and grizzled tight end, playing the hero. Lewis provided memories of McNabb's early days, like in 2000, the first year the Eagles made the playoffs under Reid, when all McNabb had was the tight end over the middle to hit, Lewis leading the team in receptions and receiving yards.

For Donovan McNabb, that victory represented requital.

Sort of.

Afterwards, McNabb's beaming father Sam, told *The Washington Post's* Michael Wilbon, another South Side Chicagoan and champion of McNabb's, "He knows people have now had to eat their words, but he won't say it. With him, it's not a matter of vindication or, 'I told you.' I taught both my children (including Donovan's older brother, Sean), 'Let your actions speak.' There's strong scripture in Proverbs that says if you train a child in the proper direction, when he grows older he will not depart. He's handled some situations better than I would have. I'm proud to see his growth and development as a man. I'm proud he lets his actions represent him. Words don't always communicate effectively. Actions take care of any uncertainty."

Moments after the game, the league rolled out that stage that Donovan McNabb so wished to stand upon. Slowly, he made his way on it, cherishing the snapshot of this moment.

He would say, "Back in 2001 when we played against St. Louis, when I went out there on the field, my idea was just to get hit by the confetti. I actually watched it happen. I watched the guys run around the field being happy. I saw them shake hands. I saw them smile. I saw them with their kids on the field. That's an exciting feeling, and I was on the other end of the deal. That was a feeling that I just could not wait happen to me. Once I got up there on the podium it was more less, Where is the confetti? Once the confetti was shot down, that's when I reacted.

"At the moment, that was the pinnacle. You have reached the pinnacle and you made it to the Super Bowl. No matter how you get there, you made it in that given time, yes. You know, it is really a dream come true, and for a lot of us, you realize now that it actually happened. The only other thing now is to go back there [to the Super Bowl] and win it. But is it really going to happen? You know, before, making it three times, the most important thing was winning the Championship Game. That day against Atlanta, we had confidence. We knew where we needed to be. Now we know where want to be. In order to get there, now we have to win it."

AND DELIVER US FROM EVIL...

At the two-minute warning of the NFC Championship Game, the outcome evident, fans began to chant what had eluded them in this very situation twice before, what had eluded them in all for the past 24 years: "Sooo…per Bowl! Sooo…per Bowl! Sooo…per Bowl!"

With thirty seconds left, Donovan McNabb looked skyward, surveying the stadium, all of those people standing and hollering, ingesting such a rapturous moment, and slowly dropped to one knee for the final play.

Bedlam ensued. Fireworks shot off into what was now night donning a glowing full moon. Silver and green confetti fell from the rafters, and light snow fell from the sky, a forgotten patch of the departed snowstorm. The sound system blared "Philadelphia Freedom."

A blissful man held up a sign that said, "There's only one Kearse in Philly."

"These people deserve this more than anyone," said that Kearse, one Jevon.

Dummy copies of the front page of the Philadelphia Inquirer were dispensed, the banner headline blaring: FINALLY.

"When you win a game like that," Jeremiah Trotter will say, reflecting back, "it's like curing a disease."

What a difference from two times ago, the heightened stillness in the stands of Veterans Stadium illuminating the Tampa sidelines, as you could hear individual yowls of delight echo from the strutting Bucs players who waved their pewter flags bearing the skull and cross-bones. Police in their black leather jackets and helmets encircled the field on their horses and motorcycles, while the people wordlessly shuffled into that cold night devoid of emotion, anesthetized by a sure thing gone awry. The scene depicted a futuristic bleakness, much like the last time, the only differences being it was Carolina, the new environs, and that lack of belly-punch astonishment at the end, the people now proficient in the descent from defeat.

Two Sundays ago, they were delivered.

All of them. Beginning in the owner's box, where before he made his way to the sidelines for the trophy ceremony, Jeffrey Lurie kissed his wife Christina, and Joe Banner kissed his wife, Helaine, both of them basking in the effulgence of Finally. For finally, after being so close so many times, the team making the playoffs now seven times in the ten years it has been under their stewardship, they were going to the Super Bowl.

Some of the players felt they were tight before last season's loss to the Panthers before the game, about forty-five minutes prior to kickoff, Hugh Douglas staged a dance party in the trainer's room. Think line dance on Soul Train. Jeffrey Lurie was in there watching, smiling at his players' chicanery, hoping against hope this day would be different. I think of Lurie who has done everything right with this franchise. Lord knows, it was a fruitful investment. The franchise is worth hundreds of millions more since he bought it from Norman Braman in '94. But sport is also a business of competition and conquest and glory. There are other wealthy men on this planet, but how many of them have reached the Super Bowl?

I think of Lurie, and I recall a conversation with Pat Croce about why he didn't want to run a professional sports team again after his experience with the Sixers. "I didn't have any control," he said. "I could make sure everything else was perfect, except the outcome on the court."

The players urged the owner Jeffrey Lurie to dance.

What the hell?

"The players wanted me to, so I did it," he smiled. "I can't say I did it well, but I did it. It was just the players and everyone trying to stay loose."

A city was delivered. From those people inside Lincoln Financial Field to those nestled in their homes, some of whom now willed to wander out into winter's arms, trekking to Broad Street or Frankford and Cottman to see the others of the flock, or trekking to the end of the driveway deep in the suburban sprawl to see thy neighbor, or maybe just to happy howl into the absorbing night.

Amen.

It's three o'clock. The tent is a bit thinned out for the pregame show, many having already set out early to Alltel Stadium. The stragglers here clutch to the belief that all of those seasons without a championship – 82 and counting, combining all four professional sports franchises in the city – will end on this breezy night in Jacksonville.

Back in Philadelphia, the callers express a similar sentiment. These are the good times. Unadulterated joy. A sanguine spell over the flock. If they were to bottle a moment, this would be it, trumping even that of victory. Because however sweet victory is, it is also shallow. For people of quality, it is about the journey.

The callers called from the road, while doing their last-minute food shopping, preparing for the feast that Father Joe spoke of, or from their living room, packed with family and friends, or for last-minute confirmation that, yes, the Eagles have a good chance of winning this evening.

Mobile Tom, a lottery winner of a million dollars on a scratch off ticket, calls to say today brings forth "the same kind of feeling. I never, ever thought I could feel this way twice in a lifetime."

Anthony from Havertown says, "I just got back from the cemetery. I put an Eagle flag on my father's gravesite."

Mobile David calls to share the news that he and Kelly got engaged after the Falcons game. "The Eagles brought us together. After the game, we're at my mom's house, and we were walking out, 12 inches of snow on the ground, and I got down one knee in the snow. I looked at Kelly and I said, Let's have little Eagles fans and live happily ever after. I don't know what's more exciting, the Birds in the Super Bowl or getting engaged."

Samantha from Cherry Hill calls to say she and her husband who met chatting in an Eagle fan forum, are already on the sofa, huddled with what brought them together.

I did receive one disturbing call, from a man named Joe, whom I deemed Malefic Joe. Malefic Joe said he lived in South Philly for 20 years before relocating to Boston. Speaking with a robust Philadelphia patois, he condemned his roots. Said how ignorant the people were. How it's the fattest city in the country. How he was embarrassed of where he came from. His phone call lingered with me until the end of the show. Why would one feel the need to puncture today? Issues of self-worth? To social climb? To thwart feelings of inadequacy? It's one thing if you do not wish to embrace the phenomenon that has swept over the city, dominating the landscape. I can understand one feeling beleaguered by it. But then why listen? Wouldn't one feeling besieged bunker from it? To be proactive, and call for the sole purpose to be spiteful and discordant, I thought him a demon.

Especially, when I think of Stephanie Phillips, who is here in Jacksonville right now, probably having just arrived at the stadium. Last August, Stephanie was inducted into the Hall of Fame in Canton upon winning a contest sponsored by Visa to find the Ultimate Fan for each NFL team. "I was so proud to be in a room with fans from other cities and say I was an Eagles fan," she will say.

Last November, she was diagnosed with breast cancer. She endured several surgeries between December and the Super Bowl. "When the Eagles won the conference championship, I just sat in my seat and cried," she will say. "But I found solace in the Super Bowl because I was feeling like everything was going wrong, then when I sat there with all the pre-game festivities and watching the Eagles warming up I just thought, this is my team and this is what I've been waiting for. Things aren't so bad. I can get through the chemo and be ready for the next season! I actually forgot about the cancer for a few days!"

Stephanie, who is 48, from Wilmington, Delaware, a season ticket holder since '89, is an Eagle traveler. She's witnessed them play in

18 different stadiums, and one of her routines is that she greets the team upon arrival at the hotel.

No greater trip, she will say, was the one here. No matter how poorly she felt, she could not miss the Super Bowl.

"Through the years I have met some wonderful people through tailgating, at away games and in the stands at the stadium," she will say. "To me, when I was diagnosed, it was like, not now...it's football season! Things were not real good, and I know this may sound crazy, but having the Eagles to think about during this time made it a little easier to deal with."

The theme of the three-hour show, right to kickoff and host Rob Charry's Super Bowl in-game party on the station, transcends football Xs and Os. I ask for those to dedicate this game to someone close, for whom you'd like to see the Eagles win. Most of the sons choose their fathers and most of the brothers choose their brother, and then they sang "Fly, Eagles Fly" and chanted, then it morphed into all singing and all chanting.

Raw emotion, without structure or profundity.

I will recall a conversation with our program director Tom Lee, who relayed a conversation he had with his wife, both of them new to the area, without any ties to this football team, while driving around and listening to the people. "For not having a lot of content," she will say, "the show sure is entertaining."

Because it was so very Philadelphian. And because The Passion of Philadelphia can be ever so inveigling.

BIG JON, B-WEST, IDIOT MAN, AND ALL THE REST

Game time nears, and I can see the locker room. I have been there moments before a game, standing amid the screaming silence, just the players and a few attendants, 60 or so men in a warehouse of a room alone with their thoughts in the company of men.

I recall a Monday night prior to playing the Giants during the last year of the Vet, how it typified the antithesis of the perception of pregame, you know, guys banging their heads against the wall and howling animal sounds. Instead the players just sat there in front of their stall, lost in reflection, some wearing headphones, others a towel over their head, donning utter blankness. How the digital clock that read 8:51 stood out, the silence such that I could almost hear the red lights morph into fifty-two, fifty-three, fifty-four, the angular numbers twisting, bleeding into one another. I recall making eye contact with Jon Runyan, a slab of a man who always bears the stare of a prison guard before the game. Our had eyes locked for a moment, and I felt strangely transparent.

I can see Jon Runyan now with that same look. Jon Runyan was born to make men feel uncomfortable, a square-headed, classic Midwest mammoth that goes six feet, seven inches, 350 pounds, as cuddly as a coffin on the football field. Jon Runyan reeks other side of football, the brutality of it, what we don't see on the play that goes for a 60-yard touchdown. He plays the thankless position of right tackle, where you only get noticed if you fuck up, where it's about guys his size beating on you, cheap-shotting you with a thumb in the eye or a fist to the groin.

Jon Runyan is the kind of man John Wayne wished he was. The Super Bowl will mark his 131st straight start in the NFL, the fifth-longest streak among active players. Playing the role of faithful body-guard to Donovan McNabb, he has played through all levels of pain. So it's only fitting that we see him now, the man who didn't play on the offensive line until his senior year of high school, upon his epiphany: "That year," he will say, "I realized I could snatch guys by the shoulder pads and put them where I wanted to."

Jon Runyan had played tight end as a junior, and then the University of Michigan put him on its radar, since he was homegrown (by way of Flint,) and had grown to such enormous proportions. It made sense to switch to protector, particularly after attending Michigan's wicked offensive line camp, which breeds less compassion than Quantico.

"Kind of how I learned to play the game," he will say. "Just the way they taught it to me. Michigan is notorious for its nasty offensive line-men. They say this is how to do it: You finish guys. You put them on their backs. One time, I had a penalty in college. I pancaked a guy over a bench. I shrugged. I thought that's how I'm supposed to do it. They wanted big dudes who friggin' killed people. That's what you wanted to be. That's where it all evolved from."

Yes, blame the Wolverines for the way he plays, with the professional indifference of an assassin. Known for his dastardly ways and dirty deeds, the reason he is an infrequent choice for the popularity-based Pro Bowl, Runyan plays devoid of emotion. Such an eerie way to play when you consider the unruly tenor of this game.

"You can't get emotional," he will contend. "Then you end up swinging at somebody. What I do is poke, poke, poke until a guy loses his cool and then he's done. He loses it and he can't think. I try to get into people's heads until they can't take it. I always love the incident in Miami. All of their defensive backs are coming for me. They're flopping when I touch them trying to get penalties. I remember I was trying to peel Zack Thomas off of Duce [Staley] and one of 'em hit me in the back of the head while I'm on the ground. I scooped his ankle and rolled over the side of his knee. I almost broke his leg and he got a 15 yard penalty.

"See, if you start swinging, forget it. I had those four guys standing over me and the dude that hit me in the back of the head is standing over me and he's like bitching me. I'm like, go ahead, how's an ACL sprain sound? People get real skittish when you're around the knees."

Big Jon will swear that he is a yes-dear bloke at home, dutifully following the commands of teeny wife, Loretta, the five-feet tall Mexican spitfire who was a street cop in Houston back in the day. He says he is a passive soul who likes when his three children crawl all over him, that he likes to manicure his sprawling yard in Jersey, that he is way, way laid back, especially now that he took care of that horrible snoring problem.

He says that football, even during Super Bowl Week, is just a job. "I don't go for all of the hype," he will say. "It's great down here, everybody's looking to party. The media is everywhere. To me, I'm working. Just doin' a job the way everybody does a job. My wife is great. She knows how it is. Like down here, she took the kids. She gave me my space so I could be by myself and concentrate. Even during the season and the offseason, she knows what I do, when I have to work out and if I'm injured or I worked out too hard and I'm sore. Having a good relationship with your wife, that's huge in developing as a player. She's got to understand it's a job, not a game. Like working out, that's part of work for me. That's part of my job. That's what I mean when we talk about the locker room and there's nobody punching the walls and the coach isn't giving us some big speech. If you can't motivate yourself, you're not going to be around. Think about it: nobody's screaming in your ears, pushing you out of bed before eleven in the morning to get a workout in. You either decide to do it or decide not to do it and deal with the ramifications."

There you have it: an O Lineman's Discourse.

They are all the same, you know, offensive linemen. You need to wield a certain disposition to play the position. It's not an ego spot the way the skill positions are, especially wide receiver. Look at the league's best: Terrell Owens and Randy Moss, two of the sport's biggest divas. Conversely, linemen get less pub than those in Salt Lake City, sans the obligatory throwaway newspaper feature in training camp, all with the same angle: Grunt does good in the shadows. Runyan's right tackle is as big as it gets and that's only due to the position's high pay, due to its importance on the field.

By nature, most linemen exist unto themselves, a big man's trait that probably dates back to when they were children coming to grips with their super size. They are usually intelligent, quiet souls who shy from attention, fine with being everyone's afterthought. When it comes to the game, most of them are like Runyan, with very little interest outside of their own world, which is to say football is not their hobby away from work. To illustrate the point, I recall a conversation with Big Jon last month during the Eagles' bye week of the playoffs.

"You gonna watch the games this weekend?"

"Who's playing?" he said, in all honesty.

"The Wild Card games. Minnesota and Green Bay. Seattle and the Rams."

"Nah. Probably go to the movies."

"Get the hell outta here. Aren't you interested in who you guys are gonna play?"

"I'll see enough of who we're gonna play when I go to work on Monday."

Big Jon Runyan is tired. Not now, not literally speaking, not after sleeping 15 hours Friday night and another 12 Saturday night, but it's been a long season. All the seasons are long in that way, but especially so for the Eagles, the last four feeling like eight. It's like that when you're an especially good team, a team that travels deep into the play-offs, to all of those conference title games without reward of champagne and a deep breath.

"You know how HARD it is to get back to the championship each year," he will say. "When I was in Tennessee, we went from 8-8 to all of a sudden 13-3. That season, we started with a game against the Cincinnati Bengals and we were getting blown out. We were like, 'Here we go again.' Well, we came back and won that game. Then the thing just clicked. It just happened. It's such a delicate thing. So much has to go right. You can't get the wrong people hurt. You're winning a game and something stupid happens – there's bad call, somebody slips, somebody fumbles the ball, it just pops out, somebody drops a pass or an interception. Stuff like that can change a whole season. You put in so much work and there's so many things you can't control.

"You do your best. You friggin' ball out. But it doesn't always happen. That other team is paid a lot of money to make sure it doesn't happen. You can only do so much. So to do what we've done? Most teams don't put themselves in that situation to play long into the season the way we do. It wears on your body. There are guys out there with a whole month's rest more than you've had and you're at the top and everybody and their mother is gunning for you. It makes it harder to be good."

Never was that more apparent for the Eagles than two years ago in Title Game Three against the Panthers. They were spared the previous week against the Packers by a fluky Fourth-and-26 conversion, and they entered the day a broken down bunch, without running backs Brian Westbrook and Correll Buckhalter and half of their defensive ends, and Troy Vincent was nicked and McNabb got busted up in the second quarter and missed most of the second half.

"People ask me about the hit in that game," Big Jon will say. "I never saw the thing. I can't react to hearsay about somebody killing my quarterback. If I saw it, I guarantee I would have been up in somebody's face. That was just a very frustrating game all around."

Following that game, Runyan voiced his frustration by second-guessing Andy Reid publicly, questioning the lack of running calls. "My thing about that was if it's working, do it," he will say. "We were running the ball well. In that game, the quarterback got hurt with a rib injury. I can take pressure off of him, buy him some time to get him fresh. That was my frustration. Andy and I talked about that. I kind of went to him. I felt bad for him. What I did was disrespectful. I apologized to him about it. He has a way of doing things. I know he doesn't express his opinions publicly. He's the boss and we do what he says. I just told him I was sorry for hanging him out like that and that we're not about that around here."

So we're back here now in the silence that followed the carousing. Runyan will talk of how the team was loose before the Super Bowl, how the room had that same feel to it, guys laughing and joking, just like the time two years ago after the Eagles lost their first two games of the season and they played bad football and they were in no mood when Koy Detmer, the resident scrounge, entered wearing a three-piece suit and top hat. "I remember that day," he will say. "Koy broke the ice. He was hilarious. And we haven't changed since then. We've always been a special group. We don't need special attention or get all crazy, amp ourselves all up in a lather, to feel secure. Sitting there in Jacksonville, before the game, I felt like we were going to win."

At six o'clock on the nose, The Caravan left the tent, walking arm and arm the short distance to a ballroom in the Radisson Hotel.

We watched the game on television.

Poor Boo, he wanted to attend the game badly. He spent all day trying to score tickets. Said he would pay two grand, if need be. Of course, all of my leads dried up like a grape in the desert. Such a hot ticket all week. Normally, the closer to gametime, prices on the street plummet, those holding fearful of getting stuck with the tickets. But not for this game. By middle afternoon, those who were selling had already sold, for a generous profit.

I had my press pass. But by the time I finished the pregame show, hightailed to the stadium in choked traiffic, I would miss nearly the entire first quarter. Blessed, I have covered numerous big events, from World Series to Final Fours to NBA Finals to Bowl Games and many, many momentous NFL games. I didn't feel right to be in a Press Box, as much I do love the Press Box, the vivacity from those on a deadline, the erudite way of watching the game. Alas, I cannot be detached today, and I believe in the sanctity of the one rule of the Press Box: No cheering. It should be treated with the same respect given a library. Besides, how could I truly leave The Caravan? I wanted to enjoy this moment in the company of those whom I loved, with whom I had shared so many of life's profound moments. I wanted sit in the middle of Joey and Vinny and Boo, and feel what they feel. I wanted to high-five with Uncle Dirt and Steve and Nick and Dave and Bubba and Brian.

I longed for an experience, and an experience is always better in the company of your people.

I can see the faces.

Position often dictates demeanor. For example, cornerbacks are usually elegant, cats prancing with their noses skyward, though Lito and Sheldon still have a long way to go to reach the polished off-field ways of Troy, who carried a briefcase on the road and donned perfect-ly contoured suits, and Bobby, a part-time male model who preferred fitted berets. Meanwhile, the other offensive tackle Tra Thomas, another mountain of man at six-seven, 349 pounds, prefers sweatsuits and makes no bones that his biggest goal in life is to "slide on through."

Though Thomas did scale an even bigger goal this season, return-ing to his Pro Bowl ways.

Glory averts the offensive linemen, the protectors of the field, and this thankless lot makes them appear so very Joe Normal, only super-sized. Like portly center Hank Fraley, the godsend from the leftover pile whose pudding tummy pouts over his pants, prompting Andy Reid to say once, "Everyone in those bars in South Philly, yeah, they love Hank Fraley, Mr. Budweiser Belly, Mr. Everyone." Thanks to everyman analyst John Madden, Fraley's belly a while back became the NFL's answer to J.Lo's rear. "Really bad body, really good player," Madden had said, and Fraley ate it up. You can tell as he waddles to the shower, resisting vanity. Suck it in? Hell, no.

He's called Honey Buns, just like the Tastykakes.

Meanwhile, lord of the game faces, Brian Dawkins sits hunched in the back of the locker room with the rest of the defense, imbibing emotion. He is still, but something seethes inside, his expression washed with wince, face pocked with tics, eyes vacant. The Transformation of Brian Dawkins that begins with a twitch when he presses the Breathe Right strips over his nostrils and slips on his beanie cap is nearly complete. Football players need to kindle their emotions in the same way cops need to be armed, so on the surface Dawkins' conversion into a creature – whom he calls "Idiotman" – might seem a bit contrived. But there is something organic about his transformation, perhaps because he craves his God so deeply and sincerely.

Talk to him any other time, and Brian Dawkins, who has been one of the best safeties in football over this run, conveys an odd peace, as though he knows something you don't. He has the aura of an old soul, certainly older than 31. "I was there," he says. "I had lots of struggles. Lots of tests. My second year in the league, I felt the pressure. I had a newborn. My wife was going through postpartum depression. A lot of things were going on in the house. I couldn't get a handle. On the outside, I'd smile and say how great everything was. On the inside, I was burning up. I was about to go crazy. I succumbed.

"Jesus has been at me for a long time. I know I am a soldier of His."

God is big with the Birds, many players partaking in Bible study and prayer groups, perhaps because of their coach, perhaps because it's a way to cope. Let's be frank, life's golden trappings are plentiful here.

I've attended their social gatherings, and there are shapely women with cascading hair and dark Spanish eyes and elegant fingernails, and they sidle to you with a seductive smile. And who are you? You're supposed to be somebody. Deep down, you're just a young lug from some backwater town, a place as cosmopolitan as a corn dog. Then there's the adulation and the cash. Everybody's calling. Everybody wants some. What to do? You lose control. Then a teammate, like say one B Dawk, who's got it all together now, nice-nice, family, finances, tells you it's good to drive slow because ain't nobody driven off a cliff going under the speed limit. He talks about God. God's nice. You feel good. You can manage.

Anyway, he swears there aren't two Brian Dawkins, though the raging one bears no resemblance to the one who will cradle the baby of a man who died in the World Trade Center attacks after practice one Saturday morning a few years back. Donovan McNabb held her first, only to have her droop from his arms, prompting the mother to say, "They're about the same size as a football. Except they don't have laces." Dawkins scooped her from him and told McNabb, "Someday you're going to have to learn this."

That day, came earlier in 2004 for McNabb. Her name is Alexis.

Anyway, lost in a state, Dawkins explains: "There's this click. It's like something hit me in the head. That's when the man starts peaking out. I find the transformation. I cross that door."

Near him is Idiotman Junior, Michael Lewis, the strong safety and the other defensive back gem of a draft pick, taken in the second round, sandwiched between Lito and Sheldon. Lewis is a hitter like Dawkins is a hitter. Lewis led the team in tackles and made the Pro Bowl. The fans go wild for him. Most of them probably don't know that on his website – Hit-em32.com – he writes in response to a question regarding which team he gets up for the most, "The Cowboys. I hate the Cowboys."

Hugh is back.

Back with the Eagles and back in Jacksonville. Prior to last season, Hugh Douglas made a score. Got six million dollars up front to sign with the Jaguars. They released him after one unhappy and unproductive season, and he re-signed with the Eagles. Butchy called it "the perfect caper."

What did he learn from the experience? "The grass isn't always greener, but the money always is," he says.

"It was not a good fit here," he elaborates. "It's a job, and sometimes you go to another job and it just doesn't work out. They didn't get a chance to see me and who I am here. I'm comfortable in Philadelphia. I have roots there."

Douglas was miserable with the Jaguars, but he says he never made those disparaging remarks about Jacksonville attributed to him in the local paper earlier in the week. I believe him. He always owns up to his words. Words are important to him. He talks like God is about to snatch his tongue. Like exhaust from a car, words just emit from him. Quotes. Barbs. Songs. Gibberish.

Hugh Douglas' game is not what it used to be, evolving into a situational player these days rather than gamebreaker he was. But it's his presence in the locker room that has always made Douglas an integral part of the Eagles, the reason Andy Reid brought him right back, though he reinstituted the Hugh Rule: Douglas must ride on a different bus than Reid because his constant jabbering drives the coach mad. I recall a playoff game years back, one where the team beat Tampa, and Douglas threw his bags in the door and said, "I got this one. Take the day off. Don't worry about this one, fellas. I brought the cavalry with me. Hop on my back."

By the way, Hugh Douglas is also mrkillyoass. That's the name he uses when he plays video games. He likes killin' folks.

Across the other side of the room is Brian Westbrook, the great find who was found not far away, on the sweet, leafy campus of Villanova University. He's not too small, after all, the first Eagle back since Wilbert Montgomery who can turn the corner on a sweep and the most dangerous multipurpose runner ever. "I love Brian, strictly in a platonic way," says Jon Ritchie, the robust fullback with the horns on his head from leading with his helmet. He's been out for the season since a knee injury in late September and walks a staff, the perfect compliment to his flowing hair and long beard. "But it's a very strong love I have for him. He's such a unique athlete. He has strangely amazing balance and speed in every direction. Stopping, starting. He is so low to the ground. He's able to run with incredible leverage. He's got great vision."

Over in the special teams coffin corner is the best kicker in the history of the franchise. After so many hold-your-breath types like Roger Ruzek and Luis Zendejas and Tony Franklin and Chris Boniol, David Akers has left the flock free of agida since he left his day job as a substitute teacher and his night job at a Longhorn Steakhouse in the summer of '99. Akers set the record this year with 17 forty-plus yard field goals. He's also a martial arts toughman. Once in the middle of a locker-room, he took down six-foot-eight Harold Carmichael.

There's poor Chad Lewis, foot in a cast. He literally gave his body to the NFC Championship victory, suffering the dreaded Lisfranc injury on the second of his two touchdown receptions, as he dragged his toes just inside the sidelines of the end zone creating the most famous chunk of dirt in the history of divotry.

There are his replacements: Jeff Thomason, the old pro who hasn't played since 2002 and took vacation time from his job as assistant project manager for Toll Brothers Construction to play in the Super Bowl, and Mike Bartrum, who has made a career out of long-snapping, who displayed his skills on a piece on the *Today Show*, where he long-snapped footballs into a mail slot and a basketball hoop from half court and fast-food drive-thru window. "It's crazy," he once said. "Nine years. Just snapping the ball between my legs."

In the coaches' room is Juan Castillo, who drove from Philadelphia to Green Bay in a snowstorm upon Ray Rhodes' firing to talk to Andy Reid about a job. Reid was preparing for a playoff game in the middle of the night with Mike Holmgren when a security guard said a man from Philadelphia was here to see him. "Bring him in from out of the storm," Reid said.

When Reid first arrived in Philadelphia and was in the middle of plotting his coach staff, Castillo knocked on his door at the Vet. Castillo had come to clear his locker out at three in the morning. He knew Reid would be working late.

"I'm leaving my keys," Castillo said.

"Maybe you shouldn't," Reid said, and hired him.

And there's young John Harbaugh, whose special teams are always among the best in the league and who you just know will be a good head coach someday. He's 42 and likely will get his chance soon.

Andy Reid's first lieutenants are somewhere close by: crabby and choleric Jim Johnson, a football lifer who's really the stereotypical softy, the grandfatherly coordinator who masterminds the defense with his creative and contemporary array of blitzes; and cerebral and sedate Brad Childress, the offensive coordinator whose brain Reid picks for playcalling and devising the game plan. Childress is another on the fast track to having his own team.

AND THE PRIEST TURNED TO THE COACH AND SAID, "BOO!"

Right about now, Andy Reid will enter the locker room deep inside frenzied Alltel Stadium with a purposeful stride, behind him the heavy doors slowly opening and closing, first disclosing the great din of the Super Bowl that shocks your system the way sunlight does upon exit from a matinee, then fetching back the stillness, the almost absolute quiet. The players will be nearly fully dressed, parked still by their stall, and Andy Reid will wield all of his girth to the center of the room with an impassive looked upon his face.

Dressed even entirely in black, from the slacks to the federal agent winged-tip shoes that will soon be scuffed white from chalk, he is the biggest man in a room of Woolly Mammoths, particularly in stature and standing. The way he walks, with short stalking strides of purpose, clearing the way like a snowplow of flesh, you know this to be indisputable. He is impervious to the whole maddening scene of the Super Bowl, in fact, because Andy Reid's biggest gift is the ability to wade through chaos armed only with dogged belief and capture man's most elusive trophy: control.

Control of thy destiny, control of thy surroundings. It is the seedling of success. For success to fully blossom, however, you must harvest enough faith in yourself to embrace such control. That is what provides fortitude and resilience and stamina.

"All right," he will say, "fall in. Let's go, fall in."

The players will stir to life and gradually encircle their coach and their coach will begin.

"Listen up," he will say. "We're here. Some of you have been here before and some of you will never be here again. Make the most of it. Enjoy it. Let your personalities show. Now go out there and play the game of your lives."

That will be it. Brief and sweet, typically Andy Reid, without any overwrought kill 'em, beat 'em, stomp 'em, destiny is your darlin', woo her and the world is yours type of harangue.

Succinct. Cool. Inscrutable.

The message: You belong here. You don't need to be prodded with a hot poker of riling words. It's just like always. Just another game. Keep your head, boys. Keep your head and you'll do just fine.

Even last night, back in one of the ballrooms at the hotel at the night-before meeting of only team members, tucked away from all the damn people and the festivities and the distractions and hype of Holy Week, Andy Reid's homily was just a paragraph highlighted by just a few footnotes.

"Remember," he said, "this is just a game. But this game is a little faster. It's a little bit harder. They'll let you play on both sides of the ball. You can get away with more. They make this thing into a big show. Don't let the hype get to you. That's for them, not us, you understand? It's just a football game. And you know how to win football games. Now let me treat you to a cheeseburger."

There is no Gipper to win one for anymore. Players today crave defined roles not unrefined rahs. Remember Ray Rhodes? Remember his notorious sermons? Remember how it worked for awhile? Then the players invariably began to slouch in their seats, hide their faces and suppress their laughter. Yes, success truly becomes a coach only when he masters the science of football. Look at The Brain, Bill Belichick, tight-lipped, curmudgeonly, passing acquaintance to his players Bill Belichick who motivates through wins, not words. "[Belichick] will never be confused with Tony Robbins but the man understands the game better than anyone I've ever met, including Parcells," one NFL veteran told me.

"You don't want big highs and big lows," Andy Reid says. "You don't want to be a screamer and a yeller. People turn that off. You don't want to be a rah-rah guy because people turn that off. If you just shoot 'em straight, people accept that. Whether it's football players, other coaches or your wife."

The Lost Gospel of Vince Lombardi just doesn't translate anymore, and wasn't part of that myth anyway. I mean, Vince Lombardi was not just some football fire-and-brimstone preacher. He was the original brain, an innovator who dissected the game on another plane. In Jerry Kramer's classic account, *Instant Replay*, he talked of a painful loss to the Baltimore Colts, spearheaded by a Johnny Unitas touchdown pass to Willie Richardson in the waning moments. The locker room was awfully quiet and he walked by the coach's room and heard Lombardi screaming, "Damned stupid high school play like that. Damned stupid play. What in the hell were we doing? What in the hell were we waiting for?" How members of the defense thought they played the play the right away and how the veterans hoped the team understood Lombardi's reaction. Bart Starr said on the plane coming home of Lombardi: "This man is one great coach. He's got a brilliant mind. He prepares us better for a football game than any other team in the National Football League. Going into the game against St. Louis, we knew exactly what we could do, what we couldn't do, how to do it. The same thing today. I've never seen a more complete book on a team than Coach Lombardi had on Baltimore. It was really a beautiful thing to see."

Back in the locker room at Alltel Stadium, the players will howl and jump in place, knocking into one another. Hugh Douglas will pant and spew, like always, words coming out like exhaust fumes from an old puttering truck. Something like: "Let's do it. Let's do it. Oooooo-haaaaa. They sayin' they're a dynasty. Don't let them say that later, y'all. Ain't no dynasty. C'mon, now. Let's do it."

That sort of thing is great. For the players.

Meanwhile, the coach is devoid of emotion. On the facade.

For the façade should always tell the same story, which is no story. You can't read what's not there.

I recall former Eagle Brian Mitchell, the longtime spitfire veteran, telling me, "If your coach is rattled, you're gonna get rattled. We players look at a coach's face. If it's droopy, well, we think, damn, how am I gonna make that play? Or, damn, how we gonna win this game? If the coach doesn't believe it's gonna happen, we think, damn, how's it gonna happen? Andy always makes you think it's gonna happen."

To this day, Mitchell, now retired, still gets a kick out of the onside kick Reid called to open the 2000 season against the Dallas Cowboys, which became a secret weapon over the years. "From that day on," Mitchell says, "I knew he had, like we say in the locker room, big balls. Players love a coach who's gonna go for it. Who's got balls. It gives players confidence. It's like, Whoa, Coach is cool. I remember that day, I went over and slapped him on the backside. You know, we players, like to hear something when we do something good. Coaches deserve the same thing. They're human, right? So I did it. I always felt comfortable doing that sort of thing with Andy.

"Andy's like Joe Gibbs. Joe wasn't a loud person but he had respect. He only yelled when he had to. He was normally cool. That was the thing. He never got rattled. And you don't understand what that means to a player. Because a team will always reflect its coach."

Now inside Andy Reid, the normal feelings churn: the rush of anticipation, some amp, some nerves, the whirling of the mind, revving with every possible scenario, plotting just one more time. Then one more time.

How hard is it for people to understand that? It's that never let them see you sweat thing. Them is the players, the rest of the staff. The leader needs to lead. A leader doesn't crack, not even a splinter. Emotion dilutes thought. Emotion dilutes control, whether it's pregame, during the game, postgame, back in the locker room, back in the office during the week. It's not about singular moments or singular games, even the Super Bowl. Acting for the singular is to act desperate. For it's solely about the institution you've built, protecting the entire infrastructure, which is as delicate as a peanut shell.

How to deal with the players is always a factor in keeping the dominoes from falling. Too soft, and you're a throw rug. Too rigid, and you're staving off mutiny for as long as possible, like Tom Coughlin, for example, a fine coach who before going to the Giants just grew weary in Jacksonville because his players just couldn't take his litany of rules, including keeping both feet on the ground during meetings. Earlier last season, he ran into a mini-revolt in New York when he fined his players if they weren't five minutes early.

"I don't have a lot of rules," Reid says. "Be on time and work hard. That's it. Everything else is based on common sense. You have to enforce the ones that are there, of course. But I don't like to fine players. I treat them fair. If you put too many rules or restrictions in there guys don't know what direction to go. It curbs their personalities."

Enter in particular a guy like Terrell Owens, the live wire who pushes locker room life to the brink of anarchy, down to his penchant for outlandish celebrations following touchdowns. "I don't mind guy letting their personalities show," Reid says. "Somewhere along the line when this game was created by a couple of chubby guys who were too big to play baseball it was meant to be fun. I want my guys to have fun. But there's a point when the celebrations don't need to be crude or incite the officials."

It's why Reid nearly pulled backup Koy Detmer from a game two years ago in San Francisco for doing his could-be-sexually-connotative "whip celebration." Other than the opener when Reid ordered security director Butch Buchanico to retrieve Owens because he thought his celebration was lingering on, the only issue during the season came in Cleveland, where Owens tore down a derogatory banner (T.O. has B.O.) following a long touchdown and received a 15-yard flag. Reid pulled Owens to his side, and pointed to the penalty. "See?" he said, "You got a flag."

"He's extremely fair, I think, judging from what I hear around the league with other coaches," Ike Reese says. "But you know what really makes him a successful head coach? He doesn't blink. This cat can stare into the eye of the storm and it just rolls off him. That's what we truly get from him. He doesn't let the players believe there's a chink in the armor, even if everybody in the world thinks there is."

Let us fast-forward all the way to the spring, on a gorgeous, play hooky kind of day, the season's first present of real warmth. The man's yawning office window paints a lovely picture of rebirth: a sun tickled, manicured field, slightly breeze-blown, encased by a sprouting shrub fence, light splashing everywhere, through everything, creating prisms aboundingly. Nary a soul in sight, it's the picture of platitude.

It's a football field, a reminder that however wonderful the journey to Jacksonville was, even for the man who rarely allows himself to feel in the moment, the games will be here in a snap.

While most of the football world slumbers, the man is working. There is so, so much to do: free agency is ongoing, the draft is approaching, the plan of course for 2005 needs to be honed. "We're way behind, you know," he sighed. "Going to the Super Bowl puts you back two weeks."

I tell you this because this is an insight into the man. The Super Bowl, while winning it is the ultimate endgame, it is almost – I stress almost – a hassle to the man. It's a singular moment, capping a singular season. An NFL season is a finite period of time for the fans, easily plotted: root, root, root, rejoice, cry, reflect, wait 'til next year. Meanwhile, it never ends for men like him, blending into the next one and the one after that. The game has long since been played, the outcome what it was, the season what it was, and now it's about sustaining the infrastructure. There really is no time to reflect, let alone, God forbid, wallow.

Let us, however, rewind and reflect.

That sort of approach is why the man got the job in the first place, skipping a step or two en route to head coach; it's what he conveyed in the interview to Eagles owner Jeffrey Lurie and president Joe Banner, who needed an architect for this thing of theirs more than simply a coach. Rhodes, the man's forerunner, was a coach, the classic tree guy. See what's right in front of you: the players, the games, the roster.

Everything in the middle suffered. Because there was no middle, which went beyond the players running amok, the liquor bottles rolling to the front of the plane during turbulence, guys falling asleep during film study, just about everybody habitually late because it was a party on a party, those merely symptoms. And so after an initial spark of success, culminating with a rousing 58 point outburst in a playoff victory over the Lions in a singular moment, the entire thing collapsed. The mark of success is progression; Rhodes' Eagles went from that dynamic Wild Card win in his first year (1995) to losing the Wild Card Game the follow year, (without scoring a point), to winning only six games the year after, then winning only three the year after that in what turned out to be the disasters of all disasters. The coach knew he was fired in October and apparently had all but secured another job in Green Bay in November.

Recalled Reese: "It was a culture shock when I got here to the NFL. Coming here as a rookie under Ray, seeing the veterans, what was allowed to go on. I just thought it was the way most NFL teams were run. Hey, guys are making millions and millions of dollars, partyin' it up, livin' the life, I thought that was the way it was and we just weren't winning. I didn't realize that was the reason we weren't winning.

"When Andy came in, he immediately laid things out. Andy said that he knew Ray and that he was a good coach, that Andy liked to have a good time, too, but it's all about winning and the good times come with winning. He made so many changes. How meetings were held. There were meetings after practice and no food in the meetings. It wasn't going to be a lunchroom or a bedroom – nobody's falling asleep. How we would run from drill to drill during practice. That was a big thing. Fast tempo. Fast pace. Not a leisurely walk. Those first mini camps of his were like playing full blown in training camp.

"When Ray was here there wasn't a lot of yelling or things of that nature. Everybody was more or less buddy-buddy. It was relaxed. It didn't feel like it was business on the practice field. Under Andy, right away, it was intense. No guys sitting in the back, jacking around. It was, 'Pay attention! Pay attention to your position. Know what you need to know from the meeting room to the field.' They tested us on it. I remember Ron Rivera, our linebackers' coach, handing us a blank sheet of paper with just an offensive book. He'd say, 'Draw up the defense. Tell me where you're supposed to be and where everybody else is supposed to be and what's going to happen.' I mean, under these guys, this wasn't no game."

So the Eagles had settled on their man, a forest thinker, from the tundra of Titletown, a hot protégé of Mike Holmgren among football people, a *Who the heck's that?* among the Philadelphia people.

Lurie talked about Andy Reid's organization. How he was so utterly prepared during the interview, so meticulous, with binders that encompassed every last detail of the job. It's only now that we understand what that meant, organizational skills suddenly not appearing as some corporate catchphrase, but coming to life in the little things. Like creating a chain of command: each position has a player captain and if anyone has an issue, he goes to that player who goes to the position coach who goes to the coordinators (Brad Childress on the offense, Jim Johnson on the defense), and if need be, he goes to Reid.

Johnson has autonomy on defense regarding the calls and the substitutions following week-long consultations with Reid, while Childress and Reid work together on the offense.

It works the same way in the personnel office, with the scouts and personnel people reporting to vice president Tom Heckert who reports to Reid.

In the beginning, however, what did organized mean?

In the beginning, during that first training camp, what Philadelphia knew of Andy Reid might comprise a paragraph: Was quarterbacks coach for the Packers. Worked with Brett Favre. Liked a physical camp. Wasn't brash like Buddy Ryan. Wasn't confused like Rich Kotite. Didn't curse like Ray Rhodes.

And yes, yes, meticulously prepared.

I recall talking to Brett Favre that summer in Green Bay. "I hated to see him go," Favre said. ``I think he's a good coach. I'm not surprised he got the job. I won't be surprised if his team does well. I just think he's a great coach. I hated to see him go because he kept me prepared but he also kept it nonchalant. Never beat me up over anything. If you made mistakes, you made mistakes. But you prepare and you play hard. That's the way he wants you to approach things. If you're prepared and you make a mistake, how can he be mad at you? He's a players guy. I think the players will respect him. He'll be hard on them but fair. That's why I think he'll do well."

Now most players will praise their former coach, especially position coaches in football, where the true bond forms between player and coach. But I never believed that Favre was offering hollow praise. That day he spoke longer to me about Reid than he did the rest of the pack that followed the Pack about the retirement of wide receiver Robert Brooks.

"It didn't surprise me he got that job after being a quarterbacks coach," he said then. "I can't say that I thought it would happen as fast as it did. But you know [former Packers quarterback coach Steve] Mariucci got San Francisco's job. He went right from Cal. When you're a good coach, people know about you. They find you. I'd be lying to you if I told you all the success I've had has been because of me."

Let the record show, for whatever it means, that Favre and the Packers never made it back to the Super Bowl after Andy Reid left, and Mike Holmgren has not enjoyed the same success with the Seattle Seahawks that Reid has enjoyed with the Eagles, losing his title as General Manager's prior to last season.

I recall that day in Green Bay vividly. I recall Favre's backup, Matt Hasselbeck, who went to join Holmgren in Seattle, saying, "You can tell his whole coaching career he has been preparing for this moment. I think he's ready. I think he will do a great job. He has a lot of work to do but he's always working. When I got here early, his truck was always here. When I would leave at night, his truck was always here. I think he's gonna do things the same way Mike Holmgren and Bill Walsh have done it with a little bit of his personal touch."

What also impressed Hasselbeck was how Reid went over the list of quarterbacks that were drafted in recent years. "He was right on," he said. "He picked out guys in the lower rounds that have turned out to be starters, like Jake Plummer, and guys who went in the first round who didn't do anything. For that reason alone, I love his pick of Donovan McNabb."

Machiavelli once opined that there is nothing more difficult to take in hand, more perilous to conduct or more uncertain in its success than to take the lead in the introduction of a new order of things, and we assume being tortured and imprisoned by the Medici family provided the inspiration, not the prospects of coaching football in Philadelphia. But that notion could make Florentine politics in the 1530s seem like a spring stroll along the Ponte Vecchio.

To wit, let us recall Andy Reid's first night here for good. Weary, famished, a snowstorm making his trip from Green Bay a trek, he found himself in the heart of frozen South Philly gristle, a near-empty Italian restaurant on Front and Fitzwater, slumped in a hardback chair in a theater of the bizarre. Only two other tables were occupied at Frederick's that night in February 1999, one occupied by a priest and his ladyfriend.

"It's the new coach!" the priest declared. "Coach, let me make you feel right at home: Boooooooooooo!"

He laughed until he wheezed, and he did it again, cupping his hands over his mouth to amplify: "Boooooooooooo!"

"Get used to it, my friend," said the priest, who later tried to buy the new coach a bottle of wine.

Then things really got weird for the new coach.

He attended the prestigious Maxwell Club dinner for football's postseason awards and then-Mayor Ed Rendell was escorting Ricky Williams. Ed has an arm around Williams' waist, and he's nodding and winking and smiling an If You Know What's Good For Ya smile in the direction of the new coach. By then, you remember, the city had decided the Eagles would select the University of Texas running back with the second pick in the 1999 draft.

"I couldn't hide," Reid recalled later. "I couldn't go under the table. Believe me, I looked to see if I could. Three weeks in town and the mayor is pointing at me from the podium. Then everybody else starts pointing at me. Then I go to a hockey game and the fans start booing me and chanting for Ricky."

They booed long through the draft. Interestingly enough they usually don't boo that soon. The pattern over the years has been that they like you first, boo you second. They boo you right out the door, because the mob has forever ruled this town.

I am qualified to explain the mob because I was a teen charter member. I booed the Bend But Don't Break defense of Marion Campbell, the Moses Malone trade to Washington and Von Hayes. So let me tell you the mob is often fickle, always restless. For the mob knows no logic. The mob subsists on uncut emotion. God pity you if the mob turns on you.

Prior to Reid, only three people ever figured out the mob: Ben Franklin, Pat Croce and Angelo Bruno.

The mob didn't take at all to Andy Reid in that first year because Andy Reid put in earplugs and looked straight ahead and clutched to his belief. Andy Reid is stubborn and a control freak and didn't care what anybody else thought.

The mob grew more agitated, offering the sentiment: Who the hell does he think he is, anyway? We know what's right. We knew more than Rich Kotite, didn't we? We knew more than Wilson Goode and Brad Greenberg, right?

Judging by the catalog of False Messiahs that predated Reid, however, it was not without just cause. On the football side alone, the last three Eagles coaches fit that category. Some of us still love Buddy Ryan, but what of substance did he bring? In the end, the fog rolled in off Lake Michigan and he didn't win a playoff game. Rich Kotite won a playoff game with Buddy's team and was 7-2 in 1994 when he brought up a contract extension. He lost seven in a row and got canned. Rhodes spoke our language, which is to say he cussed and talked of defending the row home front, but the players suddenly went deaf to such rhetoric and the village fell quicker than Ireland's Armagh at the hands of the other Vikings.

So there was this one day following practice that I chatted with Andy Reid. It was pleasantly quiet, a cease-fire Friday from the catcalls and barbs. Fridays are good days for football's forlorn. The howling is gone from the previous week's game and hope for a new Sunday begins to percolate.

Fridays, unfortunately, are always fleeting.

Three games and three losses into his first head coaching job, the mob was angrier than ever. It had already tired of Doug Pederson playing quarterback, especially with the offense going eleven straight quarters without a touchdown. Because Pederson was with Reid in Green Bay, as Favre's backup's backup, fans levied charges of favoritism toward the coach. Meanwhile, it was hard not to pity Pederson, a gentle fellow, a good fellow, who knew the game like a professor, and unfortunately played like a math professor. Yet in order to be saved, this team needed a Doug Pederson to be hurled into the volcano. It needed the sacrificial quarterback who could endure a flogging behind a severely thin green line and dress like table scraps until the team could embrace the youth of Donovan McNabb.

But the mob, fatigued from relentless feeble football, had no wick left, and it was anxious to see if the kid Reid selected over Williams could play a lick.

"Full speed ahead," he said that day. "I knew coming in it was going to be a major overhaul. I know it's going to take time. The hard thing, by nature, is that's not me. I don't like to lose. I'm going to find a way to make sure we get this thing turned around and going in the right direction. I think we are going in the right direction. We have to put the finishing touch on when."

When is the simplest of questions, but the toughest to answer.

"In the narrow-mindedness, I want it right now," he said. "I don't put a timetable on it, I just keep trying to bite chunks off it everyday. I know if I approach it that way, one day it's going to be right."

That day, Reid admitted to feeling the heat. Funny to recall, as he sits here almost fully insulated now.

"I see it. I hear it," he said then. "People come up to me and talk to me. People yell stuff. I'm aware of what's going on. But it's a hard enough job getting this thing turned around, without outside influences. We talk about an attitude of a team. There are fifty, sixty guys on a team, and that attitude has to be right. That's where my focus lies. I don't have time to have outside distractions hinder me right now. Everybody has an opinion, I understand that. But I have to have tunnel vision on what I want done."

Just that night before, the phone rang repeatedly at the Reid home, first Mike Holmgren, then Bill Parcells, then out of football, then Reggie White. Reid and White grew close in Green Bay, and that night White, like the other coaches, wanted check up on him. Reid recalls that call, and he took White's recent passing hard. "He was just a good man," Reid will say. "It went beyond football with Reggie, he was just a good, decent man."

Andy Reid ended the conversation that day by saying, "I've gone into losing programs before. In time, we have been able to turn those programs into winning programs. This city, these people, deserve a winner. By nature, I am stubborn and I will keep fighting. So it's full speed ahead."

What has marked his tenure has always been that sort of mindset. Full Speed Ahead, and what the fans don't like now – the offense, the receivers, the playcalling, the middle linebacker, whatever – they'll come to like later. Oh, the offense…in the beginning, the mob howled about the horizontal nature of it, how it went dink and dunk, screen to the back, over the middle to the tight end, six yards, three yards, five yards. Oh, how they howled about stretching the field, loosening up the defense, and how they didn't get the complicated nature of the offense, all of those varied pass plays in the game plan, sometimes nearly two hundred of them on any given Sunday.

At the time, Reid told me, "IF you've counted how many times we attempted to go deep it's as much if not more than most offenses in this league. Now whether or not the ball is checked down or whether or not it's thrown to, say, Pinkston, and he doesn't catch it, that's another story. The mark is how many times you complete the deep ball. We'll do that better in time. This offense, what people don't realize, is built off the vertical game – Twenty-four, double do: Both receivers hauling tail down the field tight down the chute, backs checked down; then you run the comeback, the dig, the square-out, the square-in, the hitch, the smoke. You run all of those things. It's all built off showing a go route."

I can't help but think of the offense now. What it looked like throughout the season, with McNabb seasoned, with Owens and Westbrook, impossible to double both, with Pinkston just able to fly on single coverage. What it looked like against the Cowboys on Monday night and later against the Packers in a conference defining game, scoring at will, with garishness, both games decided by the halftime gun.

A year and change from that forlorn Friday, with success beginning to blossom, I am with Andy Reid in his old dungeon office in the Vet. He leaned back in a leather chair from the comfort of the right side of controversy.

Earlier in that week, the high-pitched ting of champagne toasts resonated inside the team's fourth floor executive offices, a hallway away from the sticky, paint-peeling walls of the stale Vet press box. Lurie and Banner had politicked hard for a home of their own and the proceedings seemed destined for peril against a stonewalling mayor.

For Lurie, the Eagles had become about the future, aligned in his mind in this order: general manager, coach, quarterback, stadium, Super Bowl. On that day, as Reid hollered "How's first place feel like?" on his way into the locker room, the present seemed to be gaining on the future.

As we look at the Linc now, fawning outward toward I-95 in majesty, finally a staple of the landscape, we recall the Eagles' deteriorating billet. With construction booming around the league, plush stadiums going up like the "Snowy Owl" housing developments in the South Jersey sprawl, complete with all the palace trimmings, the Eagles, by comparison, lived in the projects. The practice facility was a giant bubble in the Vet parking lot and the outdoor field was adjacent to people's homes in Packer Park, separated only by a chain-link fence and some cheap shrubs. Players had to drive back to the Vet locker room to change following practice, sweaty, still in shoulder pads.

The real Doppler of the stadium, of course, was the infamous concrete turf that burned when you slid on it, that bruised when you landed on it, that might as well bore the mark of the devil in between its ligament and tendon tearing seams. Back then, free agents like John Randle and Lomas Brown opted for less money elsewhere than sign with the Eagles.

Donovan McNabb, in fact, didn't want anything to do with the Eagles prior to his pre-draft visit to Philadelphia. Reid had to sell McNabb on the Eagles.

Before he came here, Andy Reid had to sell everyone who cared about him on the Eagles before he took the job.

"I had very few people that supported me on this decision," he said with a sourceless smirk. "It was like a, What are you doing? Are you crazy? All the way to my two sons who analyzed it all. They said, 'Dad, what are you thinking about? I was not even going to take the interview here."

Reid's stock had soared around the league during that time. Jon Gruden and Ray Rhodes and Steve Mariucci had all previously courted him to be their offensive coordinator. Several teams had approached him about possible head-coaching openings, including the St. Louis Rams, who were considering firing Dick Vermeil. The Rams eventually gave Vermeil one more shot and won a Super Bowl, and Reid opted on the Eagles because the Eagles provided him with a can't lose scenario. If Reid turned around the Eagles, like what happened, he was and is set for life. If he had failed, he could blame the awful climate, arming him with a solid alibi for another head coaching position.

Smart rule: Always start at the bottom.

Reid will wink. Only one way to go.

"You mention the bottom," he will say. "When I came here Jeff and Tom were very honest. They felt that's where the football team was at. For whatever reason, that's how they felt and they weren't the only ones. Bob LaMonte, my agent, did his homework. He said a lot of things here were misunderstood. He said the notions that Jeff Lurie didn't have enough money and Joe Banner would cut your throat were wrong. So I took the interview. I asked a ton of questions, I wrote down all the answers and I left with a very comforting feeling. You know I'm a hunch guy and my hunch told me to take the job."

So we are back in his old dungeon inside the old Vet, and he mused, "Imagine my office in the new stadium?"

Andy Reid's grand office is in the NovaCare Center, and it's everything he could have imagined, with his secretary, Sweet Carol, across the small hallway diagonally across from the door. The outer part of the office is the size of a high school classroom, decorated with more of an eye toward function than elegance, though it's not without its law firm furnishings and feel. Directly behind the expansive desk and high-powered executive's chair is a shelf with four game balls inscribed and encased by glass. They read, going from left to right:

Eagles 30, Cleveland Browns, 17, September 2, 1999, Veterans

Stadium [First preseason win].

Eagles 13, Dallas Cowboys, 13-10, October 10, 1999, Veterans Stadium [First regular season win].

Eagles 27, Seattle Seahawks, 27-3, September 23, 2001, Husky Stadium [Significance: victory over Mike Holmgren].

Eagles 17, Packers 14, November 10, 2003, Lambeau Field.

His library of binders, filled with plays upon plays, and books stacked inside the shelf. Andy Reid is a reader, mostly nonfiction and self-help. Right now he's reading *The History of the Pythagorean Theorem.* He just finished, *Whale Done,* about a CEO whose company is not faring well. The CEO is at Sea World and he sees the trainer get the whale to do tricks. He waits for the trainer, befriends him and asks how he accomplishes the feat. "The animal can eat me," the trainer says. "You have to respect the whale." The story is a basic philosophy of respect and finding ways to communicate with your employees.

Before that, it was *Gung Ho,* about a female CEO and her spree into the forest to watch how beavers work together to build a dam.

One of his treasures is a compilation of works by the late Jim Murray, the renown sports columnist for *The Los Angeles Times.* Andy Reid grew up reading Jim Murray, and has talked openly about his admiration for the writer and how he might have been one in another life. So Murray's widow sent him the book a little while back, with the inscription, "To Coach Reid, Wannabe for *Sports Illustrated.*"

Andy Reid writes. Keeps a journal.

Journal keepers respect the story of life.

See? He reaches into his work bag and pulls out his journal with the lighthouse on the cover, the one he always writes in it when he flies.

On this spring day, the yawning window in the man's office sells serenity. So we talk of it. "Know what I'd like to do?"

"What?"

"I like working with wood. I like making Clipper ships. Gotta big one I did at home."

He likes to build things. He likes to create.

Makes sense.

Let us go back to that 2000 season. I recall being at the Vet, a little before nine on a Wednesday morning in the middle of November, and the Eagles then were the surprise team of the NFC and they had Arizona on deck that Sunday, a trap game with the Redskins looming the following week. Andy Reid walked to the front of a room of sixty or so men who had wedged themselves into wooden elementary school desks for the first formal team address of the week, the players having been given off that Monday and Tuesday, reward for a gripping, most inexplicable overtime win in Pittsburgh.

That was the address that set the tone of practice for the week, and it lasted for nine minutes and twenty-three seconds, and he made direct eye contact with all sixty or so men at least once.

He praised them. He criticized them. He cautioned them.

He did so without raising his voice above the engine hum of a BMW; if he had written his words, he would not have inserted a single exclamation point. He inflected certain syllables and certain letters – like the "Keh" in kick, as in "I want you to KIck their tail."

"All right," Reid said, "you have to understand you're playing a high-caliber opponent. I want you to come out and kick their tail from the beginning of the game this time."

His voice was raspy, and he began to enunciate every word.

"You've got yourself a nice little record," he said. "But you've got to understand, you can't look ahead to the Redskins. The media's gonna want to try to bait you into talking about the Redskins. Or the playoffs. Well, you haven't won anything just yet. Don't go there."

The talk is brief and sweet.

Succinct. Cool. Inscrutable.

"Our personality is a little different over here," Donovan McNabb said. "You don't have to yell at anyone. We're all men. Of course, whenever I hear him say, 'Five!' I know he wants something now. All coaches yell, but he doesn't do it to the point where it gets annoying."

Rarely does Reid filet his players with words. But there was one time I recall after an uninspired loss to the Colts, that he employed his kind of shock treatment. The Eagles had rolled to a 6-2 record at the midway point of the season, when Indianapolis limped into town struggling on defense and without star running back Edgerrin James.

The Eagles were terribly flat from the start, and Peyton Manning passed the defense dizzy, while a muzzled McNabb ran for his life much of the game. Resignation seeped in early in the fourth quarter. The players stood there on the sidelines withdrawn, with empty eyes, McNabb mired in a slouch, following a myriad of mistakes, Duce Staley biting his lip, Brian Dawkins shaking his head back and forth in disbelief. The banner from Sign Man that streamed across the middle of the 500 level of the old Vet wouldn't shut up: CHAMPIONS DON'T LET DOWN. A mass exodus from the stadium ensued, spilling boos. The game ended without mercy, with Reid, accompanied by Butchy, being rousted at the tunnel by the gargoyles that appear after losses like this one. "You fat slob," a man of ample flab spewed. "You stink." Reid refused to acknowledge him, though later Butchy would return to the scene and shoot back, "Come back next week. We'll make you happy. You should lose some weight yourself."

Shame overcame the man. "I'm sorry," he said.

Butchy then directed his security staff that there would be no one but team members allowed in the locker room. "No kids. No friends. Nobody. Lock it up."

A silence filled the room, the kind that comes with calamity, where you felt guilty to feel anything but dishonor. "Bring it in," ordered Reid as he stepped into the center. "Let's go." A few stragglers dawdled and Reid's voice flared, wielding an uncharacteristic edge. "Let's go! Let's go! Get over here!"

The masses moved closer, forming a circle of beaten flesh, and Reid declared, "We've got seven games. SEVEN GAMES! It's time to do it. We can't play three good games then let down. We need seven straight. It's time! We can do it. There are a lot of veterans in this room. It's time to be leaders. It's time to reach down! I'm talking to everyone. The players, the coaches, everyone. We lost this game. It wasn't the offense. It wasn't the defense. It was us. Everyone in this room. It's time to dig deeper! We can't have that [kind of performance] again. We're not going to have that again. We're better than that. I know it. You know it. Let's show it. Let's prove it!"

Reid's verbal flogging of his team was conspicuously PG. His voice spiked in a manor of menace, but the words streamed sanitized, depicting his Mormon faith. Andy Reid flexes his message through his

enormous girth, posturing his point. The sentiment of a veteran referee comes to mind. He told me, "Never once has Andy said anything
off-color to me, or to any other referee. Usually, he doesn't say a word.
In fact, if he argues, we probably made a mistake."

A hunch told Andy Reid the call would come that fall. Part of him
surely felt proud that this snowy-haired icon of college football, and of
The Religion, too, would handpick him as the successor. If human, the
other part of him felt a twinge of dread, the phone ringing through
him, wondering if it was him, rehearsing alone in the car what he'd say,
how he'd say it. Reid knew he had to refuse LaVell Edwards when he
would suggest Reid's return to Brigham Young University in his place.
After all, NFL prestige, money, commitment, particularly to his players, remained in Philadelphia.

It takes courage to deny someone whom you admire and love, even
if that person knows he will be denied. If it had been another time in
his life, there would be no decision the other way. He had always
thought about that job at that place that forever altered his path. In
many ways, BYU chose Andy Reid. He had always planned on
Stanford, protecting one of the great quarterbacks. It wasn't until he
suffered a knee injury his senior year at John Marshall High in Los
Angeles and all of the Pac Ten schools backed off him that he considered Utah.

He entered Mormon country a part-time Lutheran, the son of
Jennifer, a radiologist, and Walter, a theatrical set designer. He was a
brawny eighteen-year-old from the mostly Mexican neighborhood
near Dodger Stadium, who embraced sports so he wouldn't wander. At
times, he did. Nothing bad, mind you, but he "got a little crazy" twen-
ty-some years ago, and the strange thing is that his face reddens when
he says this when I supposed mine should when I think about last
night.

Anyway, LA in the early seventies was a place ripe with things to
go bad for a teenager. "I grew up in downtown LA," he says. "I saw a
lot of things. Life was a bit chaotic. I grew up as a minority in my area.

There were a lot of factions. A lot of directions I could go. I grew up in a different lifestyle. I was not living my life the way I'm living it now. My mother and father both drank and smoked. You know, the city is just a different lifestyle. Everything was available ten-fold. We were just coming out of the sixties. Whatever you needed or wanted, drugs, booze, whatever, you could get. I just tried to hang on to sports.

"BYU wasn't No. 1 on my list of places to go. I took a visit there. Everything revolved around sports. That's where the money is. Then I found out later about the Church. It was just first class. There weren't a lot of distractions. People at the university weren't in a hurry to go party. If you're on the football team you're consumed by football. It absorbs you. I enjoyed that. I guess I felt like the ultimate gym rat."

Andy Reid just wanted to play football, and he found a wife, Tammy, the Barbie blond who always had this innate sweetness, and he found his God.

We talked about the misconceptions of Mormonism. If you live in the east, outside of New York, you might think Mormons still collect wives and the Donnie Osmond is their spokesman. In truth, the Mormon belief is based on the Thirteen Articles of Faith, which are axioms not radically unlike other religions that worship Jesus Christ. "People know us as Mormons and wonder if we believe in God and Jesus Christ," Reid shrugged. "We're not into bashing other churches or badgering people about the Church. We believe in family values and the family unit." What Mormons don't believe in is cursing, caffeine, alcohol or tobacco, which KO most NFL coaches and certainly many of those who made The Pilgrimage to Jacksonville.

Contrary to belief, Reid has never outlawed cursing on the sidelines. He does not expect Hugh Douglas to sack quarterbacks, then come off the field and become Joseph Smith.

According to Butchy, who spends more time with Reid than Tammy, Reid never slips, though he may repeat one only if he's quoting somebody else. Especially Buchanico, who explained to Reid why he curses in a hysterical bit:

"I'm a former Philly cop," he cracked in that husky voice. "It's like a steam release valve God gave you as long as you don't say His name in vain. When you say it, it releases the pressure. Ah, fuck...you see?

You can't say, geeze or shoot. Watch – Shoot!"

Buchanico shook his head and shrugged.

"You see? Nothin'."

"Now…fuck. Ah, I feel better."

So LaVell Edwards called, and Reid pondered life again in Provo, if only for a moment, if only, he said, "because of your religion, your family, the environment, and then your head coach whom you respect that much. That's as far as it ever got. BYU's a great job. I love the university. I love the head coach. I acknowledged it for a minute out of respect, but I have a great job. What happens is it takes place during the season and that's not good. I couldn't let it become a distraction. So that's as far as it went. I made an obligation here. Somewhere in this crazy business there has to be a sense of responsibility."

Fast-forward to this sun drenched day earlier this year. Gary Crowton, whom BYU settled on as coach, was asked to resign, but LaVell Edwards didn't call Andy Reid this time, not with Reid firmly entrenched in Philadelphia with a contract extension. Other teams around the NFL had wondered if he'd opt to coach out the rest of his deal and hit the free agent market, since right now, the man could just about name his job in football, whether the NFL or college.

We talk about wanderlust, about itinerant eyes, about other situations, with other players, with the thrill of newness. How so many great coaches were lured by it all, how they rarely reproduced totally their success, how Parcells never won it after the Giants and Holmgren never won it after the Packers and Riley never won it after the Lakers.

How Reid's quest to reach the level of the aforementioned is still not yet complete, but even if it were, even if the outcome of Jacksonville had provided a parade to end all parades, he could not envision starting over for the sake of starting over.

"The grass isn't always greener," he said. "I've seen it. I know what these players are going through [with free agency]. I had a chance. I told Bob, Listen, let's just get this done, I don't need to be the highest coach in the NFC East. I don't need to make headlines with my salary. How much is enough? I mean, it's great, and of course you want to earn a great living, but what's really important in life?

"I have everything in place. I don't want to go through putting my system in place. Going through all of that again. Having the players run 'til they drop. That Hegamin thing was bad. Some ugly stuff. It needed to be done, but I don't want to do that. I want to win championships here. It's one thing if you're fired because you were losing. Or if you weren't treated fairly. But to leave just for money. That's no good."

This is a topic of conversation because nary a moment ago, president Joe Banner entered Andy Reid's office with a voice of vexation: "Anthony," he said, "would you mine excusing us for a moment?"

After fifteen minutes, Banner emerged shaking his head with troubles. "Thanks."

Upon reentry, Reid's face had suddenly drooped. "You're going to find out tomorrow. T.O. changed agents. He's now with Drew Rosenhaus. "

Which means Terrell Owens, who made record recovery from ankle surgery and played superhumanly in the Super Bowl, who helped the Eagles' offense become the most potent in the league, who appeared to have shed his divisive ways, is going to present a huge problem: He wants to renegotiate his contract.

Owens, now with the notorious Rosenhaus by his side, wishes out of the contract he signed exactly one year ago, amid a web surrounding his free agent status after his former agent failed to file the necessary paperwork with the league.

So as we speak, Corey Simon is unhappy with the franchise tag placed upon him and desires a long term deal. Brian Westbrook is unhappy with the middle tender offered him and desires a long term deal. Hollis Thomas desires a raise. And now there's the potential bombshell with the noisy Owens.

Thus the new hurdle heading into Year Seven for Andy Reid: Keeping players content.

"When you go to the Super Bowl, it's important to keep people's egos in check," he said. "Everybody has to check their egos. Particularly money wise. What they want. You have to make them remember how they got here. Sometimes when you go to the Super Bowl everybody thinks it's about them. That they are the primary reason you got there. Everybody can't feel that way. Everybody has to keep it all in perspective. Hard work is what got you there. Team is what got you there."

You are invited to a typical day in the man's life. Because living a day with him will grant you insight into just who the man is.

In his colorless Sunday suit, the man could be going to services, if not for the police escort that surrounds his Danali all the way to the entrance of the parking lot. He motors through the gates and veers into the darkened tunnel of this house of worship, right through the autumn Sunday morning, hushed and clean and windswept, the backdrop of the city beneath the low-hanging sky appearing in high def.

The man climbs out of the SUV that will be stationed by security in one of four papal parking spots inside the stadium – next to the team owner's, the owner's wife's and the president's – and confers briefly with the attendant, who dutifully asks, "Need anything?"

"I'm fine," grunts the man, awash in Sunday reflection and Sunday sternness. He's been up for hours, and it's not enough. Like now, he's thinking about how quickly he can reach his office and resume last-minute preparations, though he never stops thinking, preparing, hatching scenarios, fishing for the outcome. He's consumed by it, consumed the way a stalker is. A big man with squinty eyes, he shrinks the corridor with his presence, the wrinkle in his pink brow spelling Do Not Disturb. It is 10:24, and only two game officials escorted by the man's camerlengo will be granted an audience before it's time, the customary meeting to discuss any trick plays or odd formations, and to synchronize watches. We will not see the man again until 12:56, shortly after the attendant bursts through the doors of the locker room forewarning, "Two minutes!"

You know the man. He's been here going on six years. You know him only in this way, by what he does, which is almost all there is to tell – sans maybe life's details, like he took his wife for the bye weekend to New Glarus, a quaint Swiss-like village in Wisconsin full of wholesome festivals, apple cider and meat, and that his mantra is pretty simple: faith, family, football.

Never has a man been this known and not known at all, oddly a stranger to genuine adulation from the flock, which still genuflects to Buddy Ryan, a coach without a playoff victory. There are pockets of warmth, especially now, and he adores this place, however starkly different from his home city of Los Angeles or the other places he's been: Provo, San Francisco, Flagstaff, El Paso, St. Louis, Green Bay. The intersection of Andy Reid, a man with little indulgence out of food and football, and Philadelphia comes with a shared obsession: the sport.

"I feel like I fit here," Reid says.

So the Eagles beat Carolina on that autumn Sunday afternoon, though to a man they rebuke the notion of revenge. And though this is their fifth straight victory by double digits to open the season, there is little merriment.

Andy Reid walks to the center of the locker room and rasps, "All right, bring it up."

Some players dawdle, including Terrell Owens, and Reid's voice deepens and grows louder. "Let's go. Let's go. C'mon. T.O., bring it over here."

Reid winks at Owens. There is a moment through the thicket of weary men, and Reid addresses the group. "How 'bout Lito Sheppard out there?"

The team hoots for the young corner who wrote in his journal the day before he'd snare the first interception of his career. He had two.

Reid beams. He's proud.

"There are no empty wins," he says. "They're all good. See you Wednesday. Now let's pray."

The players drop to one knee and clasp their neighbor's hand and recite the Lord's Prayer in unison. Unbeaten and easily the best team in the conference, it looks very promising right about now for the Eagles. The NFC Championship Game looms in the foreground, still months away, and, no, it's not too soon to pray.

So now the man, in rapid fire succession, will address the media, shower and change, kiss his wife, Tammy, and hug his five children, three boys and two girls, all of whom were born in a different state: Garrett, the oldest, followed by Britt, Crosby, Drew Ann and Spencer.

Then he will hop in the Danali and drive to his office at the NovaCare Center, grab a burger and watch the tape of the game over and over and over, working the remote like a salesman does a cell phone.

Perhaps he will a get a few hours of shut-eye on the couch, before waking up, watching the game again, discussing the game with his coaching staff, meeting with expert trainer Rick Burkholder to discuss the injury status of his players, meeting with trusty aid Derek Boyko, the director of media services who has wondrous sensibilities of the forthcoming questions and how fairness is played in the other aspect of this game, and addressing the media once again. After about twenty-five minutes, he return to his office and begin work on the game plan of the following week's game, first settling in for hours and hours of watching film of his opponent.

Sometime after midnight, he will finally leave the complex, turn right on Pattison Avenue, past FDR Park on his left, drive through to Penrose Avenue, and with the Platt Bridge in front of him and the junkyards to his left, hook a right onto the Expressway, taking it all the way to the exit for Villanova.

Soon, he will be home.

Home? That's a laugh. The Main Line is nice if you ever get to see it. A football coach's life is spent in his office, closed off from the world, from things like movies and the mall and television shows and the yard and a sitdown supper with candles in the dining room. He can't tell you the last movie he watched, only that some Friday nights the kids rent their videos and he may stumble upon a scene or two.

People ask about the money, the newfound riches.

The money? It's for them, God bless them, the family. It's good that he's secure now, more secure than he'd ever imagine, and Tammy deserves to be secure and have some nice things now. Through all of the towns, she was there trucking beside him, raising the children, being the strong one. She didn't have a problem when dinner at San Francisco State was the free hot dogs at the school's barbeque or when a date for them was walking from their tiny apartment to Fisherman's Wharf and sitting down on a bench arm and arm, maybe treating themselves to an ice cream cone.

"I give these little talks on family, faith and football," he says.

"How you balance it out and make it work together. I look at football and I believe it's very important to our family, to me and the people I've been around. It is a way of life."

For a moment, he will reflect on his life, how he got here, how he picked up little items from every coach he's been around. Like the bulging binders and the notebooks, which came from San Francisco State Coach Vic Rowen, a gridiron lifer who spent forty years on the job. Andy would walk into his office and Vic had notebooks everywhere, like walking into a library. He had notebooks on every team in the country, both college and pro. He'd sit and watch games on Sunday and take notes and write down plays and then call the coaches that Monday and ask about them. "For a coach, it was a shrine," Andy says. "It was the greatest place to learn."

Jim Johnson gave him an education on defense and LaVell Edwards gave him philosophy, particularly how to treat players. "I try to guide kids," Reid says. "At the end of the day you have to look in the mirror. You have to see the kind of person you are."

It's why he's such a stickler for character players. Because, he says, good people reach deeper during tough times. They don't let the bad times get them down."

The NFC Championship Game, this one, the fourth, yes, that was a good time, made all the sweeter by the tough times.

"I didn't think about the Gatorade," he says, remembering the best time, the clocking ticking down, the fans deep into bliss, and Ike Reese and the guys dumping the bucket on him for the first time in his career, the cold not even cold, not even then, his head and shirt soaked. "I didn't have enough experience with the Gatorade. That's the part you enjoy in this business. Because you have the fans around, it's in your atmosphere, your stadium. You get to celebrate with your people. It's different than when you go down to the Super Bowl. The jubilation is greater when you win the NFC Championship and share it with your people. However, the longevity of joy is phenomenal after you win the Super Bowl."

Andy Reid likes the islands. He likes the sand and the solitude and the sea breezy suppers with his wife. He likes to wear oversized Hawaiian shirts and walk the beach holding Tammy's hand. He likes to read those books by the rippling ocean and feed his soul with serenity. You can't get further away from football than the islands, an alternate universe of tranquility, away from the tundra and the tension.

The more remote, the better, away from anything football, anything Eagles, away from everything and everyone. So shortly after the Super Bowl, he will escape to Peter Island, an exclusive hockey puck of an island in the Caribbean, totaling about eighteen hundred acres in all, consisting mostly of lush mountainous terrain. To get there, you have to fly to St. Thomas and take a puddlejumper to Beef Island Airport in Tortola and then a ferry four miles to Peter. There are no phones or televisions in the only hotel resort on the island and no privately owned vehicles.

"There's a beach on one side of the island and a beach on the other side and a giant hill in between," Reid will say. "You're pretty much shut off from the world. I loved it."

So one starry night, Andy and Tammy will sit down to a dinner at a romantic beachfront restaurant, when a dinghy from one of the catamarans anchored in Deadman's Bay will roar up on the beach, plopping down on the sand with a loud thump. A bunch of guys will appear, hooting and hollering, rum soaked and duly unruly, obliging the few diners to survey the commotion.

"They were loud," Reid will say, "really, really loud. So they see me. It's Andy Reid. They tap each other on the shoulder and point, and they go right into it: E-A-G-L-E-S, EAGLES! They start freakin' out. 'Yo, Andy!' They had a few pops. They're all pumped up. They grab me. They say, "We're from Jersey. We're taking you with us on the boat!"

Tammy, the football wife, will say with sweetness instead of bitterness, "Happens everywhere we go. At the airport. On the plane. That never doesn't happen. The fans are little more boisterous here, for the lack of a better word, without saying a bad word. They're very loud and they're very passionate."

Reid will continue, "After about a half-hour of taking pictures, they're causing all kinds of commotion. People are looking. It's a pretty exclusive restaurant. I said, 'You guys better get some dinner.' So they're sitting down. They're still all pumped up. We get up to leave and I hear it again: E-A-G-L-E-S, EAGLES! Go Eagles! They got me pumped up."

Suddenly, Andrew Walter Reid will no longer be impassive. He will be a man brimming with emotion, overwhelmed by thoughts of that wonderful week and what it might be like to top it. He will feign dialing a phone on his palm recounting the story.

"I'm so fired from those guys that I call Donovan on the phone," he will say. "I said, 'Yo, Donovan! We're going back there. We're going to Detroit! And this time, we're gonna win it!'"

ON THE FIFTH NIGHT, UNDER A STARRY SKY IN THE RIVER CITY

Soon they are summoned to depart the locker room, the fighter with the grand entrance into the ring. An NFL coordinator informed them they would have to walk all the way around the other side of the stadium to come through for pregame introduction. The Eagles clearly were hometown Jacksonville's choice, and as the players made their way through the bowels of Alltel Stadium, the worker moles applauded them.

"Go Eagles!" they yowled intermittently.

The players walked at a leisurely pace, spread out through the shadowy tunnel. Butchy was among the first to arrive at the entrance to the field that assails the senses with fabulous light and the din of the crowd. The coordinator from the league flagged him down.

"Where's the team?" the man said.

"They're coming out now," Butchy answered.

"They gotta go on the field. NOW!"

"What are you nuts?" Butchy said. "Take it easy. They got spikes on. There's a flood back there. It's wet and slippery. They're hurrying. I'm not getting one of my guys hurt over this."

So many people in charge at the Super Bowl. They appear out of thin air with their curt directives, always contradicting one another, and they resemble sideline coaches, with their headsets and walkie-talkies, and all they know is that you needn't be here. And who are they? From the league? From television? The teams? Which one? Security? League or local? Pregame extravaganza? Halftime extravaganza? National anthem production team? "God Bless America" production team? Alicia Keys' assistant's assistant? They won't tell. Because they don't know. They are deputized and told to stand here, wherever here is.

The field of the Super Bowl is like a European train, controlled chaos in every compartment. Especially after Gretchen Wilson, the Charlie Daniels Band, the Black-Eyed Peas, Earth, Wind & Fire and the Florida A&M "Marching 100" Band have just finished performing, and Will Smith is introducing a Ray Charles tribute leading into Keys' rendition of "God Bless America," and that will precede Michael Douglas introducing a joint-service choir performance of the National Anthem and former Presidents George H.W. Bush and Bill Clinton calling for donations for tsunami relief in southeast Asia.

The teams finally took command of the field. The kid football player from Jacksonville ceremonially flipped a coin rather flatly and then officials did so for real. The Eagles guessed the outcome right and elected to receive.

After more television delay, for more of those million dollar, sixty-second commercial spots, Adam Vinatieri kicked off at exactly 6:38 Eastern Standard Time amid a strobe light of flashbulbs. "That's what I'll remember most from the game," Jeremiah Trotter said. "All those flashes at one time. That's when it really feels like you're in the Super Bowl."

Donovan McNabb raged with adrenalin. He needed to get hit. All quarterbacks, especially in the Super Bowl, need to get hit to let them know that it's really just another football game. Knowing that McNabb would be overly anxious, Pats defensive coordinator Romeo Crennel dialed up two blitzes on the first series, the second one by linebacker Tedy Bruschi that resulted in a sack. McNabb fumbled on the play, but the call was reversed following a challenge by Andy Reid.

McNabb's knee was down before the ball was wriggled loose.

Crennel employed a different look for the game, moving line-backer Willie McGinnest to end and changing from 3-4 defense to a 4-3.

Meanwhile, New England quarterback Tom Brady, normally Tom Cool, eerily similar to Joe [Montana] Cool, looked equally jumpy. Following a sixteen-yard completion by Deion Branch, in which Corey Dillon effectively picked up a Trotter blitz, the Pats' first possession resulted in similar ineffectiveness.

Two more possessions, two more punts, before the Eagles mounted the first serious scoring threat of the game. Behind a fourteen yard screen play to Brian Westbrook, a thirty-yard strike from McNabb to Owens and a subsequent roughing penalty on the Pats' Roosevelt Colvin, the Eagles had a first and goal at the New England eight. But on the next play, McNabb, under great pressure, retreated and retreated and couldn't perform another "elusion trick," the way he has so many times during his career. He lost sixteen yards on the sack, then threw a pick along the right sideline that was nullified by an illegal contact penalty on the Patriots. But with new life and new set of downs, McNabb forced a throw to Westbrook downfield into double coverage in a play eerily similar to the one against the Falcons that was intercepted and dropped. The ball floated in the coastal night air, and Rodney Harrison, providing safety support from the backside in the Pats' zone, held on for the interception.

When McNabb reached the sideline, Reid stopped him.

"What happened?" he said.

"The wind took it," McNabb shrugged.

With the Patriots' backed up at their own three, the Eagles defense, playing spirited football, held once more and gave the ball back to the offense in New England territory. But once again, mistakes proved costly. This time, it was a fumble on third down by LJ Smith following a reception over the middle, the ball stripped by Pats' corner Randall Gay.

Jim Johnson's defense continued to frustrate Brady and the Patriots, forcing them into their third straight three and out. In its first four possessions, New England managed just thirty-seven yards, one first down and zero third-down conversions.

Afterwards, tight end Christian Fauria would say the Pats were "tight early on offense" because of concern over Johnson's deadly and confusing blitz packages.

The Eagles finally found the end zone with Smith thanks to two big plays by the oft-maligned Todd Pinkston, including a forty-yard reception on a great leaping grab deep in the middle of the field. Though he proved a valuable role player as the fleet, deep threat opposite Owens, leading the conference with an average of nearly nineteen yards per catch and leading the team with five plays over fifty yards, Pinkston endured the ire of the flock for a lack of fortitude that began with the championship game against Carolina and continued this season with two mortifying short-arm attempts for the football. Alligator arms, they catcalled him, especially after the one in Washington that he said he lost in the lights, though replays showed he was clearly skittish of charging Redskins' safety Sean Taylor. Pinkston would leave the Super Bowl in the second half with muscle cramps.

The Eagles' 7-0 lead marked great hope for the flock and the first time New England had trailed in the postseason. It was just the second time in twenty-seven games the Patriots didn't score first.

It was clear. This would not be a rout, even after the Patriots responded quickly behind the running of Dillon. They drove to the Eagles four before Brady botched a play-fake and lost the ball, recovered by tackle Darwin Walker. A three-and-out and a short punt by the usually dependable Dirk Johnson set up the Patriots' game-tying touchdown just before halftime, a four-yard catch by David Givens, who imitated Owens' patented foot on the football, arm-flapping celebration.

So the Eagles entered the long halftime tied and cursing so many missed opportunities. Football is a fickle game of rhythm and flow, especially when the combatants are so evenly matched. So if fortuity is frittered away early, it usually haunts a team in the end.

"In the first half, I thought Five forced some things and rushed some things," Reese would say. "We should have been up. The one they got back before halftime was cheap. Guy standing out there alone…cheap. But we made too many mistakes. We let them hang around."

"We should have been blowing them out," Runyan added. "It was a tale of two halves. Something you learn from if you get back there again."

The Patriots came out energized in the second half. After a suspect first half, Brady again resembled the money player he was in the play-offs. He hooked up with MVP Deion Branch three times amassing sixty-three yards on the opening drive of the third quarter, setting up a two-yard blip to linebacker and goal line touchdown-maker Mike Vrabel.

The Eagles did make an impressive stand midway through the quarter, proving the disparity between the teams nil. McNabb settled down, concentrated on his mainstays, Owens and Westbrook, and embarked on a ten-play, seventy-four yard scoring drive.

And that was it. With dreamy visions of a parade coming to life throughout the Delaware Valley and down here in Phillyville, the ballroom at the Radisson Hotel erupting in carousal and conviction, the Patriots put forth the rest of their offensive halftime strategy and answered with another killer touchdown drive.

Utilizing the extra long halftime, Patriots offensive coordinator Charlie Weiss scripted the first ten plays. He opted to go with four wide receivers – which elicits a nickel defense and pressure from the defense – and spread them out to see where the blitzes were coming from.

Weiss, who had just accepted the Notre Dame head coaching job, making the Super Bowl his curtain call with the Patriots, confused the Eagles defense by running out of pass formations that he showed in the first half (and for most of the season) and throwing out of running formations. The four wides also took Trotter out of the game. Weiss drew the Eagles pressure and then ordered Brady to hit the defense's soft spot with screens, either to Dillon or third down specialty back Kevin Faulk, resulting in huge gains.

The Patriots' first four possessions of the second half yielded two touchdowns and a field goal, and the two longest completions by Brady on the game-winning drive came on screens to Faulk.

"I still the say the one advantage they had was being used to the length of halftime," Reese said. "Suddenly we were in that locker room for twenty-eight minutes instead of twelve minutes. We went into the halftime on a high emotional pitch and we left it there. I don't know if we expected them just to lay down or what. But we didn't have the same fire on defense. We kind of sleepwalked through the third quarter, and we got hit with some adjustments they did. They're good but they're not THAT good. We weren't the same team. It didn't feel the same out there on the field. We didn't feel the same."

The Patriots pushed the lead to ten with eight minutes and forty seconds to go on a twenty-two yard field goal by Vinatieri. The Eagles marched right into New England territory following a dramatic play by Owens in which he caught a short pass, broke through Gay's tackle attempt and sprinted thirty-six yards down the sideline. But any momentum Owens provided died when McNabb overthrew Dorsey Levens in the flat, the ball hitting Bruschi square in the numbers.

The Patriots were now in clock-killing mode.

Which brings us all the way back to Five Minutes and Forty Seconds.

Looking back on it later, Ike Reese said: "People talk about the last 5:40. To me, I thought Five was hyped to start the game. He didn't seem OK to me on the first few drives. He got pressured a few times and that made him a little insecure in the pocket. He didn't look right then. Some of the throws he made weren't the type of throws he made the previous two postseason games. I can't put my finger on it. But early on, he was jumpy.

"I do remember him making a statement earlier in the week during a players' only meeting that he felt some of the other guys might be nervous. I thought that was an odd statement to make a couple of days before the game. 'Some of you,' he said, 'look nervous. Some of you are behaving nervous.' Nobody felt that way. I thought it was a little odd. I thought maybe he was speaking about himself. I thought everybody was straight. Guys all seemed the same. Having Eighty-One out there helped."

Months later, Reid said, "The end result that took place was a touchdown. When you play in the game it isn't all going to be perfect. We got into a hurry-up offense. Donovan got the stuffing knocked out of him. If you want to stop a two-minute offense, that's how you stop it. He got hit a couple of times and he battled his tail off to get back off that ground and get in the end zone.

"For whatever anybody says, that was the end result and there was time left to go down and win the game. We didn't take care of business after that. We needed that onside kick. We've been pretty good with those onside kicks. We practiced onside kicks all week and it was working really well. It just didn't happen. Donovan knows better than everybody what he'd like to do if he had another shot at it. I'd know what I'd like to do if I had another shot at it. Every player does that. You go through that self-analysis. Donovan's far enough in his career that he knows. He knows what he did good and what he has to do better. But our guys battled throughout the game. There was no quit in them. I'm proud of them and the season they had."

Trotter put it more succinctly in hindsight. "You have to play good enough to take the title away from the champs. If it's a draw, you lose. We just couldn't deliver the knockout punch early."

Harrison intercepted the Eagles' final gasp, Brady took a knee and the Patriots officially became a dynasty. As the clock bled to zeroes, Brady tossed the ball high in the air and reporters and the sidelines spilled onto the field. Andy Reid maneuvered through the throng of humanity and all of those television cameras to shake Bill Belichick's hand, and barely escaped unharmed as a league crew worked feverishly to set up the postgame ceremony.

"When you lose, the NFL abandons you," Butchy said. "The NFL adopted my idea of using a perimeter set up by a rope. Now they're pushing us. I know they don't know what they're doing. One end is going faster than the other and the rope was beginning to wrap around Andy."

Butch became deep in the streets Butch.

"Yo! Hold on! You're strangling people! You're strangling Andy Reid!"

"I almost cold-cocked this guy," he said. "I'm trying to get Andy out of there. It was like a cattle drive. Andy had a rope burn on him."

Back in the locker room, the Eagles dressed quickly and somberly, did their interviews and hurried to the buses that would carry them back to the hotel. Silence reigned.

Back in the tent, Professor Glen Macnow had the duty of the postgame show for the radio station.

He arrived there at Five Minutes and Forty Seconds. "The tent was packed when I first arrived," he said, "filled with desperate people hoping for the miracle that never came. As soon as the game ended, they filed out like zombies. I started the show with about fifty fans left, sitting dejectedly in folding chairs. Within a half-hour, they all slunk away, except for a half-dozen diehards."

The tent was worn and muddy, dark and dank, strewn with empty plastic cups, torn-up banners and the remnants of revelry.

"It reminded me of hosting a New year's Eve party and looking around at four in the morning at the mess that was left after all the guests had left," Macnow said. "Plus, you knew it was gonna hurt worse in the morning. I remember they turned out the lights in the tent around midnight, leaving Brian Robbins and me sitting under the glow of the WIP spotlight. It was kind of spooky.

"Occasionally, an angry drunk would pass by us on his way back from the game, presumably to his hotel room. The drunks would scream some invective and just keep walking. The half-dozen diehards just sat and listened. They were more numb than anything else. The calls I got that night weren't angry as much as fatalistic and confused. 'Why us?' was the recurring theme. I felt like the shrink walking victims through a grief-counseling session. And, it was one of those moments when WIP serves a real purpose – sharing the collective pain so that we can all get through something together. We seem to serve that purpose a lot."

A Patriots fan near the River Walk stood upright, and said, "We walked around town all week and those Eagles fans called us names and made fun of our team. Well, we got our just due, right here."

One of the last stragglers in the tent was Phil From Mount Airy. Wandering out of the stadium, feeling lost, he had taken a river taxi and cut through the tent to get to the parking lot.

"I hugged Glen and started crying," he said. "When the tent emptied that's when it hit me: There's no guarantee we're getting back next year. We were fifteen minutes from heaven. The next morning I cried again waiting for train to Orlando."

Jeffrey Lurie planned a lavish reception for the team back at the hotel. A king's welcome, it was, furnished with elaborate decorations and the finest of food and spirits, spanning the entire bottom floor of the Marriott, encompassing four different ballrooms.

Those in attendance estimated the cost at "millions."

Few felt like reveling, especially the players, who spent the first hours of the party huddled away in their own private ballroom. As the players wandered in, those within the organization offered consoling words. Reese said, "We just sat in there by ourselves. Trying to rehash the game. Figuring out what went wrong. In the mind, trying to change what happened. Some of us who knew we were free agents. That type of talk going on. We didn't get started until near one in the morning. Around two-thirty, we kind of snapped out of it a little. Hell, we just played in the Super Bowl after all of those long years. We lost, but hell, by three points! Then we sort of celebrated the year we had until about four in the morning."

We are now just men bemoaning the fate of our team. The Caravan has assembled on lounge chairs by the small pool at the motel. Somebody lights a cigar. Somebody burps open a beer. The motel is hushed. A soft wind sweeps through. It's actually very placid, almost quixotic, if not for the topic of conversation. Surely, like the players, we recount what transpired in the River City to the last detail. We perform an autopsy of the game.

A lot of sentences begin with, "If only…" If only they had capitalized on ONE opportunity in the first half…if only they had scored then…made it 14-0 or even 10-0…it's a different game…the Patriots might have felt desperation.

If only Donovan would have played better and if only they could have defended a couple of those screens better and if only they had gone to TO more and if only they scored just a little quicker, before the two-minute warning…Then they could have kicked it deep and gotten better field position on the last gasp.

"Akers can hit one from fifty-five," Boo says. "We might still be sitting there. In double overtime. How great would that have been?"

"Can you imagine if they had won it?" Uncle Dirt muses.

Silence overcomes the pool area, as if each one of us does just that to ourselves, and who knows? Maybe everyone else is imagining what it would be like if only they had won. I do. We are lost in that dreamy state, when an old crotchety man breaks our trance.

"Pool's closed," he barks. "Gotta leave."

The man must be seventy, and he wields a nightstick.

"Sir," Boo says politely, "we're Eagles fans. Just talking about the game, you know? It was a tough loss."

"I don't give a good goddamn who you're a fan of," he shoots back. "Pack up and leave now! The pool is closed. What don't you understand?"

Are you serious? Go away, pal.

Really. Kindly leave us alone. Let us stay here and enjoy commiserating. We're not doing anything wrong. We're just groan men bemoaning the fate of our team. I know the brown uniform with the polyester pants and the faux badge give you a power rush, but it's time now to take it a notch down and be on your merry way. Crimefighter Superhero, go hassle a crackhead in one of those broken down rooms.

I'm in no mood. The Eagles lost.

"We'll be in leaving in a few minutes, sir," Vinny said, resisting the temptation to say what I am thinking.

"You'll leave NOW! You DEEF?" he says, meaning deaf.

He stares at us with his best I-mean-business face. We don't budge. It's a Jacksonville standoff outside the Roach Motel. Nine angry Eagles fans and a seventy-year-old man.

Finally, he leaves in a huff, muttering something about calling the coppers. Steve runs to talk sense to the motel manager.

Joey, who never does anything inappropriate, flings the lock and chain to the pool area into the pool.

The man comes back in a bit, hardly chagrined. "All right you boys can stay for five more minutes," he says. "Anyone see the lock to the gate?"

3
MONDAY

Monday morning brings forth more luminous sunshine and gridlock at the airport, as the great deflation of Jacksonville begins, the mass exodus of the weekend revelers underway. The chartered flight tarries on the tarmac awaiting takeoff clearance from the tower. Those inside are restless.

When you lose, a player once told me, you just want to get home to your family. You want to be around the people who love you. You want to heal. You want to decompress. You want to forget football for as long as possible. In the case of the Eagles, time is the players' friend. The offseason seems boundless right now, the future presenting visions of a palm tree.

THE AFTERMATH

The Caravan has dispersed. Joey and Boo are driving the rental car to Orlando, the closest airport from which they could garner a flight back to Philadelphia. Vinny, who had security clearance to fly in the jumpseat with the crew from Jacksonville, is already in Chicago, awaiting his connecting flight to Appleton. Boo calls Vinny. Says they're lost and stuck in traffic on one of the Florida highways. Vinny dials up his GPS, and directs them to the correct route.

I am with Steve, Nick, Dave, Brian and Bubba back at the tent doing our last show from the Super Bowl. The producers will drive the RV back to Philadelphia, while Steve and I will fly back to report to work tomorrow morning.

The tent is even more depressing in the daylight. It is soulless and disheveled, with garbage overflowing from the hefty trash cans, the grass and dirt floor matted with rotting food and cigarette butts. The men who ran the food stand pack up their supplies and leftover inventory in silence.

Prior to the show, I sat on a bench on the now deserted River Walk watching the St. Johns, feeling wistful. I feel this way not so much due to the outcome of the event, but because the Pilgrimage is now over. A sudden emptiness always follows such an experience. For what awaits back in Philadelphia is only the rest of winter, with its cold and dreary days.

The mood of the callers is as expected: dour and embittered. And that is to be expected, the game still too fresh, The Morning After too soon to reflect upon the journey.

"I'm angry," says a man, whose name escapes me, as all of the names now seem to run together. "My twelve-year-old son is crushed. My wife baked brownies and he head-butted himself with the plate."

Most of the conversation centers around Five Minutes and Forty Seconds, the overall performance of Donovan McNabb and some of the coaching moves by Andy Reid. It's why sportsradio became a hit: to bitch and moan and Monday Morning Quarterback.

Why didn't they run a hurry-up offense? Why were they lollygagging back to the line of scrimmage? Why did McNabb appear so defeated with that towel draped over his head? Was he sick? Was he exhausted? Why didn't Andy Reid try to score before halftime? Why didn't he kick it deep at the end instead of going for the onsides kick?

The five-hour show feels like a wake, the polar opposite of the past weeks. The callers project the mood of the town, an assortment of bitterness and entitlement. They are irrational and fatalistic.

We'll never win…

The charter flight lands in Philadelphia, where a group of fans have gathered to greet the team. Wielding perspective, they cheer the effort and the season and a ride they will forever remember. The spirit of the players is lifted, though a part of them still imagined a different home-coming, one that celebrates conquest and adorns champions.

Yes, yes, they imagined the ticker-tape parade that would have taken place the day after tomorrow. Oh, what a spectacle it would have been, millions in merriment lining the street, the party to end all par-ties. The parade route had already been planned. It was going to start at Washington Avenue and go north on Broad Street, curling around City Hall and onto the Parkway. The ceremony was to take place on the steps of the Art Museum.

Accompanied by a police escort, the team now reaches the NovaCare facility, where the members file into the practice bubble to retrieve their luggage. The bags are lined up on the Astroturf, arranged in alphabetical order.

Andy Reid thanks the team for the wondrous season that fell just three points short. He talks about doing this next year in Detroit, and next time winning the Super Bowl.

"God bless you all," he says, and disappears out of the practice bubble doors.

On the plane ride home, I sit near a woman, salt of the earth type, ooz-ing simple sweetness. She talks of her husband who plowed the stadi-um for nearly thirty-six straight hours and what this journey meant to them. She lives in a modest home in Jersey and she uses words like cool and awesome and she professes to "UUUGE" Eagles fan. She's friendly and honest.

I think about the role this experience played in her life. What's wrong with that? Does this make her life less enriched that she extract-ed such joy and fulfillment brought forth by a football team? Isn't it all about taste? Can't I marvel at beauty – whatever the art form? There is always this war to feel superior, to diminish what others find gratify-ing. It rolls through us. Dross runs downhill, we say. But why is it when you push it down, you don't feel any better?

Enlightenment only comes when you inspect all facets of what is before you. What I witnessed in A Sunday Pilgrimage was the collective delectation of a city and its surrounding environs, a spiritual togetherness that momentarily combated the hardships and adversity of everyday life. I regaled in the individual stories of the people in and around the Philadelphia Eagles and how this affected and impacted their path. And I long to revisit this place of Elysium on earth again, perhaps in a place like Detroit.

Photo Credits: